Waldwick...Greed

Kenneth Linde

Waldwick Books
www.waldwickbooks.com
McHenry, Illinois

Waldwick: Greed

Kenneth Jon Linde

Waldwick Partners, Inc.
dba Waldwick Books
www.WaldwickBooks.com

August 2024

Printed in Wisconsin, United States of America

ISBN: 979-8-9852613-8-7

Down the Rabbit Hole:

'Down the Rabbit Hole' refers to Lewis Carroll's famous book, *Alice's Adventures in Wonderland* where Alice follows a white rabbit down a hole and enters a fantastical world called Wonderland... a strange and surreal world where Alice gets deeply absorbed in an unknown and complex situation until she loses track of time and her own existence without ever realizing it.

This is a story about going down a rabbit hole into the peculiar world of money and power. It's a summary of what happens when enough is never enough. Some call it avarice. Others, including myself, call it greed. My name is George Terrill. I went from nothing to everything to nothing again. As George Terrill the Fourth, I was known as 'Q' when I was young and Mister Terrill when our net worth exceeded three billion dollars, winning a Nobel Peace Prize and wealthy beyond most people's imaginings who's now broke, alone and cold with only nightmares for dreams. How do I begin...make that where? Perhaps a quick comment on how it all began and then, just perhaps, how it will all end.

I was born on a farm in Waldwick... a small town just outside Mineral Point, Wisconsin. It was, is and will always be what I call home. I grew up farming with my dad. God, I miss him! Nothing fancy! Nothing great! A way of life that could be considered straight and narrow just like the rows of corn he planted each and every spring.

Dad had one goal for me, go to college and get a degree and so away I went, all the way to Madison, 52 miles from home. Dodgeville, Ridgeway, Barneveld, Blue Mounds, Mount Horeb, Verona then the University of Wisconsin. For four years I toiled to get a Bachelor's degree in Journalism. I always wanted to write, perhaps become famous. Instead my destiny took a different path filled with untold riches, incredible wealth and what many consider profound achievement all to have it go 'poof' and with it the aspirations and dreams as if they never existed.

As my last year in school was about to end my roommates and I decided we needed to go on one last bender...one more time for good old days... to giggle and laugh in stupid ways. We went to the Hochunk casino because the drinks were cheap and along the way played rock, paper scissors to see who had to remain sober and drive us all home. I lost, yet, won.

To this day I ask myself what the consequences would have been if my hand had opened for paper instead of two fingers for scissors. Would life have been different? Would I have found happiness? Would obscurity meant satisfaction? Instead, fate had it that I'd meet the man who became my greatest friend. There's no way to explain our bond except to say that either one of us would die for the other. There's no way to comprehend our friendship other than to accept that he, a Native American, and me, some skinny, white farm kid, became brothers. I, who nearly died, introduced him to Ann, a nurse, who became his wife. She in turn introduced me to Amy who became my wife. Four people living lives disparate and yet parallel, always bound together by love and respect, honored by the knowledge that we would always have each other.

As Amy and my relationship evolved secrets slowly became known, none more prevalent than the fact that her father was one of the wealthiest and most powerful men in Wisconsin who could make or break a person simply because he could. Called 'The Duke' his empire was such it made dreams seem like reality.

While The Duke was the alpha male in my life, it was Amy's mother who served as the bedrock. A woman of African descent from St. Martin whose mother sold straw hats on the beach, Grandma Marie, as she was called by our children, became a doctor and world-renowned pediatric oncologist who gave of herself until there was nothing left to give.

With Amy's and my marriage came children...twin boys named George Terrill the Fifth, better known as 'V' and his brother, Derrick, named after what would have been his uncle had he not died of a drug overdose and then our daughter, Melia, wonderful, wonderful Melia, who only wanted one thing in life, to be happy and live a normal existence.

Times were good...very, very good. We had money, investments, property and luxury...things most people only dream about. For decades we lived the good life...private jets, multiple homes, luxury and opportunities to take part in any indulgences we ever wanted, whenever we wanted. Catered to, looked up to, bowed down to, we had It all.

With life the way it was, other than health, there were few times when we didn't have it all. For me, when those other times arose, I simply went home to the farm and a small spit of land we call The Forest. There, where pure spring water flows from the ground, I could get my bearings and bring myself back to reality.

Amy and I were sitting on top of the world with more money than we could spend and thought our world would last forever. Little did I realize that, with a few strokes of a pen, Amy tied our houses, cars, jets and belongings to our company instead of to us and those few wisps of ink will probably wipe us out.

I really don't know if I was ever happy. I don't know if what I achieved was ever enough. I certainly don't know how in hell our family ended up the way it did. What I do know is that, along the way, we did something wrong that I'll always regret. I started out as a dreamer who wanted to conquer the world. I found there was no joy in the world of business and began a Foundation...a great Foundation...that helped countless people lead better and healthier lives. My team and

I won a Nobel Peace Prize for our efforts. I 'retired' and went into business with my brother using the family farm to grow prime beef, distill prime bourbon and then premium wine.

A few years ago, I almost died. There are days when I wish I had. Instead, I gained the one thing we all have in common and that's time....time to think...time to feel...time to ponder, where I learned the one thing we all have in common besides life and death is time. After that I was diagnosed with Stage Two prostate cancer and had surgery.

Before almost checking out my life was measured in minutes. We purchased helicopters to save time commuting from Pine Lake to Waldwick, Wisconsin. We purchased jets to save time flying to St. Martin and when faster jets were available we spent more money simply to save time flying to our home in France.

When death left my doorstep and then my life-changing surgery, I realized there was more to life than saving time and began to ponder what time really was and why it had been so important to me and finally realized that I incorrectly equated time to opportunity. Time to enjoy life. Time to experience the inexperience's that had been deferred simply because time had always mattered and, finally, to realize that the concept of 'now' is transient as an ever-receding present moment that serves as the dividing line between the past and future. But how wide is that line? Is it an infinitesimally small point or a brief duration? This fleeting nature made it hard to grasp. I ask myself does 'now' only exist in relation to past and future simply defined by what has happened and what is yet to come? If so, doesn't that raise the question, does the past and future truly exist or are they just products of our minds relying on the present moment?

Going through what we are enduring 'now' changed my entire concept on life as measured by the seconds, minutes, hours, days, months and years that we are 'here'. To me, whether wonderful or catastrophic 'now' isn't just a point in time, it's the duration of our immediate experience. 'Now' is simply the present moment that includes not just the instant but also the echoes of the recent past and the anticipation of the immediate future in terms of people, places, events and circumstances. 'Now' only gains significance because it's the only time we can truly act and experience our true existence. The past is set, the future uncertain but the present offers the potential for engagement and change, change that can alter our life path for better or worse.

The fleeting nature of 'now' stands in contrast to the perceived solidity of the past and the open-endedness of the future. This contrast can heighten the significance of the present moment, making us appreciate what's happening to us right now.

What we find important and meaningful in life shapes how we experience 'now'. If we're working towards a goal the present moment takes on meaning as a step on that journey. If we value connection 'now' becomes an opportunity to interact with others and rise us up from the valley of despair.

So much...almost too much...life has been more than anyone could ever expect. But, as Steven Hawking once postulated, the net sum of the universe is zero. For every positive, there must be a negative. For every good, something bad. For every mountain there must be a valley. This is my story. I call it 'Greed' and believe you'll quickly resolve why.

For my adult life I've attempted to emulate The Duke and be motivated by a rational desire for a better life, without an irrational and insatiable craving. I sincerely attempted to build a sustainable future for Amy, me and the kids without focusing on the immediate gratification and accumulation. I did so through hard work and responsible financial management without prioritizing self-interest and disregard for ethical considerations and always, and I mean always, attempted to give of myself without negative emotions like envy and anxiety. What did it get me except another reason for this book?

Perhaps, it's my personality and the fact that I acquired wealth and wasn't born into it. Perhaps, there really are psychological differences between wealth acquisition and greed which can vary depending on conscientiousness, agreeableness and openness to experience. All I know is that for some of those in our family our financial wealth is, or make that was, simply not enough. For one child, it's because they wanted more notoriety. For another child, it's life's simplicity. For the third...well, I guess that's one more thing this story is all about.

They say that hindsight is always 20/20. As I've looked back on where we've been and where we're going, I realize now I made a mistake. If I'd understood the psychological differences between wealth and greed perhaps we wouldn't be in the mess we're in. While wealth can be a positive force in individual lives and contribute to societal well-being, greed can truly lead to destructive behaviors and negative consequences not only for us, but for so many others.

I sincerely feel that in my life I've fostered values of hard work, responsible financial management and social responsibility with the belief it would promote healthy approaches to wealth and contribute to a more just and equitable world. Sadly, so sadly, something incredibly bad has gone wrong.

How did all this happen? Well that's what this story is all about.

The Beginning of the End:

While many days simply blend together to create the past some turn white hot and are burned into your heart and soul never to be forgotten. Such was a Sunday nine months ago. It was early December and the gray winter Wisconsin sky was underscored by the black branches reaching out like an old lady's fingers trying to grasp any sense of warmth and resurrection. The holiday decorators had come and filled our yard and house with the reds and greens to make us merry.

Sadly, forlornly, it wasn't working. Even the Christmas songs had become nothing more than anvils of angst intended to do nothing more than make one feel guilty for not being more, giving more, doing more with the underlying promise that material things equate to love and more than a just feeling. So much for the Christmas spirit.

More succinctly, it was breakfast time which had become the only opportunity Amy and I would sit silently facing each other. My God, we'd grown distant. As I sat eating, the phone rang and I watched Amy's expression morph from one of inquiry...to concern... then to one reserved only for profound distraught. Tears welled in her eyes as she simply nodded at the receiver and finally offered, "Thank you for calling," before collapsing in total emotional terror.

"What?" I asked, irritated and somewhat impatient.

"Uncle Frank."

"What?" I inquired as my tone morphed to one of concern.

"He died."

"What?" I exclaimed, now almost incredulous. Uncle Frank had been our beacon of love in St. Martin, our most gracious host, who made anyone and everyone feel welcome as his broad smile caressed his soft brown skin and made us relish his lust for life.

"He had a heart attack last night and died."

"Oh, no!"

Unlike the past several months Amy rushed into my arms and I held her as she sobbed. Her parents were gone. Her brother was gone. Aunt Julia was gone. Now the last vestiges of yesterday simply evaporated and she was singular... alone, empty of the past. There's no good time for death but to do so right before Christmas seemed profoundly cruel.

"Arrangements?" I asked.

"Not yet and why now?" as Amy's hands went to her face in terror as if I would have the answer.

There was a pause as Amy turned to me and said, "I think we need to talk."

I knew this was serious. I thought it would be about 'us'. Instead I was about to find out how bad things really were at Wilco, our family business.

We sat at the kitchen table as Amy began. "George, things at Wilco aren't going well."

"What do you mean?" I inquired.

"When The Duke was alive everything he touched turned to gold. In the end the company over-extended into things we should have never started.

I felt like an ice pick was being jabbed into my soul as I self-admitted all the expansion had been at my behest simply to show the world I didn't marry Amy for her money.

Amy continued. "When the initial team began to retire we didn't have the same wisdom as my dad and the leadership we put in place didn't have the drive and expertise it should have. As we grew, other specialists came along who duplicated our efforts in every single arena and, instead of being great, we became good. As we attempted to compete we began cutting corners and evolved from good to average as those competitors began eroding both our business and passion until we evolved into mediocrity."

Amy took a deep breath and continued. "Derrick thought the best thing to do was sell off some of the assets and expand into different areas. In the end we over-extended the company to the point that, right now, the assets are less than the net worth of the corporation.

"But things are going to be Ok, aren't they?"

"I don't know. We've pledged everything, and I mean everything, to keep the company afloat and it's like we're playing Monopoly with pup tents when everyone else has hotels."

"Is there anything I can do?" I inquired.

"Not really, unless you can come up with a few billion dollars."

"Oh, my God!"

"What's at stake?" I inquired.

"Everything."

My hands trembled in frustration as I requested, "Define everything."

"Wilco, our houses in France, St. Martin, Pine Lake, airplanes, car dealerships… everything."

"What?" I challenged as I slid back in my chair, incredulous to think that all the chips were on the table as I selfishly asked, "What about Terrill B&B and the farm?"

"They're part of Wilco."

I took a deep breath and, as I exhaled, simply whispered, "Jesus."

Amy continued. "Things have been bad for a long time.

"Why didn't you let me know?" I demanded, now churning in a maelstrom of anger and pain.

Amy looked at me with tears welling in her eyes and simply said, "After all you've been through I didn't want you to worry."

"But!"

Amy saw the look of frustration on my face and offered. "George, you've had blood clots and cancer. You've been at risk and all the material things we have will mean nothing if you don't have your health."

"Why now?" I asked.

"Derrick got involved with some people he shouldn't have. He wanted to take the company public and show profound growth. Instead the scheme collapsed and with it all our money and, now, the company.

"Oh, my God." I felt as if I'd been hit in the chest as I sat in disbelief.

The deafening silence was broken by the ringing phone. It was the Emerald Funeral Home in Saint Martin. Amy took the call and discussed arrangements. Cremation? Yes. No funeral. No memorial. Just as Uncle Frank wished.

Amy looked at me and inquired. "George, can you go down there and take care of everything? I really need to stay here and help try to save everything…anything!"

I quietly nodded in the affirmative and asked when she wanted me to go. Amy indicated they wanted me there as soon as possible as they needed someone to pay for the cremation. I really didn't know if she wanted me out of town to protect me from the pressure or because she was so ashamed of what was happening.

I indicated I would go the next day.

Amy hung up the phone and I called Wilco Ops which controlled our 30-plane private jet fleet and told them what was going on. The flight was scheduled for the next morning. I didn't sleep well and drove to Mitchell Field with the plane sitting on the tarmac. I was told our plane, designated as Amelia^X, was in for regular maintenance and I'd be taking Amelia III. I climbed on board and opened the liquor cabinet only to find it empty.

My flight was solo and I was alone to think about life and, particularly, Uncle Frank and how gracious he'd always been. We landed at Princess Juliana and I looked at the spot where the Rover normally would be waiting with Uncle Frank having everything prepared and realized I already missed my dear friend. I went through customs and took a taxi reflecting on the joy of life for those who came to visit but never take time to actually experience Saint Martin."

As a tri-national who repeatedly traversed between Wisconsin, France and Saint Martin I'd become 'blended' in terms of my outlook on life and hoped I would be able to take the best from all three and mix them together in terms of lifestyle, social standards and tolerances…yes, tolerances, as each has its freedoms and limitations…socially, politically and ethically.

From America I took the enthusiasm that comes from being in the land of opportunity. From France I took the joy of the moment where clocks tick slower and life's more casual. From Saint Martin I thought about assumptions and how the one thing I'd learned, above all else, is that you never should assume anything. In so doing each day can be filled with the majesty of something new and exciting to store in the memory drawer you carry in your mind, heart and spirit.

A few years ago I built our dream retreat called the Lighthouse on the top of Bell Hill, above Anse Marcel overlooking Bell Point and Anguilla to the north. I arrived, stood on the deck and looked out at the ocean below and listened to the afternoon plane take off for Saint Lucia from Grand Case–Espérance Airport. When the sounds of the plane's departure ended and I watched as it became a tiny spec in the Caribbean sky, my mind became ensconced in the deafening silence of singularity, alone with nothing but the wind whispering to me its profound sadness.

I made my way to our bedroom, opened the closet and took out a pair of dress shorts and golf shirt, got in our Range Rover and made my way to Auberge Gourmand in Grand Case which had always been our special spot. I rationalized.

'If I'm going to have dinner alone, it will be at my favorite place, filled with so many memories.'

I arrived and the staff, who were my friends, made me feel welcome. I sat alone at table number one as Pasquale, the owner, poured a glass of wine and we toasted Uncle Frank and his memory. Word spread fast that he was gone.

I ate my dinner staring blankly at the quivering candle and realizing it's a metaphor of life that will slowly burn down and finally flicker out or suddenly be whiffed out before its time. Either way the cold, dark pallor of death will ensconce itself, as it does us all.

My trance was broken when the check arrived. I opened my wallet and offered the Wilco card. Mary our favorite server, smiled took the card and returned with an embarrassed look on her face. "Mr. Terrill, the card has been refused," in her French intonated English accent.

A look of surprise and then embarrassment flushed across my brow.

"There must be some mistake," I offered.

"I tried three times and it wouldn't go through."

I opened my wallet and offered my rarely used personal American Express card.

Mary, our favorite server, accepted it, went to the desk and returned with the same look on her face telling me there was a problem as my heart sank.

Pasquale came over and offered. "You and your family have been good to us for so many years. Tonight the meal is on us."

"I'll send you the funds. I just don't know what's going on."

Pasquale waved his hands as if to indicate it wasn't necessary. I shook my head in an apologetic way and slowly walked back to the parking lot only to see my Rover being towed.

"My God what's going on?"

I hailed a taxi and went back to the Lighthouse. The tram wasn't working and so I made my way up the stairs as despondency crept into my soul. Sleep did not come!

The bright sun greeted me and I made my way to the funeral home. Uncle Frank's remains were there but the cremation needed to be paid for in advance. We'd always kept cash in the Lighthouse vault and, after dinner and the Rover being towed, I knew there was an issue and so I paid the three thousand dollars needed for a proper cremation with directions and agreements that Uncle Frank's ashes would join Grandma Marie, The Duke and Aunt Julia in Bae Marie, a small inlet between St. Martin and Anguilla where Amy's grandmother would take her mom when she was a little girl.

I made my way back to the Lighthouse only to see a strange car parked in front of the driveway. I asked myself, 'Who would be so inconsiderate as to park there?'

I made my way up the stairs only to find the door open.

"Can I help you?" I asked the two gentlemen standing in my living room.

"Mr. Terrill?"

"Yes."

"We're here to serve eviction papers and escort you off the property."

"What?"

"Yes. The property has been seized, as well as the House on the Hill, the Saint Martin auto dealership and property on Orient Beach."

"What?" I offered incredulously.

"Sir, here are the documents. We know this is an unfortunate surprise and we will work with you to remove your personal belongings but we need to have you vacate the house as soon as possible."

"Let me call my wife, if you don't mind."

I picked up my cellphone and the line was dead. It was my Wilco issue and I realized things had gone terribly wrong. I sat down at the kitchen table, took a deep breath and asked to see the documents. While not a lawyer I could tell the gentlemen had every right to be there and I needed to move out.

I took another deep breath and asked if I could use one of the gentlemen's phones. They nodded in the affirmative and called Wilco Corporate only to have that line dead, as well. I called Wilco Ops to schedule a plane home and it, too, was dead. Jesus!

I had no other credit card and only $800.00 left after paying the funeral home. I asked for one more phone call and contacted Delta Airlines and made arrangements for the next flight from Princess Julianna through Atlanta and back to Milwaukee. I told them I'd pay when I got to the counter. Airfare was $786.00. I needed more cash but there was none.

"Gentlemen, here's what's going on. I just made arrangements for a flight home and need a ride to the airport. I'm willing to trade four bottles of some of the most expensive wine in the world simply for a ride."

The men looked at me and frowned and so I added. "Obviously, something has happened that's affecting my credit cards, as well as ownership of our property here on Saint Martin. All I'm asking is for the dignity of leaving. Is that too much to ask?"

They realized I had a quandary as their position softened and one offered. "Mr. Terrill, we know how generous your family has been to those in need here on Saint Martin. We also have our instructions. You don't need to give us wine for the ride. We'll call a taxi and make certain it's paid for.

I went to the guest bedroom closet and got down the only suitcase we'd ever used simply because we always had our 'St. Martin clothes' as Amy called them. With each drawer, I simply placed a few personal belongings in it. I paused and looked at The Duke's gold Cross pen and wondered if it was mine. I looked at the gentlemen and they nodded in the affirmative. With the little suitcase full I set it on the dining room table and inquired. "Do you mind if I take one last tour before I go?"

"Ok." One of the men agreed, realizing this was a very sad moment in my life, when they saw that my dreams and aspirations were similar to Uncle Frank in terms of existence.

I went up to the tower and looked at the ocean and pondered if I needed to simply follow Uncle Frank and go to Bae Marie.

I wondered what was happening at home.

How's my wife?

How are my kids?

What's going to happen?

I stopped in our bedroom and realized that someone would be sleeping in my bed, not realizing or accepting their world could someday come crashing down.

30B

Finally, I made it down to the main level and offered to show the two gentlemen the control center and provide the code for the vault. They already had it. It came with the seizure, along with everything, except what I was carrying in one small, brown suitcase. They checked to make certain it didn't contain anything that now belonged to them.

"I have one last favor."

"Yes, sir."

"Would you mind calling my daughter in a couple of hours at this number? She can let my wife know my schedule."

"Yes, sir."

"Thank you."

I slowly walked down the steps to the waiting cab and took a silent ride through Marigot to the airport. I went to the economy line and waited my turn to pay. I placed eight one-hundred-dollar bills on the counter and received $14.36 in change. I made my way through security and out to the gate. No seat was assigned until everyone else had boarded and I was given seat 30B…the center seat of the last row in economy.

I boarded the plane, stuffed my bag in the overhead and sat down in a place I'd forgotten existed. Yet, there was congruence that pervaded my nature. We took off and I listened intently to the safety instructions and then, as I peered out on the memories, the man sitting to my left pulled down the shade as if to draw the final curtain on a life once lived. We became airborne and for the next four hours and forty minutes I simply stared at the seat back a few inches in front of me.

I closed my eyes and thought of all that had transpired. I wanted to write a few sentences but had no paper. Instead I began reiterating my thoughts over and over and over until they were seared within my memory for later reiteration that came out as. *"The universe is large to the point of being beyond comprehension. Mankind has evolved taking it from a point of simply being a member of the universe to being its guardian. Along the way humans have fouled, despoiled and profoundly upset the delicate balance that has been in place for millennia. Our progression now sees mankind consuming itself socially and environmentally - changing our culture, changing our society and changing our world - homogenizing it and reducing its scope and luster to a single finite point called 'now'."*

"We must respect all living beings who share this universe with us. We must honor their dignity and ensure their survival. We must lead others and those with the power to change and rearrange the world to the same point of acceptance that we're not alone on this planet or in this universe. We must realize and, more importantly, admit that we're here on an interim basis to share the graces of God and all that He or She has provided.

We must assume that today is our last and make of it what we can for we never know what tomorrow will bring and always, always, always cherish the moments for they, too, are fleeting."

I made it through the Atlanta Hartsfield maze to my gate and got in the Basic Economy line on Delta Flight 7125 to Milwaukee. A sense of relief flowed through my veins when they told me I'd been 'moved up' to 24E. I was still in a center seat and my knees were still against my chest but at least the guy at the window left the shade open.

The fellow next to me was reading a book by someone named Jordan Peterson. He got up to use the bathroom and left the book face-down on his seat. I glanced at the back jacket and read, 'The book's central idea is that suffering is built into the structure of being and although it can be unbearable, people have a choice either to withdraw, which is a suicidal gesture, or to face and transcend it. Living in a world of chaos and order, everyone has 'darkness' that can turn them into the monsters they're capable of being to satisfy their dark impulses in the right situations. Scientific experiments show that perception is adjusted to aims, and it's better to seek meaning than happiness.

My seat mate came back and I pretended not to have noticed his book. I was offered a soft drink for free and beer for $6.00. I took a pass. After wearing $2,000 shoes I'd forgotten the empty feeling of having no money and nowhere to get it. With $4.06 in my pocket, no telephone and no one to call, my next concern became getting to Pine Lake and that had me anxious.

The man sitting on the aisle seat had been writing on an old-fashioned yellow, lined, tablet and I asked if he'd mind giving me a sheet of paper which he reluctantly obliged. I knew I wanted to simply outline of my thoughts on relationships while realizing they were the only thing that really mattered if a person REALLY wanted to have a joyous life. As we were making our final approach over Lake Michigan my thoughts turned to Amy and how she was enduring all that had transpired. I glanced at the Wilco terminal and saw all the planes parked on the tarmac and wondered what it felt like when you're to blame.

I thought of Horatio Alger the 19th-century American author renowned for his rags-to-riches stories featuring impoverished boys who, through hard work, determination, and often a bit of luck, rose to positions of middle-class comfort and respectability. I wondered if Amy and I weren't actually the 21st Century version of the same story in reverse. Asking myself, "how can we comprehend going from everything to nothing?" While pondering what are the consequences and what about tomorrow?

We landed and I made my way down the terminal escalator towards the exit door with my mind hidden in thought about how I was going to get home. I looked up and wondered if my eyes were deceiving me. It really couldn't be, could it? I saw the smile and knew it wasn't a dream. When friendship turns to love and love to brotherhood those in need are magnificent in the glory of those who care.

I looked and a soft smile creased my lips as tears gathered in my eyes. The person who'd always been by my side was there. I walked up to him and simply nodded.

"Little brother, let's go home." My best friend, Rodney, had heard the news about Wilco's default and called our son 'V'. My dear friend simply stopped his world and came to mine. His big hand was placed upon my shoulder as he spiritually carried me back to my reality. We drove to Pine Lake and I was allowed to gather a few personal belongings. I offered my keys to the man who watched my every move. He indicated the locks and security code had already been changed. I looked for the family photos on the fireplace mantle and it was bare. We'd already been removed…wiped clean in the name of commerce.

I took one last look and understood that gone would be all the trappings of wealth… the fancy shoes, fancy clothes and perks we'd come to expect. I entered Amy's study and looked at the almost barren shelves.

A dejected frown crossed my face as I realized that my first gift to Amy, Amelia Earhart's model Lockheed Electra 10E I'd made as a kid, sat austerely alone where it had always been as a reminder of a time so long ago when only tomorrow stood before us without the chains of yesterday.

I took the Lockheed down and carried it with me like a child hugging their most-loved teddy bear and made one last pass through the great room where the professionally decorated Christmas tree sat alone, isolated, abandoned in the corner, a dark, stark reminder of the counterfeit way in which we lived.

I wondered if Wang Huning's hypothesis about America was correct when he wrote that America had traded its soul—the connective tissues of community, tradition and family—for the glory of wealth and power. Strong but weak-spirited, individualistic but lonely, rich but decadent - a paradox headed for disaster.

I turned to Rodney and simply asked, "What now?"

"Well, my friend, thanks to Melia purchasing the condo in Madison and having it in her name, you have a place to live. The structure has been frozen but not the apartments."

"What about the research Foundation?"

"The Foundation is under the control of the government, as well as the rights to Mediglove."

"And the Forest?"

A smile crossed Big Brother's face as he looked at me and said. "The Forest is still ours…yours and mine and will be forever."

Bookends:

Rodney and I headed west towards Madison with me sequestered in the wretched silence of defeat. As the drive progressed I thought back to when Rodney and I met...working at the casino, the cottage, Jeepers Creepers, Amy as the UPS driver, proposing to her in the Capitol rotunda and the glow of memories that started it all that made my life worthwhile. I had a hollow feeling in my heart. All my dreams were shattered. So much work! So many hours! One assumes it will last forever. Poof! It's gone! Yet a strange sense of peace shielded me as I paused and thought about the blood clots and how death really did save my life.

My eyes sought something – anything that would give me a sense of now and, yet, it was all a blur. From my brush with death I'd changed. I know I had! First, I learned that when you fly you need to stand up periodically to prevent blood clots. Second, I learned that a simple PSA blood test can save a man's life. From that day forward I did everything I could to abide by my own prioritized mantra and did so in that order and no other. It hadn't been easy! With each contemplation, deviation and consternation I attempted to see if I could derive another way... some other set of dynamics or different order that would create a greater level of happiness and satisfaction. In the end I always came back to the same series and always in the same sequence realizing that death not only saved my life but gave real meaning to the concept of tomorrow - no longer assumed - no longer taken for granted - allowing me to cherish each today as if it were my last. I remembered glancing at the reflection in the passenger window and observing an old man looking back who readily admitted he's not perfect. I pondered if there's anything that actually is.

My mind wandered as I accepted the treatise that the net sum of the universe is zero and believed it's true for each person...good and bad, happy and sad...resulting in the same consequence... namely an individual with strengths and weaknesses, aspirations and foibles, where the only constant is time... something everybody and everything shares, until there is no more time, except the time to go. Sadly, in America today, our lives, our existence and our legacy is measured in dollars. Not in what we've done. Not in what we've accomplished but in what we've acquired. Yet, they still don't add trailer hitches to the back of Cadillac hearses.

The only sounds within the car were those of the tires humming on the frozen Wisconsin winter road and the incessant wind pressing against our destination. I realized life's like that...cold at times, with wind that makes nothing easy, yet, makes us stronger. Rodney turned on the radio to divert the deafening silence. I glanced at my dearest friend and silently nodded. It was as if divine intervention had come into play as SIMON and Garfunkel's 'Bookends' began. ...*'Time it was, and what a time it was. It was a time of innocence, a time of confidences. Long ago, it must be! I have a photograph! Preserve your memories, they're all that's left you.'*

I closed my eyes and thanked God for what he'd provided...a life, unlike many others, affirming I'd been loved and hated, admired and admonished as a leader and a fool beyond my wildest dreams. Yet, in the end, neither the top of my mountain or its deepest valley mattered. Not the money, perks or material things. Had it not been for the people who gave my life meaning I would have been nothing...done nothing... accomplished nothing. Rodney took his eyes off the road for an instant and glanced at me before his attention returned to the blackness ahead as he simply stated. "You're a great man, Little Spirit. While there are dark clouds on the horizon your sun will rise again."

Rodney's soliloquy entered my heart, compelling me to bathe in the warmth of his compassion. It had been a long, sad day - from the funeral home to Atlanta and then Milwaukee and not knowing how I was going to get home, then Rodney and Pine Lake and, now, the ride to Madison tightly grasping my little plastic plane. How sad to even have to ask someone now in charge if they minded you take your own childhood memories.

I squinted to hide my sorrow as exhaustion overtook me remained ensconced in the obscurity of my grief until Rodney pulled up in front of the condo and, in the softest, quietest, most gentle way, whispered "Amy's waiting for you."

Perhaps, just perhaps, from the darkness of defeat would come the glistening of love that had slowly cooled until, like strangers in the night, we existed but no longer lived.

I got out of the car, shook my dear friend's hand and gave him a hug and made my way towards the door into the condo garage.

Who's Sorry Now:

As I made my way towards the condo elevator I glanced the empty parking slot #805. With no key I buzzed our apartment and the speaker came on. In a voice so soft and so sad I heard a monotone "hello."

"It's me, George."

There was no response, just the rumble of the steel cauldron as it made its way down to meet me. The doors opened and I stepped in. I pressed the button for the eighth floor and watched the doors close taking me slowly up to my new reality.

The condo doors opened and I was back to where it all began 30 years ago. Our daughter, Melia, had remodeled when she lived there and, yet, it was still home. I heard crying in the bedroom and made my way in to see Amy lying on the bed. I touched her shoulder and she simply looked at me with sorrowful eyes that need not say more.

Slowly Amy arose from her supine position such that I could hold her and feel her angst. The powers of regret made her convulse in sadness. "I'm sorry," she whispered.

I stood in silence and allowed the torrent of gloom to trickle down upon her cheeks. For a long moment there was nothing and nothing needed to be said. Gently, I slid my hands to her shoulders and decompressed our bodies such that our eyes could meet and I could peer deep within her soul as I whispered, "It's Ok!"

More tears convoluted as she trembled in disdain.

"It's Ok."

"But..."

"We've been here before and we'll make it again."

"But..."

"Trust me. We'll make it again."

"But I'm...I'm so ashamed."

For the second time in her life my wife was expressing shame. For the second time I simply inquired, "About what?"

"About how you...you've been treated," she offered.

"Treated? I've been treated with dignity. I've been treated with friendship. I've been treated with love and compassion. What else could any man want?"

There was a long pause as Amy wiped her tears and then her nose as a sense of reality regained its momentum. Still holding her, I simply asked, "Are we bankrupt?"

Amy shook her head, "No."

"We're not?" I inquired with more consternation and confusion than before.

"We're...I mean, our assets have been frozen."

"Frozen?"

"Uh...huh!"

"What does that mean?"

"All our assets are frozen. We can't withdraw money from our bank accounts, sell our investments or transfer ownership of property without permission. They've taken our company cars and our phones don't work."

"Does this mean they've liquidated everything?"

"No, George, it means there's been a court order put in place to ensure assets are available if a judgment is passed against us."

I was angry, I was hurt but, above all else, I was incredibly frustrated and confused especially when I learned that we could no longer pay bills, access any income whatsoever or try to maintain any form of lifestyle, let alone, that which we'd enjoyed for so many years.

"What happens when we win?" I asked, assuming this was an error.

Amy had a sorrowful look on her face as she simply shook her head from side-to-side and quietly replied with a profound sense of regret. "With the way things are I don't think that's going to happen."

"How can we afford to live? How can we do anything? This is crazy!" I lamented.

"It's the system, George. What's critical is the Wilco asset freeze and its reconciliation. If we can get this resolved quickly we could restore some of the revenue streams, liquidate some of the unproductive divisions and reduce our overhead. But that's based on the freeze and how long it takes to go through the courts."

I was getting perturbed regarding the freeze. I knew that The Duke ran a clean ship and couldn't understand how all this could be happening as I simply asked. "Why, Amy? Why the freeze?"

Without emotion, Amy frankly stated. "To prevent us from fleeing the country or obscuring assets before the trial."

Now I was both terrified and concerned..."Trial?" I had no idea we were doing anything illegal.

Amy took another deep breath and clinically proclaimed. "Everything is frozen to satisfy judgments against us and prevent us from engaging in further criminal or fraudulent activity."

My heart sank. "Oh, my God!"

Amy looked at me and it was if she was aging in front of my eyes. Gone was the youthful swagger. Gone was the aura of self-confidence that had permeated her since she entered the world of business. Instead was a frightened, insecure, terrified soul who was simply drowning in remorse.

"How do we live?" I asked

Amy shrugged.

"How do we pay for anything?"

Again, Amy's response was one of not having the answer to the most basic questions.

We were in a deep hole and the only thing we seemed to have to our name was a shovel - SHIT!

Acclimation:

It's now September and the life we lead has become one of financial, legal and emotional pressure - always culminating in anxiety and remorse. While our marital life had been cool before it all began, it has reached a point where it appears neither of us have any feelings left for ourselves, for the world and, sadly, for each other.

It's 10:40 AM on a Wednesday. For many, it's 'hump day' half way to the weekend. For me, it's Monday and I've got five straight days, or make that daze, of work ahead of me. I grab my backpack and neatly fold my orange apron. I stop and glance at my name hastily scribbled in magic marker. Sadly, I missed the first 'E' and became "Gorge". My rush! My error! My consequence! Yet, there are days when I feel I'm in a gorge, down deep, unable to see the horizon, wondering if I'll ever see the sun shine again.

My paper sack with a peanut butter and jelly sandwich, apple, bag of Fritos , napkin and two bottles of water are on the kitchen counter. We buy our water at Costco at fifteen cents a bottle versus two-dollars in the machine at work. Every penny counts these days!

I need to walk up Wilson Street to South Hamilton and then to West Doty and downtown Madison, Wisconsin's capitol square outer ring and finally, the bus stop. Monday through Friday, the bus comes at 11:05 and heads out East Washington Avenue. When I was in college the bus went out Williamson Street. With all the apartments on East Washington they changed the route and the bus will make seven stops to the East Towne Mall where I'll get off.

The bus arrives. It's half full. The bus driver has begun to recognize me and gives me a familiar nod. I return a slight smile, scan my pass, reflect his gesture and head towards the back of the bus. I don't like riding sideways. Never have. Never will.

My favorite seat in the corner of the last row on the driver's side, away from opening doors and prying eyes, is open. Today's my lucky day, an empty seat on a city bus...my how my world has changed.

I make my way past strangers who have familiar faces simply because we all seem to have the same schedule and destination. I crawl into the corner and sit looking out the bus window at the world going by.

For months, this has become my 'quiet time', thirty-minutes when I could be introspective. I'm a long way from being a scientist or philosopher, just an ordinary guy who's lived life and wondered why. Along the way, the one thing that has repeatedly struck me is how something once so special, once so exciting, once so unique, through repetition becomes commonplace. I've looked high and low and can't find an explanation anywhere and so I've begun calling it 'The Theory of Acclimation' my social premise that simply states, *'Through repetition, what was once special becomes commonplace. What was once commonplace, through repetition, becomes mundane. And, what was once mundane, through repetition, becomes boring or meaningless.'*

Applicable to many things including homes, cars, jewelry, vacations, intimacy, people and experiences, acclimation affects how and where we live, what we drive, how we dress and even our job, lifestyle, romance and daily existence until we become numb to it all as we seek out new and exciting people, places, events and things to rekindle our spirit and our tomorrow.

With more time than money, I have decided to begin compiling the random thoughts I stored in my computer and go back to my childhood passion which was writing. With my 'theory' floating around in my brain I've decided to write about acclimation - acclimation to wealth and what happens when it no longer has meaning before, one day, it's gone - not gradually, but in an instant, like a flash of light. Poof! And with the 'poof' arrives the darkness of despair, the sagacity of regret and craving for retribution made more difficult simply because of the profundity that comes to have and lose than never have had before.

One would think that enough would be enough. Sadly, our acclimation to wealth created a distorted view of our existence where enough was never enough. How many homes, how many cars, how many pairs of custom shoes is enough? Was it greed, I ask. Was it nothing more than being driven by an obsessive and insatiable desire for more? Regardless of need or consequence, did our acclimation result on us focusing on immediate gratification and accumulation without regard for long-term consideration? Tragically, was it a lack of concern for ethics, fairness, or social responsibility riled with emotions like envy, discontent, and anxiety? Who knows?

While normally associated with things or experiences when you have so much wealth, does wealth's consequence become mundane and physical possessions, exceptional experiences and personal liberties become muted as you reach the point where nothing, and I mean nothing, is special anymore.

I shudder at the thought as I sit on the bus and ruminate audibly ensconced in one of my few remaining luxuries - my noise cancelling headphones that allow acoustic privacy. I simply close my eyes and dream the nightmare we're living will soon be over.

We begin the journey and I feel the vibration of the bus engine beneath me. I plug in my headphones into my used I-phone, scan my music list and hit random play. To my surprise.... Pink Floyd's song 'Money' rambles into my ears. My mind wanders and reflects on bygone days as the song digs deep, penetrating my brain and finally landing in my heart in spots where I thought dreams and fears could no longer hide. The words ricochet....

Money, it's a gas
Grab that cash with both hands and make a stash
New car, caviar, four-star daydream
Think I'll buy me a football team
Money, get away. Get a good job with more pay and take the pain away.
Money, it's a crime Share it fairly but don't take a dime
Break the bank with a smile and add it to your style
A penthouse suite in the sky is calling out your name
Live it up in the fast lane, champagne and endless fame
If you can find a money tree, let me know
Money, get away Get a good job with more pay and take the pain away
Money, it's a crime Share it fairly but don't take a dime
All you need is love But you can't buy that with money, can you?
It's a gas Gotta have it somehow if you wanna keep on breathin'
Money, get away Get a good job with more pay and take the pain away
Money, it's a crime Share it fairly but don't take a dime
Money, it's a hit Don't give me that do-goody good bullshit
I'm in the high-fidelity first class traveling set And I think I need a Lear jet
Money, money, money Must be funny In the rich man's world

Becoming Wealthy:

Seven stops and the bus ride is over depositing me at my new reality. I'm simply a clerk. Nothing more, nothing less. For one who had the honor of a Nobel Prize, who counted dollars in the billions, the fall from grace has been profound.

I make my way across the asphalt desert punctuated by white stripes that denote space and do so with enticing signs blaring at me...come in...come in...bring us your dreams and your money. I make my way in the front door. It's 11:55 and time to punch in, I put on my apron, my happy face and pretend, yes, pretend, all the problems of the world belong to others.

I invest my eight hours for the grand sum of $120.00 before taxes and social security and walk across the now empty parking lot and wait for the bus to take me back to reality. As 'now' slinks back into my mind I pause for a moment and examine the dark vestiges of oneness while staring at the black ink where a golden pond once shimmered before my time. Tonight the bus is full, stuffed with fellow workers going home because the stores have closed due to the fact that someone, somewhere determined its cheaper to have an empty store late at night than keep it open. I'm reluctant to stand, yet, make my way towards the bus's open door.

I pause and ponder. Perhaps I should wait twenty minutes and catch the bus out to Sun Prairie, accepting it will return and bring me back while providing my coveted rear corner seat and more time to contemplate. I have more time than money, yet, I crawl in with the masses and simply stand, my right hand tethered to the plastic strap that keeps me upright within the twists and turns of reality. Veracity creeps in, intercepted by the sound of the motor on the bus humming its monotonous tome.

My left-hand slides to my phone and beg her to play something - anything - to bring me back from my funk. Sadly, it begins to play as tears roil within my soul. It's SIMON and Garfunkel's 'Sounds of Silence' I don't want to listen but can't stop.

Hello darkness, my old friend I've come to talk with you again
Because a vision softly creeping Left its seeds while I was sleeping.
And the vision that was planted in my brain Still remains within the sound of silence
In restless dreams I walked alone Narrow streets of cobblestone 'Neath the halo of a streetlamp I wandered Past buildings tall and white
People hurrying past each other Not a sound to break the spell I saw the signs and I saw the wonders In the colors that they held
In restless dreams I walked alone Narrow streets of cobblestone 'Neath the halo of a streetlamp I wandered Past buildings tall and white
And in the naked light I saw Ten thousand people, maybe more People talking without speaking People hearing without listening
In restless dreams I walked alone Narrow streets of cobblestone 'Neath the halo of a streetlamp I wandered Past buildings tall and white
And touched the sound of silence And felt that it was wrong For the lonely crowd to murmur And the gnashing of teeth to go on and on and on.
Within the Sounds of Silence.

The sordid bell rings notifying the driver a fellow rider has reached their end. My eyes remain affixed on my corner spot and when it opens I make my way back and sit ensconced in the solitude of singularity. Seven total stops and my ride culminates with the State Capitol ablaze in all her glory. We're on the outer ring as it's called, one block off the Square where my day began. I arise from my seat, my eyes blurry from the consequence of reality while pondering all I've been thinking anticipating simply getting off the bus. Wondering if someone, anyone will ever contemplate what I've dug from within my heart and splattered upon my soul. I take a deep breath and vow that my self-ordained homily will serve as my motivation for what follows. I have but one goal...to understand and comprehend how and more important why...why it all happened but then, I guess, that's what's about to transpire.

We reach 'my' stop and I make my way to the bus's open back door. I step down upon the pavement and begin the trek back to the condo. With each step the pressure of the day slowly dissolves until I reach our condo's garage door. I put my key in the lock and it turns. I see all the cars and SUV's nestled in their appropriate spots and observe spot #805 and its vacancy, tacitly reminding me of all we've lost.

I make my way to the elevator and place my key in the slot. I listen to the groan of the elevator as it makes its way down from where it's been perched. It's nearly eleven o'clock and I'm wide awake. The doors open and I step inside to the cornucopia of stale grease, stale food and stale people and turn the key to allow me to press the top button. Slowly the door closes and my journey begins until I come to a gradual stop. The door opens and the condo entry door greets me with a solemn reflection of a time gone by. I insert my key and the door opens as the sounds of silence permeate my ears. I'm home to solitude as I make my way into the kitchen, open the refrigerator and take out a bottle of beer before making my way back to what became our office and, lately, my bedroom.

The primary bedroom door is closed and I assume Amy's asleep. I sit at the computer, turn it on and begin writing what I'd pondered on the bus about what it's like to be rich. Once again, I simply need to write myself to sleep and begin again, not knowing why I need to share my thoughts with myself when there's so little interest anywhere else.

When you're wealthy you focus on your net worth and overall financial health by prioritizing long-term financial security through diversifying your portfolio and minimizing debt to the point you're less reliant on income and more on income-generating assets like investments, businesses or real estate even if you don't actively work. Amy and I believed we had a long-term perspective and plan for our financial future, including retirement and passing our wealth to our children, grandchildren and, if lucky, great grandchildren.

Newton's Third Law of Motion states that for every action, there's an opposite and equal reaction. The same can be said about wealth where the emotional consequences of going from average to extreme wealth can be just as significant as those experiencing a fall from grace.

While the specific emotions experienced will vary from person to person, some common themes emerge. In my life there have been some incredibly positive emotions. The initial acquisition of wealth was a thrilling experience that opened new possibilities and opportunities in a world I really never knew existed. I remember the first time I drove The Duke's Mercedes, that first fancy meal and my first private jet ride. I remember the taste of a $1,000 glass of bourbon and my custom-made shoes. God, they were wonderful.

As life went on the financial worries faded away, replaced by a sense of security, comfort and entitlement. No matter what I always felt a sense of gratitude and appreciation for our good fortune and was motivated to share it with others through the Derrick Williams Foundation. Never one for self-aggrandizement, with the wealth came an increased level of confidence and self-esteem and a sense of self-worth and accomplishment, as well as, empowerment and freedom with greater control over our lives and the ability to pursue our passions.

I'm not going to say it's always been easy. There were days when I felt guilty about our wealth. Then there were the meetings, the God damn meetings, to hear about all the money we had and how much more there was than the year before. Never once did I ever fear losing it. Probably the biggest adjustment was the social aspect. High school and college friends, with whom I'd shared so much, became distant as the accumulating dollars generated walls between us simply because it was difficult to connect with others who can't or won't share your lifestyle.

Once I had the honor of multiple friends, now they're all gone, leading to feelings of isolation and loneliness. I thought it was just me until I studied and learned I certainly was not alone, just experiencing it at a young age due to my ability to financially sustain our family.

What it means to be a man in the 21st century is to live in a time of social changes and challenges — from medical issues to social connections to divorce rates — that deeply affect life. Men like me and older can experience a kind of psychic bifurcation. We came of age amid the social upheavals of the 1960s and 1970s but our formative years were deeply planted in the traditional, patriarchal world of suburbs, segregation and sexual stereotyping.

As we've aged our roles in the family and society have become less obvious. Those who retire no longer have jobs to define themselves .For many their health begins to deteriorate as relationships outside the home fray and their position in the family erodes as wives and grown children assume greater responsibilities.

Sadly, we're basically stuck in the 1950s model of masculinity who spent our childhood with 'Leave It To Beaver' and 'Father Knows Best' as role models. Now we're retired or under-utilized and are seeing the social consequence of women's lib and the major social change of their employment going from single digits in the 1950s to 50% of the labor force today while, for many of us, our social world has simply stood still.

I'm trying really hard to shed my expectations of what it means to be a man that I learned when we were children. I spent 30 years in the working world and came to think of my job and myself as one-in-the-same. But due to retirement or the immediate repositioning of one's financial position, like me, resulted in the reality I was no longer one of these. On a good day I'm the retired executive who won a Nobel Peace Prize. On a bad day I feel like a nobody wearing an orange apron, riding a city bus, hoping and praying it will all go away.

With no social or family network I've become singular, immersed in the profound sense of guilt that has come from the realization that my wealth didn't come from something I did but from someone I married, which has haunted me from day one.

In speaking with a priest I met when I had my episode with blood clots, Father Pat allowed me to bare my soul. In so doing I'll never forget that he assured me that being wealthy was all right. He noted that individuals with a strong sense of self-worth and healthy coping mechanisms are better equipped to handle the emotional challenges of wealth where my establishment of the Foundation led him to conclude that I had a strong sense of self-worth. Until a few months ago I'd maintained that strong sense. Sadly...no make that tragically...that has all been taken away which is how and where what I now write all begins.

In the end, it's the materialism that drives our economy and our society simply the need for more and more and more. Unfortunately materialism morphs into greed because it creates a never-ending cycle of wanting. You buy something new, it brings temporary satisfaction but then you see something else you want even more. Greed fuels this cycle by making you constantly dissatisfied and pushing you to acquire more.

And so, I think I have it...a changing definition of the concept of success and how that definition affects, controls and dissipates roles as parents, teachers and mentors, as well as the mental self, by controlling our own self-concept.

Yet, in order to succeed a definition must be developed if I'm to refine not only what I am but who I am, as well. From these self-concepts I believe I need to develop a plan to ensure the remainder of my life's journey and that of our children such that it is wrought with pleasure, joy and satisfaction. If I can achieve this my final destination will be blessed with a profound sense of fulfillment called joy, that includes, or results, in the creation and nurturing not only the mental self but my spiritual self, as well.

It's almost three in the morning. Time to try and get some sleep. I look at the icons upon the screen and wonder if I'm creating thoughts for someone else or simply me. Time will tell. I turn off the computer and the lights and crawl into bed. I know that when I awaken the house will be empty in so many ways. Amy will be gone. And so it is! And so it is!

The Rich:

Another round trip to nowhere and then my day ends as the bus deposits me while my mind vacates my employ and settles into my reality. I take my left-right, left-right steps down Hamilton Street to Wilson and near our condo, oblivious to my motion, deep in thought. If our daughter Melia hadn't changed the condo ownership, I don't know where Amy and I would be living I ponder where I was physically, mentally, emotionally and financially and how it all had changed. We had it all! I mean everything and yet, in the end, we really had nothing! Nothing at all! I pause at the corner to allow someone in a hurry to blow by me in their car as if I was nothing more than an insignificant marker on their racetrack of life.

I take a deep breath unable to take yet another step as I start to examine what makes a rich person dissatisfied. What is it that makes them continue on? I look to my left and then my right and finally cross Wilson Street. I'm nearly home and stop to watch a car enter our underground parking garage. It's a neighbor who's a stranger but then aren't we all?

I think about our kids and mentally categorize them concerning wealth. For our daughter Melia, money never seems to be the case. In fact, she's just the opposite. If it were the sixties, she'd probably would have rebelled and become a hippie. It's not and she didn't. It's our boys....Derrick and George V, better known as "V" that the characteristics - high levels of dopamine and low levels of serotonin that create the insatiable hunger that are so prevalent, so preponderant and so socially debilitating that I look at my own sons as strangers... individuals who are a part of me and yet, so different - so distant - so, so strange.

I can't totally fault genetics. Not when I look back at how they were raised in a materialistic household and taught to value money and status above all else. I thought we were alone and yet it's America - a culture built on one thing - money. A society more materialistic that has established a value on wealth and status more than any other society on earth. It's no wonder why other's despise us, don't understand us, and scorn the role the almighty dollar plays in our daily lives. Beyond the basics and our culture we live in a competitive society where our children...make that all children, feel pressured to acquire more and more in order to keep up with their peers.

Finally, it's our family history where the pinnacle of wealth was equated to the pinnacle of power which caused stress in our kids and, quite honestly, in Amy and me, to the point we all made impulsive decisions and took risks simply to say on top - financially, socially, emotionally or at least, that's what we thought.

I look at where we're at as a country, society and family and realize there's no one answer. It's a complex behavior influenced by a variety of factors where there is no single cause, and why it's likely that different people develop greedy tendencies for different reasons yet the net result is that our family is in the position it is and the pain we are suffering because of one thing...greed.

For many of the rich, money is just how they keep score. It's the rush they get when they're risking something... everything... that keeps them aspiring to get bigger and bigger and bigger regardless of who or what they affect, destroy and injure along the way.

Their net worth is their way of measuring their achievement, orientation and drive for success that involves setting specific, measurable, achievable, relevant, and time-bound goals and working towards them with time-warping dedication and perseverance. This may be driven by a desire to maintain their wealth, prove their capabilities, or achieve social recognition. Wealth can afford these individuals a greater sense of control over their lives that can manifest itself in a desire to control their environment, relationships, and even their own destiny.

Sadly, as Newton so accurately states, there's the downside which seems to evolve into two key areas, namely, reduced empathy and altruism, where some studies suggest that wealthier individuals may have lower levels of empathy and compassion for others. This could be due to their limited exposure to hardship and suffering or could be because of their focus on their own individual needs and goals. They may also tend to be altruistic where they may be less likely to engage in spontaneous acts of kindness or help those in need on a personal level.

As I've seen, the rich frequently develop a sense of entitlement, believing they deserve more than others due to their success. This can lead to a lack of respect for others and a disregard for social norms and subsequently they form social circles primarily with other wealthy individuals like themselves that leads to a sense of social distance from those who are less fortunate, thereby, exacerbating the differences they have in perspective and understanding of others.

When it reaches the ultimate pinnacle, the rich move beyond their social strata and use money and its subsequent political power as a lever to adjust the system in their favor in terms of not only the financial aspect but what they sincerely think and feel is what's best for them legally, socially, and ethically as well.

In so doing the thought of the Renaissance depiction of the blindfolded Roman goddess Justitia, becomes no longer fitting simply because the concept of uniform justice is simply a facade. In one hand, Justitia holds a balance or scales, representing the weighing of evidence and arguments on both sides of a legal case where the scales being level symbolize a fair and impartial judgment, that is, until the wealthy hire expensive lawyers who have both the ability and influences to unbalance the laws in their favor. In her other hand, Justitia often holds a double-edged sword to signify the power to enforce justice and carry out the punishment deemed necessary where, once again, money affects those who rule and does so without concern or consequence to and for, those who naively believe in the Constitution's Fourteenth Amendment, which guarantees "equal protection of the laws" to all citizens.

Humpty Dumpty:

Humpty Dumpty sat on a wall.
Humpty Dumpty had a great fall.
All the King's horses and all the King's men
Couldn't put Humpty together again.

Day three of my work week comes and is about to go. While others are celebrating the weekend, I'm realizing the two busiest days of the retail week are in front of me. My ride home has become commonplace to the point I have no recollection as has my walk from the bus stop to the condo. I stand in the condo garage wondering how I really got here. Instead of taking my key and pressing number eight, the top floor with a button less worn simply reminds me of those below who don't share a floor or a life with us in so many ways.

I stand, with key in hand, looking at the closed beige elevator doors covered with scrapes and bruises from too many people in a hurry to get in or out, indifferent to the majestic simplicity of a simple painted elevator door. It's then I conclude that the true meaning of Humpty Dumpty is a satirical commentary on the dangers of ambition, where his fall symbolizes the collapse of wealth, prestige and social position. As such I, too, seem to be Humpty Dumpty, having gone through the evolution from comfortable - to wealthy - to rich - to a walking, talking, crying example of what it's like to crash into pieces where the psychological consequences have been both multifaceted and devastating.

Losing our wealth made me feel like I lost a part of myself that triggered a grieving process similar to the loss of my dad. Feelings of sadness, anger, denial, and bargaining all have been wrapped up in a profound sense of remorse where I no longer know who I am. For over thirty years I had an identity and then it was lost as our wealth and possessions were deeply tied to my self-concept leaving me feeling lost, uncertain, and without a clear sense of who I am, resulting in levels of depression and anxiety that have led to significant levels of melancholy, anxiety, and even suicidal ideation.

Every day I fight. I fight for the right to be me. I vow I will not allow myself to succumb to Post-Traumatic Stress Disorder. I will not permit flashbacks, nightmares, and hyper-vigilance. As I look in the mirror I'm ashamed and aware of my new humiliation knowing that, in America, poverty is often stigmatized thereby further compounding the psychological impact I now must bear. The idea that five days a week I must put on an orange apron with my misspelled name written in magic marker, makes me cringe, as I wonder how and why it all has happened.

Next has been my wife Amy and my relationship strain where the financial anxiety and emotional distress caused by our financial demise has put significant tension on our relationship. Daily I see it. Daily I feel it. Daily it scares me, as any small instance leads to conflict while days turn into weeks and weeks into months and the distance between us grows greater and the feeling we once shared becomes weaker and weaker and weaker to the point my only hope is that it doesn't result in divorce.

I ride up in the elevator and listen an instrumental rendition of Fleetwood Mac and "Landslide". My mind pauses as I relish the words and mentally follow along.

I took my love, I took it down
I climbed a mountain and I turned around
And I saw my reflection in the snow-covered hills
Till the landslide brought me down
Oh, mirror in the sky, what is love?
Can the child within my heart rise above?
Can I sail through the changing ocean tides?
Can I handle the seasons of my life?

Well, I've been afraid of changing
'Cause I've built my life around you
But time makes you bolder, even children get older
And I'm getting older too
I see the fire in your eyes
And the way the truth just flies around you
Like leaves on the wind, you take it all in
And dance with the devils in your head
Oh, mirror in the sky, what is love?
Can the child within my heart rise above?
Can I sail through the changing ocean tides?
Can I handle the seasons of my life?
Well, I've been afraid of changing
'Cause I've built my life around you
But time makes you bolder, even children get older
And I'm getting older too
I've been afraid of letting go
But I can't hold on forever
You've got to let me go, baby
I can't keep holding onto you
And if you see my reflection in the snow-covered hills
Well, the landslide will bring it down

The elevator doors have opened and closed three times and I still can't get out. The song has me mesmerized and frozen my thought and emotion. I wipe the tears from my eyes and began again contemplating, pontificating, rationalizing, trying to understand simply why. Why so much has changed! Why so much has happened! Why dreams have become nightmares and tomorrow is simply an illusion replaced by only one goal and that's to make it through another day.

I pull the brass key from my pocket once again and take a look at it. No longer bright and shiny, dulled by time and years, a token of time gone by that has lost its luster as it appears life has, too. Gone is the laughter and the levity as I admit to myself that the most critical of all aspects of our financial demise are the changes in personality and behavior where both Amy and I have become more withdrawn, irritable and impulsive as we cope with the psychological consequence of our situation. I cannot remember what it sounds like when my wife laughs. I cannot remember the last time she smiled. I cannot remember when there was joy in her heart.

All I can see is what I feel and that's regret, remorse, sadness and sorrow. What once was, is no more, where the loss of hope and motivation has permeated our minds, erasing any optimism and replacing it with feelings of powerlessness and hopelessness. Feelings which have eroded life by simply making it overwhelming, thereby leading to today's lack of motivation and impetus making it difficult to dream or construct any plans regarding the future beginning with today.

Finally, I have the courage to stick the key in our lock. The door opens and I'm in our entryway. I pause to place my key in the small dish that has served as its reservoir since God knows when. My head rises and I look deeply in the mirror. I see an old man peering back. No longer thinking about tomorrow or even today, only relishing yesterday.

I ponder and wonder not about me but about Amy. Will our financial turmoil be a detriment to her health? Will her leukemia rear its ugly head and seep the marrow from her soul? She was blessed with a portfolio of T-cells harvested and implanted every year like a fountain of youth until her garnered T-cells were gone and the fountain ran dry. I fear that the stress of poverty will negatively impact her physical health. I sense an increased risk of chronic diseases, immune system dysfunction and unhealthy coping mechanisms that have been at bay for so long making their way deep within her until she can no longer function. I can handle my own demise. However, each night I pray it won't happen to Amy as I whisper, *"Lord God, please save my wife from the sorrow we now share."*

In the end, whether you have millions, billions or very few, the real goal is simply to be happy. But what does happy mean? Is it an elusive and much-desired state? Is it a multifaceted concept that's been pondered by philosophers, psychologists, and everyday folks alike for centuries? There's no single, universally agreed-upon definition but there are some perspectives that seem to be the ultimate goals we must strive for.

It's nearly eleven and Amy is asleep in her bed. My eyes are wide and I make it to my room, turn on my computer - my link to the outside world and my warped reality. I need to find an answer to my deepest thought, "what is happiness?"

I seek the truth and find what I'm looking for. *"In its most basic form, happiness refers to positive emotions like joy, contentment, satisfaction and fulfillment which can be fleeting moments triggered by pleasant experiences or a more enduring sense of well-being."*

My mind wanders back, back, back to the day Amy and I were married and then skips forward to the day the kids were born and finally, the day we received the Nobel Peace Prize. Those were some of the happiest moments of my life and finally to the day everything changed.

My internal peace lasts but a fleeting moment as I realize there's also the subjective sense of well-being that encompasses how I evaluate my life overall. To be on the top of a mountain and then crash into the sea takes one's level of satisfaction and slams it into a wall, shattering all that was, replacing it with what would have, should have and could have been that now challenges my life's satisfaction, meaning, and purpose.

I turn off the computer and head for bed, too tired to do anything but lie down in a devastated pile of nostalgia and regret as my psychological well-being is shattered, battered and bruised simply because what once was, is no more.

I try to sleep. Please let me sleep! Instead there's a war raging between my heart and mind as my hedonic well-being has been challenged and defeated, leaving me broken of body and spirit, unable to rise up and strike back, nothing more than a withered remnant of what had been. I now know, realize and recognize that ultimately, what constitutes 'happiness' is unique and subjective influenced by my personal values, experiences, and circumstances. Sadly, today I live in a singular world devoid of strong social connections where I no longer engage in activities that feel purposeful and contribute to something larger than myself.

Fortunately, so far, I believe I have my physical health and well-being simply because I exercise and try to have healthy eating habits, orchestrated by my primary comprehension that, to live life to the fullest, means to 'stop and smell the roses.'

While they've taken away my wealth, power and authority, they can't take away my sense of self that I diligently protect through a series of relaxation and sensory exercises to keep me grounded and away from the emotional abyss of self-depredation that results in allowing me to practice gratitude for what I have, while living in the present moment that enhances my appreciation for life's joys. I know and accept that happiness is transitory and therefore a journey, not a destination and is about cultivating a positive outlook, embracing life's ups and downs, and living in accordance with my values.

I lie in my bed staring at the ceiling. I listen to the soft hum of the refrigerator where my self-soliloquy requires I admit to myself and accept that things have changed including me, where the element that has changed the most is my dignity and the fact I no longer feel in command. Instead, I look at life from a different perspective...almost helpless, like being pulled down a river by life's current, incapable of reaching the safety of permanence that once was taken for granted.

I was once told that the person who has the most power is the one who has the least needs. The reverse would then be, the one with the least power is the one with the most needs and that's me...financially, socially, and emotionally. How did we get here? How did this all happen? This is what the story I'm about to divulge is all about. It's not pretty and God only knows if there will be a happy ending. Yet, it must be written, not so much for me but for those who are taking the time to read it so that they have a perspective regarding what they think is so grand... money, power, prestige! Let me proclaim! In the end, all that matters is to be happy!

We all aspire to be totally 'free' and with that liberty would come our perceived happiness but the bitter truth is we simply are not and never will be. We are and will always be limited on every side...by government, corporate giants, physical and mental frailties, genetic shortcomings, even the boundaries of time and space and the burdens of our sins and pending demise, all of which bound us to here and now...today and not tomorrow.

Regardless of our wealth, or lack of, we are perhaps, particularly aware that we are not free to disconnect from the technocratic rulers of the air who open electronic doors that allow us to escape from here and now, both good and bad, joyous and tragic as we wallow in the mire of life and death of others so far, far away. My eyes close and I enter the world of dreams closer to death than at any other time. Will I awaken in the morning? Only God knows. Sleep comes and the long day turns into darkness. Sleep, glorious sleep. I welcome you as you authorize me to forget reality and thank you for the respite from my oblivion.

Wheels:

The wheels of the legal world don't turn as fast as those who need answers want them to. Instead of decisions in days or even weeks, it's now June and our world has changed dramatically as the past six months have been a living hell. From penthouse to outhouse sounds like an old adage but that's what happened. If it weren't for our daughter Melia's independence concerning disassociating herself physically, socially and financially from Wilco by putting her funds in a separate trust and purchasing our condo in Madison, we literally would have been out on the street. Instead Melia and her family are secure while Amy and I are back where it all began, 231 West Wilson in the same condo her dad purchased when she was going through leukemia treatment 30 years ago.

Take it from me, to have it and then lose it is much more painful than never having it at all. Besides all the baubles, the next thing to go is the kiss-ass respect. No more $2,000 pairs of shoes! No more luxury yacht! No more yes sir, no sir! All of a sudden you're just another walking face in the crowd of common folks where perks don't exist and smiles are real.

I guess I went through all the phases. First it was the shock, disbelief and coming to terms with the fact that we were no longer wealthy and needed to make significant changes to our lifestyle. It was also my loss of identity that hurt. It was as if I lost a part of myself that led to a feeling of shame, guilt, and embarrassment. Why had I been so foolish? Why had I been so ambivalent and assuming? Over and over, I asked myself 'why' until I realized that, when you lose everything, it's similar to when my dad died. I went through the same stages of denial, anger, bargaining, depression and finally acceptance.

I'd never been the breadwinner. I'd relied on Amy for that. Now, what could I do? I hadn't really had a job in 30 years and had no working experience and certainly no marketable skills. Elderly journalists who hadn't written a printed word in over thirty years weren't high on the list of employment agencies needed projects.

For the first time since college, there's financial stress that results in anxiety. Perhaps Amy believes I'm blaming her! Perhaps, when you've never even counted hundreds, to all of sudden having to count pennies simply because you're struggling to make ends meet, worrying about paying bills, providing for each other, the stress and anxiety can begin to take a toll on your physical and mental health as well as your relationship. Gone was the sense of partnership, replaced by the silence of depression and sense of hopelessness to the point our partnership was beginning to unravel as Amy blamed me and I blamed her for the slightest of things.

A few months ago, Amy elected to sleep in a separate bedroom. She said it was because I got home from work so late. The chill in the air had frozen what little joy was left and created a slippery slope of sadness neither of us wanted to endure. As each day began with the stark closing of the condo door I would be enveloped in solitude before leaving for work. I vowed to share what all transpired that had taken Amy and me from the mountain peak of prosperity to the deepest valley of despair and, along the way shattered what had been of our marriage. In so doing, I realized that life is like writing a book. Each day represents one more page that's finally amalgamated into chapters...youth, young adulthood, adulthood, maturity and finally the last years. Sadly, for some, the book is thin due to malady or calamity. For others it's long and filled with joy and sorrow, laughter and love until that day when they, too, join those who've already departed.

When there isn't work, I think the saddest thing is waking up and, as reality makes its way into your brain, realizing you have nothing to do and no money to do it if you wanted to. You can only watch so much TV and go for so many walks until the depression sets in and beneath it the thoughts that perhaps, I, too, should join Uncle Frank and simply check out, only to realize that would be the chicken shit way of taking care of things.

As the days evolved into weeks and then into months, Amy and I grew further apart. The cold stares! The foreboding silence! The last flickers of love seemed to be diminishing as tears stopped flowing replaced by the angst that comes from living with a stranger. I think the most tragic thing was the distance between us and our kids. Guilt with Melia, having to live in her condo, unable to pay rent. Awe of "V" whose life was so hectic making the world a better place, he had little time for us. Admonishment for our son Derrick. Always distant, now to the point he'd literally walked out of our lives, too busy trying to become more important to have time for the two people who still loved him, nurtured him and wanted nothing more than to support him in any way. Perhaps it was his feeling of guilt for he's the one who made the decisions that brought our company and so many people's lives down.

As the bills piled up and the silence deafening, I wondered who would crack first. My concern was Amy. Her last set of 'T-Cell' transplants had been given over a year ago and we both knew that the ticking time bomb within her body could mean her death deferment could be over. We always had the assurances that one more treatment would mean one more year without fear. Now there were no T-cells left and she was on her own. Each day I saw a small change as the wrinkles that had never been appeared. I watched as her once-firm, youthful body began to soften. As she aged before my eyes her skin appeared thinner, looser, and more wrinkled. Her hair was growing more slowly and had become thinner. While it had been a long time since I'd seen them up close, her breasts appeared to lose some of their fullness and firmness while her chin and then around the eyes and then her waist all appeared fuller than before. The only question was, "Was it the T-cells or the pressure causing it?"

On my days off, I would go for my walk simply to have something to do. The biggest challenge would be which direction. East and up around the square. South along John Nolen Drive or west down Wilson to Bedford over to West Washington Avenue and back to Broom Street before stopping at the mailbox and reluctantly seeing who was demanding this, threatening that, challenging life, while slapping reality across my face. Who we thought were friends no longer recognized us. Our family is in shambles, and we're living from hand-to-mouth trying to get by on the income I earn working as a clerk at Home Depot while Amy spends her time using her education as a lawyer fighting the countless lawsuits against the company and us simply because we can't afford anyone else.

I guess I can claim innocence or ignorance but neither one of them gets me anywhere. Unbeknownst to me, before that December day, my wife had used personal assets as collateral to acquire and then guarantee the company. In a heartbeat, Wilco Corporation, the jets, the homes in France, St. Martin and Pine Lake, as well as our car dealerships and finally our investment portfolio, were frozen and with it, so was our way of life.

If you've never been there and I hope and pray you have not, to have your assets frozen means you can't access or dispose of them without permission from a court or government agency including your bank accounts, investments, property, and other valuables. What was the biggest shock to me, was the fact that asset freezing is a legal process typically used in criminal or civil cases or to enforce sanctions against individuals. For the government and creditors, it's just another case where the litigants get up in the morning and go to work. What gets done, gets done. For them, there's going to be a paycheck and money once or twice each month. Money to pay the utilities. Money to buy food. Money - money - money for them to keep on living but not us.

When your assets are frozen, there's nothing. No money! No support and therefore no freedom. American society isn't a social organization, it's a big business that fuels itself with cash and when your cash is frozen so are your opportunities. For many it's the end of the financial line. Financial problems are a contributing factor in seven percent of all suicides in the United States making it the fourth most common contributing factor, after relationships, mental and physical health problems.

When you've had everything and now nothing the impact is profoundly greater than those who have always been there. Sadly, in America thirty-eight percent of American families have financial issues such as affording basic necessities including food, housing, and healthcare, compounded by paying off debt such as student loans and credit cards while saving for retirement and covering unexpected expenses, such as medical bills or car repairs. These issues can have a serious impact on a families' physical and mental health and lead to stress, anxiety, and depression that can lead to divorce or homelessness.

For Amy and me, take your pick....food, we get by with the basics where casseroles have become a main dish. Housing exists only because our daughter Melia owns the condo. Healthcare? Amy's T-cell transplants cost $20,000 per session and we had to sell our jewelry to pay for her last treatment. We have no credit cards because we have no credit and all our retirement ideas are locked up, waiting for someone somewhere to put us on the docket as we attempt to unfreeze what we have or at least think we still have to our name.

As for our mental health...do tremblers count? Do arguments over anything and everything count? Do nights sleeping in different beds count? Stress has a way of stripping away dignity and leaving emotions raw, waiting for the next assault that will remind us both that we are in jeopardy.

I used to savor speed simply to save time. I now savor anything that will use up all the time I've got. Thank God for the internet as it's helped me learn so much about so many things and I guess that's where I need to go next in my story I simply call "Greed".

The Box:

It was after my western walk one day that I stopped and gathered the mail in our mailbox with all the threats, challenges and warnings. Nestled within the thick pile was a letter with the logo and return address of Farmers Savings Bank, 305 Doty St. Mineral Point, WI 53565. I thought 'what now?" As I slid open the envelope I found a typed note indicating the rent on our safety deposit box was due and needed to be paid. As life had thrown so many curves, one thing I'd never considered was that box. My mind was a tither. I had no idea what was there except the original copy of "Waldwick" and wondered if I should take the Lamers Bus and clean out what remained of our family, one last time.

My days off at Home Depot were Monday and Tuesday and so plans were made to take the bus down to Dodgeville and then UBER it the seven miles to Mineral Point, go to the bank, then UBER back to Dodgeville and head home. I would have loved to go to the Forest, hoping it would help me get my emotional balance but, like everything else in life, there was too little time between the bus going to Dodgeville and the one heading back to Madison to make the visit.

I had chatty Kathy as my driver from Dodgeville and the seven miles seemed to take forever until we reached the front of the Old Royal Hotel on High Street, where I paid the lady in cash, got out just as a gentle summer breeze stroked my face and entered my soul. God, it was good to be home! I walked up High Street as memories flooded my mind. I paused long enough to admire my old friend Pointer the zinc dog still standing strong, looking down High Street and then made my way to Wisconsin Street before turning right, walking past the post office and then the block to Doty Street before entering the bank. In a town where any building that isn't at least 120 years old is considered new, the contemporary look of the bank with the drive-through seemed a little out of place.

I walked in the front door as eyes quickly looked my way. In a time of electronic banking, there weren't as many folks making deposits and withdrawals as I remembered. I made my way to the front counter and looked at the clerk.

"May I help you?" the young girl inquired in an almost suspicious way as she could observe the front parking lot and there wasn't any car parked there and I was definitely a stranger to her.

"I need to open my safety deposit box," I quietly offered.

"Do you have the key?" the young girl inquired.

Sadly, I shook my head 'no'.

"Sir, you need the key, to get into the box."

With that I opened the letter sent to me and offered it to her before adding. "I'm sorry, we've had some personal issues and I don't have the key."

With a perplexed look on her face the young clerk offered. "Please stay here," as she excused herself and went to an office with a glass wall looking out into the lobby with my letter in hand.

I watched as a conversation took place and then saw the lady behind the deck stand and come out.

"George? George Terrill?"

I nodded in the affirmative.

"George, it's Ann Mitchell. We went to school together."

I smiled an embarrassed smile and replied, "Sorry Ann, it's been a long time."

I don't know who had aged more, her or me and yet, the eyes gave it away. It seems they always do. Faces change as does hair and posture but the eyes remain the same.

"You need to get into your safety deposit box?"

"Yes, please."

"I know this will sound a bit ridiculous but do you have any identification on you? It's the law and bank policy."

"Sure." I said with a smile as I opened my wallet and offered my driver's license.

Ann handed it back and instructed me to follow her. Down the steps we went into a holding room where she opened an old three-ring binder and said to herself "Terrill... Terrill... Terrill" as she flipped through the pages. "Let see, George and Thomas Terrill. Here we go. Box 206."

Next, Ann opened a large filing cabinet and began thumbing through the signature cards as she once again spoke to herself...199, 200, 201, 202, 203, 204, 205...206"

Pulling out the card Ann got a strange look on her face and offered. "George no one has signed this card in nearly 30 years."

"I know. It's been a while."

"Can you please sign here? I need to make a signature match."

I signed and Ann smiled as she added. "Well, we've got a match. Now I've got to go to the vault and get another key. Please stay here."

For the next five minutes I stood listening to nothing, looking at nothing, thinking of nothing except wondering what in hell was taking so long until Ann reappeared and apologized. "Sorry! With customer traffic as low as it is, we're short-handed and I had to answer a couple of questions.

"No problem." I offered as we made our way to box 206 located on the bottom row in the corner.

Ann knelt down and inserted the two keys and opened the door. Looking up, she instructed. "Please remove your box and you can go into one of the privacy rooms and when you're done call up and I'll come down and lock it up for you."

I knelt down, pulled out the long box and made my way to the Privacy Room as Ann excused herself and went back upstairs.

As I sat at the small desk and faced the wall, I slid open the small metal clasp and opened the long top. On top were a bunch of papers. Below was the original copy of Waldwick. Chills went through my body. I was in touch with my great, great, grandfather and it was his thoughts that were moving through my body and into my soul.

Quickly, I spread the envelopes out and began looking at the contents. First, was my birth certificate. Next, came my Social Security card and then my will. Finally, I opened a thick envelope with no label to find Amy and my pre-nuptial agreement. A slight smile pursed my lips as I thought back to a time so long ago and how ridiculous it all seemed for me to require Amy to agree that what was hers before we got married remained hers and what little I had was mine.

I shook my head as if reading sick humor. "Nothing to nothing" I thought but one hell of a ride.

I opened my small leather satchel and stuck the documents inside not knowing if I'd ever be back to store anything again. I didn't know what to do with the copy of 'Waldwick'. It was nearly 200 years old. The historical society? The Mineral Point library? I simply shrugged and decided I needed to bring it home as I carefully slid it in my satchel, stood and called for Ann to come down again.

As Ann returned, I told her that we wouldn't be needing the box anymore. What I was tacitly saying is that I actually couldn't afford it.

The Red Rooster:

It was just after noon and the Dodgeville bus didn't leave for Madison for three hours. I made my way back to High Street and then walked down the hill called Henry Street and glanced across Jerusalem Park at my grandma's old house on South Street.

Like everything else in life, it, too, had changed. When grandma lived there, the house was white and had a big front porch with twenty-three stairs to the sidewalk below. The porch was gone, as were the stairs, the house was gold colored aluminum siding and the only thing preserved were my memories. Once again, I thought of SIMON and Garfunkel's song..."*a time of innocence, a time of confidences*".

I was tempted to walk west to Graceland Cemetery and visit mom and dad but didn't think I could handle it. Instead I headed east on Fountain past Hank and Kat's old house to Chestnut Hill and climbed up to the corner with High Street and the entrance to the Red Rooster Restaurant. It had been a long time since I'd had home-made Pasty. I entered through the door and it was like going back in time. The same rooster wallpaper. The same counter with the old fashion twirling stools that Tommie and I used to spin on. The same sweet smells of home wafting through the entire place as if nothing had changed in over 50 years.

As was always the case, the place was busy. Sadly, being gone for 30 years meant no friends, only strangers. I guess it was Ok, simply because I was certain folks in town knew there was trouble brewing and I really didn't want to talk about my business.

I took a seat at the counter in the corner next to the soft drink dispenser and in front of my Uncle Hank's picture. Seems as though even after a couple generations, he and his wife Kat were still revered for all they'd done for our little town.

Debbie, the waitress, came over with a smile on her face and offered. "How you doin' George?"

"Not bad." I lied.

"How's that wife of yours?"

"Not bad." I lied again.

"Pasty?"

"Yup."

"Anything else? Got some home-made lemon meringue pie. Just came out of the oven."

I smiled. Debbie knew she had me, as I nodded in the affirmative.

"Anything to drink?"

"Got any home-made lemonade?"

"For you George, of course."

I sat and watched the others going through life. A little smile here. A little frown there. Every now and then even a chuckle. Life's great when it's so simple you can even smile. Soon, the counter was full except for the seat next to me as I'd placed my satchel there simply to provide a little distance between me and reality.

As I sat there waiting for my lunch, Tank Kennison walked in. Now, having the nickname 'Tank' certainly stood out. Tank's birth name was Thomas Anthony Kennison III as he was named after his dad and grandpa. With so many Toms running around and Tank being somewhat large as a little kid, everyone and I mean everyone in town, called him Tank. I guess when you're a lawyer, it's good to have a unique name and so it was, a big guy with a big heart and a loud laugh who could figure out almost anything when it came to the law. Tank had been the local lawyer since God knows when and knew everyone in town's business. He was a relatively large man with ruddy red cheeks and an always-present smile.

As he closed the Rooster's front door, he paused and checked the counter and tables to realize the only seat in the house was the one next to me. I picked up my satchel and placed it on the floor to my left as he sauntered towards me.

"Hello, George. Didn't expect to see you in town."

I shyly nodded and replied. "I had a little business to attend to and needed some home cooking."

"Heard you were in the bank."

"Word travels fast."

"Well, George, it's a small town and I was there right after you. Had some business with Ann and she mentioned you'd been in."

"Yup! Needed to get my social security card out of the safety deposit box."

"Ann said you closed out the box."

"Yup. We don't get down this way much anymore."

"Sorry to hear about all the issues going on with your family."

Now I was getting a little perturbed. The one bad thing about a small town is when you fart, everyone in town can smell it as I replied. "Well, shit happens."

"How about the farm?"

"I don't know, why?"

"Well, if you remember I represented your brother for the closing and unless I'm mistaken you paid for his share out of your own money and not the company, didn't you?"

I'd completely forgotten, as I nodded in the affirmative.

"If I also remember correctly, didn't I fill out your pre-nuptial agreement?"

Again I nodded in agreement and offered. "Yup, I've got it here in my satchel."

"If it's my standard agreement, which I think it is, the farm is yours and your brother's and not part of the corporation."

A glimmer of hope rushed through every vein in my body.

"Do you have the agreement with you?"

Once again, I nodded in the affirmative.

"Want me to take a look at it?"

Another nod as I reached down, opened the satchel and handed Tank the pre-nuptial.

"My! I don't know who wrote this but he sure was a smart lawyer." Tank offered with a smile. "Based on what I read here, the farm and its operations were freestanding and not part of your corporation unless you sold it to your company...Wilco, wasn't it?"

Another nod, affirming that the farm was never part of the corporation but still concerned that, in my absence, Amy had pledged that, too.

Debbie delivered the pasty and it smelled delicious. I know, smell can't be delicious but the aroma and the relief that were permeating my body in such a way she could have served a cow pie and it wouldn't have mattered to me.

"You really think the farm is ours?" I asked.

"I think so." Tank nodded, shrugged his shoulder and replied as he stopped for a moment and looked around, realizing the man sitting next to him had left and so he felt more comfortable talking as he whispered. "George, you're a good man. You've done a lot for folks around here. I know what's going on and trust me, I smell a skunk in the woodpile."

"You mean the farm?"

"I mean the whole God damn thing."

Now both fear and anger were roiling through my body as Tank added. "Someone's trying to squeeze you dry by freezing all your assets. Something's going on."

"What do I do about it?"

"First, you need to hire a lawyer."

"But, Amy's a lawyer."

"You need to hire an outside lawyer. Someone outside the family."

"Why?"

"George, you never mix business and family. Emotions can get in the way."

"But I don't have any money." I whispered.

"I know but you can get a lawyer to work on a contingency."

"You mean a percentage?"

Tank nodded in the affirmative with a cautious stare as Debbie delivered his food.

As we sat eating, Tank inquired, "How'd you get here?"

"The bus from Madison to Dodgeville and then I used Uber."

"How about I give you ride back to Madison and we talk? I've got a two o-clock that won't take long and then I can drive you back."

"Ok," I affirmed.

Debbie brought the check as I reached for my wallet but Tank's mouth was faster as he told Debbie to add it to his tab. Seems Uncle Hank's deal of accumulating and paying at the end of the month was something a lot of the regulars were doing at the Red Rooster including Tank Kennison.

"Can I take the agreement with me?"

Again, I nodded in the affirmative and asked, "Still in the same office over on Jail Alley?"

"Yup," Tank replied as he stood while looking down at me.

Looking up, I smiled for the first time in months as I offered. "I think I'll walk off lunch by going to visit grandma and grandpa and mom and dad. Is it Ok, if I come to your offices about 2:30?"

"Sounds good, George. I'll see you then."

Debbie brought my pie and I ate it as I watched Tank glad-hand his way out the door only to look back and give me a nod.

I left the Rooster and headed west walking to Graceland Cemetery. It had been a long time and I had a lot to say to mom, dad and grandma. Every time I came, I'd look at grandma and grandpa's headstone and think of her and always felt guilty, I couldn't think of grandpa other than a photo mom had of him sitting in a chair, smoking his pipe with his hat on. When I arrived at mom and dad's grave, I knelt down and slowly pulled the flattened grass from around the headstone edges. Mom always kept our house so tidy and I felt she'd want her marker that way as well. As I stood with head bowed, the first thing I said was "sorry it's been so long". Next, that I missed them more now than ever before. Finally, that they helped me through the times of trouble simply by keeping me in their prayers.

I made it back to Tank's office on the button and walked in. Tank was just finishing with another client who nodded on her way out.

"Come on in," Tank announced as I entered an office piled high with paper in virtually every possible horizontal space.

"Before we leave, let's go over a few things," Tank offered.

"OK."

George, we need to find out why this is an asset freeze and not a bankruptcy or if the freeze is going to eventually lead to a bankruptcy.

I nodded in agreement, hoping neither would be the case and simply asked, "Why do you think this is happening?"

Tank looked at me and replied, "There are a number of reasons why the government might freeze personal assets. Some of the most common reasons include criminal activity. If the government believes someone's assets are the proceeds of crime, or were used to commit a crime, they may freeze those assets. This is done to prevent the person from hiding or disposing of the assets before they can be used to pay restitution to victims or fines to the government."

I cringed at the thought as Tank continued. "Another reason is tax evasion. If the government believes someone is evading taxes, they may freeze their assets to prevent them from transferring their wealth to other people or countries."

Just when I thought it couldn't get worse Tank added, "If the government believes someone is a threat to national security they may freeze their assets to prevent them from funding terrorists or other harmful activities."

I wondered if this had anything to do with the Foundation but simply shook my head as it was too small and too innocent to shut down everything, especially when we cooperated with them regarding SIMON, our quantum computer.

I simply shook my head in disbelief as Tank continued, "It could be civil forfeiture which is a legal process that allows the government to seize property believed to be connected to criminal activity, even if the owner of the property has not been convicted of a crime."

Once again I had no idea, only growing fear as Tank added, "The government may also freeze the assets of people or businesses that are subject to international sanctions typically imposed on countries or individuals who are involved in terrorism, human rights abuses, or other illegal activities."

Tank could tell I was deeply concerned as he looked at me and consoled, "George, it's important to note that the government can't simply freeze someone's assets without justification. In most cases the government obtains a court order first that will only be granted if the government can show there is probable cause to believe the assets are connected to criminal activity which is necessary to protect the interests of the government or the public."

"What do I do?" I asked.

"Well, my friend, you need to talk to Amy and see what she knows."

Tank smiled and shifted gears as he went into his legalese. "Let's talk about the prenup. I've looked it over and believe that whether or not a pre-nuptial agreement will protect you from a bankruptcy settlement depends on a number of factors, including the specific terms of the prenup, the state in which you live, and the type of bankruptcy your spouse files. Generally speaking, prenups are enforceable in bankruptcy court but only if they are fair and reasonable. This means that the prenup cannot be used to defraud creditors or to leave one spouse in a destitute financial position."

Tank continued. "If Amy files for bankruptcy under Chapter Seven, her bankruptcy trustee will likely review your prenup to determine whether it's enforceable. If the trustee finds that the prenup is fair and reasonable your premarital assets will generally be protected. However, if the trustee finds that the prenup is unfair or unreasonable, it may be set aside and your premarital assets may be used to pay your spouse's creditors."

"If Amy files for bankruptcy under Chapter Thirteen she'll be required to submit a repayment plan to the bankruptcy court. The plan must be approved by the court before it can go into effect. If the plan provides for the payment of any debts that were incurred before the marriage the bankruptcy trustee will likely review your prenup to determine whether it's enforceable. If the trustee finds that the prenup is fair and reasonable the court will likely approve the plan. However, if the trustee finds that the prenup is unfair or unreasonable the court may not approve the plan or it may modify the plan to exclude the payment of any debts that were incurred before the marriage."

Tank looked at me and inquired. "When you bought out Tommie, where'd the money come from?"

"Me," I offered.

"Where did you get the money?"

"From Wilco."

"Was it a loan?"

"No, it was money I earned."

"Did you claim it as income and pay taxes on it?"

"Of course."

"So, the money was no longer Wilco's. It was yours, correct?"

"Yes."

"Then, theoretically, you own the farm."

"I guess so."

"Who paid Tommie since then?"

"Wilco did."

"Where did the profits go?"

"To Wilco."

"What about Terrill Beef and Bourbon?"

"Part of the farm."

"The profits?"

"There haven't been any. It takes a long time to build a cattle and distillery business."

"So, no money was paid to Wilco?"

"None."

"Who paid for the cattle and the facilities?"

"Tommie and me."

"In other words Terrill B&B was set up as a separate corporation on the land theoretically leased by Wilco but owned by you and Tommie?"

"Sounds about right."

Tank thought for a moment and then added. "Right now, I believe you and your brother own the farm and for wages and benefits paid to Tommie and the staff by Wilco, they technically were leasing the farm from the two of you while the profits went to them."

"And...?"

"Then we can fight to say there's no reason why the farm assets should be frozen if it's not part of Wilco."

"You think Tommie and I might be clear?"

"I'm not saying that. Not yet anyway. It's really complicated. The first question is ownership. The second question is whether Wilco was, in effect, leasing the farm for the wages paid. The third question is what steps do we need to take to claim ownership and unfreeze the claim."

Tank paused for a moment and asked, "You wouldn't have any papers on this would you?"

I looked at Tank and smiled. Buried within the stack I took out of the safe deposit box was the agreement between Tommie and me where I paid him the money for the farm, which I handed to Tank.

Tank looked at the document, saw that it had been notarized and smiled before noting..."This says it all."

With that, Tank went to his scanner and made two copies...one for his use and one to replace the original. Then Tank looked at me and inquired. "Do you want me to draw up an agreement between you and Terrill B&B to serve as your counsel?"

I nodded in the affirmative realizing I needed someone I could trust who wasn't involved in Wilco in any other manner before offering, "The problem is, right now we don't have any way to pay you for your services."

"We'll work on that when I figure out what in hell is going on. Let me put the original in my safe. Now let's head for Madison and get you home. While Amy is your wife, you need to keep this under your hat until we find out who's the skunk in the woodpile."

"You don't think Amy's involved in this do you?"

"No, George, I don't. But, it's better to be safe than sorry and you need to keep this between the two of us?"

"What about Tommie?"

"Between the two of us."

I understood, as Tank and I walked out into the warm summer air and headed for his truck and then the ride back to Madison.

As we settled in I looked at the interior of his aging Ford and wondered if the law business wasn't as lucrative as I thought it was. Tank caught my inspection and added. "When you're a lawyer and people see your fees they think you're rolling in dough. If you buy a fancy car and live in a small town like Mineral Point they're offended. I like my truck and it keeps folks thinking I'm giving them a fair deal."

"Do you like being a lawyer?"

"Less than half of all lawyers are satisfied with their work. This is lower than the satisfaction rate of workers in other professions, such as, doctors, dentists and architects which is probably because we mainly deal with people's problems while throwing in difficult clients, managing high levels of stress and working long hours. I keep track simply to justify why I do what I do and where I do it. Fortunately, for me I like what I do. I'm not getting rich but I'm helping a lot of my neighbors and friends and try to be fair about what it costs them."

"George, you ever thought about writing a book or taking Waldwick to print?"

"Huh?"

"George, look at all the things you've seen and done and the people you've met."

"And the lessons I've learned," I added.

"How about fiction? I bet you could write a great novel."

My mind slipped into the novel mode. I had the time. I certainly had the memories. It wouldn't cost anything except the price of paper. The seed was planted. The only question was, what do I write about?

We agreed to meet in a week in the Capitol Rotunda as I had Tank drop me off in the four hundred block of Doty Street, thanked him for the ride and heard his promise that he'd see what was going on. I nodded and smiled. It had been a long time since I smiled and it felt good. I walked the two blocks home thinking about the day and how one thing led to another.

The walk did me good and I rationalized the distance simply because I didn't want any chance someone saw me with Tank.

I made it to our building and looked up at the blue sky above. The building was aging gracefully. I entered the lobby and opened the mailbox. Again, several threatening letters to add to the pile. When there are so many, they lose their impact. I pressed the button for floor number eight and inserted my key. The slow growl of the elevator was a forlorn sound as I rode up to our condo and flipped on the kitchen lights.

The Meeting:

The week slowly dragged on as my city bus rides and orange apron with Gorge scribbled in magic marker was repeated five straight days. Tank and I agreed to meet at two and I made my way up Hamilton Street and into the majestic precipice that stood before me. I looked down at the Capitol rotunda floor and the intricate designs representing the history, culture, and values of Wisconsin put there as an aide-mémoire of the state's natural beauty, commitment to democracy and spirit of innovation.

Tank was waiting, appearing as nervous as a whore in church. "Let's walk," he offered and so we went out through the south or M.L. King exit to an empty bench away from the walkers on the Capitol side of Main Street who passed by.

Tank began. "George, I don't know what in hell happened but it ain't pretty. There are so many different laws that might have been broken. Let me just name a few."

"First, is the International Emergency Economic Powers Act which gives the President broad powers to impose economic sanctions on foreign countries and individuals involved in terrorism, drug trafficking or other illicit activities. These sanctions can include asset freezes which prevent the person or entity from accessing their funds or other assets."

"Next, is the Trading with the Enemy Act which is a World War I era law that allows the President to impose economic sanctions on countries and individuals that are designated as 'enemies' of the United States. Asset freezes are a common type of sanction under TWEA."

"Third, is the Countering America's Adversaries Through Sanctions Act which is a comprehensive sanctions law that targets Russia, North Korea, and Iran."

"Fourth, is the USA Patriot Act which expanded the government's authority to freeze assets in a number of ways.

For example, the law allows the government to freeze assets of suspected terrorists without a warrant."

"Fifth, is the Drug Kingpin Act which allows the government to freeze assets of individuals and organizations that are involved in drug trafficking."

"Sixth, is the Bank Secrecy Act which requires financial institutions to report suspicious transactions to the government. The government can then use this information to freeze assets that are suspected of being involved in money laundering or other illicit activities."

I could feel the blood running out of my face. This was serious stuff as Tank added. "George, the government's authority to freeze assets is a powerful tool that can be used to combat terrorism, drug trafficking and other illicit activities. However, this power is also subject to certain limits. For example, the government must have probable cause to believe that the assets are involved in criminal activity before it can freeze them. Additionally, the person whose assets are frozen has the right to challenge the freeze in court."

I looked at Tank and asked, "Who did they notify or how?"

Tank looked at me, took a deep breath to give himself both time and air and noted. "The US Government has a number of ways to freeze a person's assets. This can be done through a variety of means, including an Executive Order from the President that would be issued in response to a national emergency or other threat to the national security of the United States. Also, through administrative action where the Treasury Department freezes the assets of an individual or entity or through judicial order where a federal court freezes the assets through a judicial order."

Tank continued "Someone had to be notified. When the US government freezes a person's assets, they're notified by a variety of means, including in-person, where government officials personally deliver the notice to the individual or entity or else by certified mail with return receipt required. They also can notify the recipient by email or even a publication where the notice is published in a newspaper widely read in the area where the individual or entity resides."

"The notification will inform the individual or entity that their assets have been frozen and they are prohibited from using or transferring them and will also explain the reason for the freeze and the procedures for challenging the freeze."

"How do I get our assets unfrozen?" I asked, almost pleading.

Tank took a deep another breath and offered. "The individual or entity has a number of rights when their assets are frozen. The right to be notified of the freeze. The right to a hearing and the right to judicial review and to appeal the freeze to a federal court."

"Let's do it!" I responded while nodding in the affirmative.

Tank shook his head, looked at a squirrel contemplating a hand-out and noted. "Unfortunately, it's not that easy. The US government has broad authority to freeze the assets of individuals and entities based on the principle that the government has a right to protect national security and to enforce its laws. However, the government must also respect the rights of individuals and entities when it freezes their assets. The key issues for the defendant are time... the government works at its own pace which can mean months and years and money. You need to have the staying power to exist and also pay a lawyer while the government uses taxpayer funds to pay for theirs."

"What do we do now?" I asked as a sorrowful frown etched into my face.

Tank looked at me and noted. "I need to find out the reason why this has all transpired and, from that, see if we can't free-up the farm so that you have a revenue stream. The big mystery is why the freeze keeps being delayed. When things are as dramatic as this with the consequences it has, they're usually accelerated. For some reason, your freeze has been delayed and deferred and we need to find out why."

"What can I do?"

"Help find out why this is happening."

"How?"

"Has anyone been acting different of defensively lately?"

I thought for a moment and realized there were two people....Derrick and Amy and answered Tank's question with their names.

"Then I'd start with them."

Tank glanced at his watch and noted he needed to get back to Mineral Point. We stood and shook hands with me not realizing that, 100 yards away, on the roof of the Old National Bank building, someone with a telephoto lens and parabolic microphone was snapping our picture and recording everything we said.

It was 4:30 when I walked into the condo and Amy was gone. Who knows where. The distance between us had become so great, the singularity of my time was almost a welcome respite from her insistence on trying to resolve everything at once and the urgency that permeated her entire genre of current existence.

Perhaps it was the summer breeze. Perhaps the glance at my satchel when I realized I didn't need to write a novel. I had one in the pile of papers stored so long in a dank, dark box in Mineral Point that my great, great grandfather had written so long ago. All I needed do was type out what he'd written and I'd have a novel that I could call 'Waldwick'. All the surprises, even the sex, was already in there.

I went out on the patio and watched the sailboats on Lake Monona and thought of The Duke and wondered how he'd get through this mess. I opened a spotted cow and it went down easy, then another and then a third when reality struck as the key to the door slowly turned and the click of the latch announced that Amy was home and with her our reality.

Exasperation:

Amy walked in with an exasperated look on her face. I could tell it had been another long day. I came in off the veranda and realized I had to pee. Seems that three or was that four beers and no prostatic sphincter will do that to you.

After I set the record for the longest pee of my life, I came out and saw Amy glancing out the window at the lake. There was no turn. There was no hello. All that existed was my staring at her back as I inquired. "Long day?"

The silence was deafening. No reply!

"Are you OK?"

Still silence as if I wasn't there.

"Amy, I can't handle this. I know things are tough but the least you can do is admit I'm here."

With that Amy turned and I saw the tears in her eyes. For the first time in God only know how long, there was regret... deep, deep regret as she whispered, "You just don't understand."

Now my ager was roiling. "Understand what?"

"What I'm going through."

"What you're going through? I thought we were in this together?" I pondered, almost hurt by her exclamation.

A slight snicker was all I got in return as my level of patience grew thin. With that, the tone of my voice changed. Gone was a soft, compassionate tone replaced by the brittle sounds of my insistence. "Assets? Frozen? Let's see...back taxes - illegal activity? Threat to national security? What is it Amy? Why has the federal government frozen everything?"

I wanted to spit on Amy as she made her way to the couch. I was so angry, so hurt, so devastated I didn't think I could handle it and then I continued. "I don't know you anymore, do I? I used to love you but more than that I respected you and you've ripped that right out of my heart."

"Please forgive me, George, please!"

"How can I? How can I forgive you when everything we built together, you threw away and now, now you won't even tell me what's going on?"

Amy was now crying even more as she gasped for air as if she were drowning in sorrow. Deep down she knew the pain I was feeling. Deep down she sensed my anger. Deep within her, she realized that all we had was gone...like dry leaves on a windy day blown from their mooring only to become memories of a splendid summer day. I knew that she realized that I wondered what all victims wonder...why? Why was this happening to me?

Through her tears, I enquired, "What are our chances of getting everything...make that anything back?"

Amy shrugged and replied, "It doesn't look good".

"Why?"

"Because the government's position is that we financially gained from this and therefore they have the right to acquire our assets as compensation."

I closed my eyes and shook my head in disbelief.

What in hell was she talking about? What did we do wrong? Why wouldn't she tell me?

Dissipation:

The anger diminished and, as the days turned into weeks, our pain receded. We still lived together but the harmony that once existed had been replaced by a required sense of singularity forced upon us by the veracity neither of us had anywhere else to go.

Woefully, one of the temptations of being rich is to continue to want more...to become greedy, also known as avarice... that insatiable desire for something more, most commonly material possessions or wealth but also an extension of one's social value, including status and/or power, characterized by an excessive and selfish desire to acquire more than one needs or deserves, often at the expense of others. To this end, I turned to the lyrics of Freddie Mercury and Queen and the song "I Want It All"

People, do you hear me? I'm talking to you I'm standing right in front of you
Can't you see me?
I want it all And I want it now I want it all And I want it now I want it all And I want it now I want it all And I want it now
I have a dream, a fantasy To have it all, to be free From the doubt and the fear
To have it all, year after year
I want it all And I want it now I want it all And I want it now I want it all And I want it now I want it all And I want it now
People, you hear me screaming I'm screaming for my life I'm breaking out, I'm breaking free I'm coming for my share
I want it all And I want it now I want it all And I want it now I want it all And I want it now I want it all And I want it now
Oh, I want it all I want it all, and I want it now I want it all I want it all, and I want it now (Yes, I want it all! Hey!) I want it, I want it Ooh, huh!

I thought about the phrase, 'I want it all' and realized it can be interpreted in many ways, depending on the context and the person saying it. Did Freddie mean material possessions and success? When someone says they want it all, they might be referring to wealth, power, status and all the luxurious trappings that come with them. They might dream of owning a mansion, driving a fancy car, and traveling the world. It's all a perspective based on what you've already got.

Perhaps Freddie was referring to personal fulfillment and happiness and achieving his full potential while living a life rich in experiences, via a fulfilling career, strong relationships, good health and a sense of purpose which are challenges to obtain and retain.

Sadly, it could also mean that Freddie had unrealistic expectations and an insatiable desire for more. Was he happy? Am I? Wanting it all can lead to feelings of dissatisfaction, anxiety, and even burnout simply because life is full of trade-offs, and we can't have everything we want.

As I pondered all that happened I realized that greed is nothing more than an insatiable longing for more...more material gain...more social value...more status or power. It's simply never having or being enough to the point one exploits others or violates ethical standards in order to achieve that next goal. It's only then they realize it wasn't the euphoria they'd dreamed about, just another step towards the oblivion of loneliness that pervades those unwilling to give the most important thing and that's themselves. Greed can lead to conflict, inequality and social destruction as exemplified by the tragic demolition of the Terrill Family.

I was also learning there are many different types of greed. Some people are greedy for money, while others are greedy for power, fame, or possessions. Greed can also be directed towards social status or recognition. No matter what form it takes, greed is always characterized by a desire for more than what's needed or deserved. I never thought that greed could lead to the exploitation, corruption, and destruction of our family. In the end, greed has destroyed it and is leading to dysfunction, distrust and profound unhappiness simply because, like so many others, our family has been consumed by greed and unable to appreciate what we had as we were always looking for more.

When time is the one thing you have a lot of, you spend interludes trying to simply answer the question why...why did our family turn out this way? Was it a genetic thing? Was it the way we raised our kids? Why is it that, what could have been so great, turned out so incredibly bad? I hope and pray that why we are a disheveled mess is because of genetics and not the way the kids were raised.

E=MC²:

Life continued on as I typed the essay my great, great grandfather had written and worked on turning it into 'Waldwick'. As I pressed the final keys and printed the final page, I felt relieved. I'd accomplished something... anything... that took my mind off our situation. It was now early September and Tank had been digging into the legal aspects and keeping me informed. I was certain Big Brother was auditing all my messages and our phones were bugged as they dug deeper into the mess we were in.

With the manuscript completed the next phase was cover design and printing, both of which required something we had so little of - money. I'd spent literally every waking non-working hour converting one of the most passionate stories I'd ever read only to realize how frustrating it is to dream and create something where you had no way to finish what you set out to do.

One day there was an email from $E=MC^2$ which I almost erased simply because I assumed it was just more spam. Instead, I opened it to find a note from Megan who had been my physical therapist in Milwaukee when I went through cancer treatment. After my recovery she'd moved to Atlanta and contacted me to help her develop a curriculum for the prostate cancer education of spouses of which I'd gone to Atlanta twice to help her inaugurate the classes.

I was intrigued by her moniker $E=MC^2$ which I remembered from high school physics. After so many years I had to turn to Google to learn that in Einstein's Theory of Relativity the letter "E" stands for energy in various forms like heat, light, or motion. "M" represents mass, which is the amount of matter in an object or how much 'stuff' it's made of and is simply a measure of an object's inertia and therefore its resistance to changing its speed or direction when a force is applied to it.

The "C²" is the speed of light squared, which has a constant value of about 186,400 miles per second and squared is nearly 35 billion miles per hour. Always hearing the term "light years" which meant the distance light travels in one year, I used my calculator to determine that a light year represented around 300 billion miles per year.

The Google article noted that light has no mass, travels as a wave and doesn't have 'rest mass', meaning it can't be stationary. However, light does carry energy. The article also noted that mass and energy are equivalent which means they are two forms of the same thing, such that, because they're interchangeable, even a tiny amount of mass can be converted into a tremendous amount of energy, and vice versa.

For many, including me, I didn't understand the concept of mass, except as it related to the Catholic Church, where the term "Mass" comes from the Latin phrase "Ite, missa est," which translates to "Go, you are sent," where Jesus Christ is truly present that has nothing to do with mass as a fundamental property of matter.

Regarding a fundamental property of matter, what I found interesting was the fact that light actually interacts with mass where, even though light itself has no mass, it can interact with objects to the point that light can be absorbed or reflected and transfer its energy which is how sunlight warms the Earth and why people get sun burned.

Finally, and what was revolutionary for Einstein was the theory that mass affects light and can actually bend light through gravity which is why massive objects like stars act like lenses, warping the path of light around them while black holes with incredible gravity simply absorb light.

I had no idea why Megan was using Einstein's $E=MC^2$ as her moniker but found it intriguing. Was she referring to her energy level? Was it in reference to all that she was doing? How did this relate to her?

Megan's message indicated there had been several changes to the meeting content and they had tried other male participants who had not been as successful as I had in terms of communicating the message they wanted presented. She noted that with the changes in the curriculum they would like to have me begin the new series to establish a standard they could adhere to afterwards.

Even with the intrigue, I was still reluctant to participate in her class simply because, when I partook in Megan's two classes, I'd simply gone to Atlanta, left my modesty at the door and helped her only to then unwillingly, accept her... uhh... gratitude the first time and was somewhat disappointed when it wasn't offered the second.

I don't know if I was shocked, perplexed, offended or aroused. I do know that after that second meeting we'd lost immediate contact until the e-mail which was probably a good thing as our perspectives on life were completely different and, quite honestly, the temptations were too great.

I read the note and pondered whether to respond. There were the concerns I'd had previously regarding how much she'd changed but then hadn't we all? Instead of an email, I called Megan.

"Hello," Megan answered.

"Hello, stranger." I replied

"How are you?" Megan inquired as the softness of her smile made its way through the phone.

"I'm fine," I lied

"How are you feeling?"

"I'm well." I said, which was physically the truth. I was cancer clear and on my way to becoming a survivor as I responded. "How about you?"

"I'm keeping busy?"

"Anyone new in your life?"

"Well, there have been some but nothing permanent." Megan replied as I thought back to her cavalier attitude after her divorce.

"How are the classes going?" I asked.

"Still doing them and that's why I contacted you."

"Really?"

"Yes, I was wondering if you'd be interested in helping refresh the class. We have a lot of post-session evaluations showing us where we need to make changes and there's been some exciting treatment breakthroughs that need to be added. We've also learned it's great to have someone who's cancer clear, to show the class there's hope at the end of the tunnel."

I offered. "Hmm, I'm interested but things have changed."

"I know. I heard that things are...uhhh...different."

I thought, 'If she only knew.'

Megan added..."George, we've tried other men and none of them have been close to what you bring to the meetings and it shows. We've been awarded a federal grant to continue the classes and now, I can offer to pay your expenses and $3,000 for the day."

I realized $3,000 would be enough for the cover design and printing 100 copies of Waldwick as well as help us get out from under some of the bills.

"When would you need me?" I inquired.

"Whenever you can fit it into your schedule."

"What's the most convenient day?"

"We've been having the classes on Tuesday afternoons."

I realized it would be my day off at Home Depot and justified how much the money would help.

"Could I fly out of Madison instead of Milwaukee? We're living here now."

"Sure."

"Same routine as last time?" I asked remembering the Q-N-A and candor that was required both physically and emotionally.

"Pretty much, except it's slotted for three hours instead of two."

My mind went into over-drive as I thought about the content and what could possibly be added.

"How about in two weeks?"

"Ok,"" Megan offered with a smile I could actually hear in her voice.

I thought it would give me enough time to review my notes and build up my courage. My greatest concern dealt with whether the funds would be taken by the government. When I got my job we had to get clearance from the judge. I remember he noted that post-action funds that were then frozen were usually only done because proven criminal activity. However, the government might claim any legally earned income if it was determined it was potentially derived either from illegal activity or simply based on their suspicion and not a proven wrongdoing. In any case, they could scrutinize its source and potentially challenge its legitimacy.

That night when Amy came home I informed her of the offer and the rationale. She indicated that, based on the fact our assets were frozen, she saw no reason why income like this could be included but would check. She was also aware I was in the process of transcribing 'Waldwick' and wanted to have it published and needed money to pay some imperative bills.

After Amy's legal summary I wanted her emotional opinion and simply asked, "Do you mind?"

Amy shrugged her shoulders and appeared completely indifferent. Ever since her declaration and my realization of what transpired we'd functioned more as obligatory roommates than husband and wife and the shrugged shoulders inferred she didn't care but asked for a day on behalf of legal clarification. Sadly, any form of emotional clarification had been deemed null and void.

The next day Amy sent me a text from wherever she was indicating there'd be no problem with the government as long as I acquired a 1099 tax form at the end of the year. This precipitated me going on line and finding a round trip ticket to Atlanta for two weeks hence. Then I sent a text to Megan to confirm the date. With no credit cards, Megan offered to pay for the ticket and I agreed, as there comes a point in time when pride is superseded by need.

The day arrived and I UBER'd out to Truax Field and got onboard the Delta flight to Atlanta. I glanced at the ticket and saw that the roundtrip airfare was $188.00. At one time I had cashmere socks costing more than that. It was my second plane ride in nearly two years and for two hours and ten minutes I relished in simply doing something I loved and that was traveling.

The Atlanta airport was rife with memories of my past trip from Saint Martin that had liquidated my self-ordained dignity. At its core, I lost my inherent self-worth and self-respect that I believed was deserved by every human being. For my entire life until my transcendence and demise, I felt that every person was born with inherent dignity, simply by virtue of their existence...to be treated with respect and consideration, regardless of their actions, choices, or social standing. Yet, here I was a fallen man, whose dignity had been shattered like a crystal vase on a kitchen floor, whose self-esteem had simply collapsed, now required to put on a show for eight strangers.

Gone was my pride, succumbing to a sense of worthlessness and inadequacy, superseded by bouts of depression and anxiety all exacerbated by the strained situation at home. It was bad enough to nearly die from the blood clots. It became worse with the cancer and the realities associated with it. The one-two punch culminated in the deep, dark, sinister belief I was no longer a man, devoid of the joys and social skills I once cherished that had all been erased in the name of commerce, replaced by a longing for yesterday, or at least some degree of culmination regarding the dread I was in.

Reflections:

As I was making my way through the Hartsfield subterranean labyrinth that would take me to the baggage claim area, I saw a reflection of myself, paused and waited for the arriving subway only to feel a tear gently ripen at the edge of my eye. I realized I had no answers as to why I was there except the desperate need for cash.

In my catharsis from constant depression, I learned how to catch myself when thinking negative thoughts and challenge them with more realistic and positive feelings. However, no matter how hard I tried this autumn day, there simply were none. Sadly, the critical thing eradicated was my pride. I'd fallen down a rabbit hole so deep and dark I'd entered personal hell and morphed to the point I'd become ambivalent, indifferent and reticent to the reality that I no longer was what I once was.

They say depression should never be a singular event and you should surround yourself with positive people but it's so difficult when the person you love is deeper in remorse than you. Sadly, so sadly, Amy's malice had become my malice to the point, like her, I no longer cared.

I looked at the old man staring back and realized I was indifferent to those around me. Gone was the spark. Gone was the need. Gone was the belief that I was anything more than what I am... a lonely, desperate, singular soul walking to the beat of an ancient drummer who wanted nothing more than to exist until the day I died, while only hoping to regain and retain some sense of dignity so closely linked to my self-respect. How sad to have one's daily goal be nothing more than to have the day end. My life had become nothing more than walking up the down escalators, where each step did nothing more than keep me in the place I was the day before.

I heard the whoosh of the subway car as the compressed air announced its arrival. I watched people exit on the other side and felt the gust on ours as the clinging masses rushed to board. I stood in the middle of the subway multitude as the doors closed and the announcement blared about the next three stops until I would reach my end. No one looked. No one stared. No one smiled. No one cared. Each person was simply enveloped in their own thoughts, objectives and destinations. I thought of the day's 'session' and how uncomfortable I'd been the last time when topics, demonstrations and discussions took place shattering my naiveté, making me realize there's a whole different world I knew nothing about.

Perhaps, just perhaps, this time, because of repetition, the shock wouldn't be there. Perhaps, just perhaps, because I'd sunk so low I'd no longer care. Perhaps, just perhaps, what's asked of me no would longer matter. Gone was my pride. Gone was my dignity. Gone was any sense of modesty. All I wanted was the money and whatever it took to get it. Like a beggar on the street I closed my eyes and vowed, whatever the day held, I'd do it, realizing my values and scruples had become gnarled and, like that homeless man begging for loose change, willing to do what it took for the currency that lured me to this destination.

I thought of my wife and wondered, 'How would she react if she knew what transpired?' Would she be mortified that now, the man, once on a pedestal, is nothing more than a paid object that struts and frets upon a stage, not for glamor nor prurient thrill, but simply to wallow in the dire need for compensation?

Our transfer from the sky to the bowels of Georgia and depths of depression ended as our subway reached its end. I disembarked and walked down to baggage claim and the spot Megan indicated someone would be holding up a sign with my name on it. What a pleasant surprise when I saw it was Megan. She was taller than I remembered and still had the effervescent smile underscoring the composite beautiful woman.

Megan remained in tremendous shape and didn't look her age which I guessed at mid-to-late 30's. As had been the case when she moved to Atlanta, her brown hair remained shoulder length but was now streaked with golden highlights. The skirt and blouse she wore were expensive and reminded me of the one's Melia purchased in Dubai. Her make-up was perfect, while her lipstick matched the color of her finely manicured fingernails. In other words, Megan looked like she just stepped off the cover of Vogue.

I did a quick survey of the social landscape and slightly grinned, recognizing that little did those secretly lusting after her beauty imagine a few minutes of bliss might open up Pandora's Box where those who succumbed might experience all tribulations of the world – sorrow, vice, violence, and more – that could plague them forever. I knew what they didn't. Beneath the physical aura was a woman whose professional drive would exhaust even the heartiest, whose perceived penchants would make most men and women blush in either erotic frenzy or total disdain.

"Hello!" was the warm greeting, accompanied by a pleasant smile, which was something I hadn't seen or felt in months.

I smiled back and offered, "You look great!"

Words weren't enough and so we hugged. Not long! Not in an amorous way but as a gesture of acceptance. As our bodies met, I felt her against me and she felt good. My God, I'd missed the sensation!

We separated to a proper distance and Megan asked. "How's Amy?" tacitly reminding me they'd met when I was going through my treatments in what seemed to be a different lifetime and the topic had been elucidated.

We stood for a moment and then a surprise as Megan offered her right hand and I clenched it in a delicate way that ladies do while electricity slithered through my veins to the point that more smiles were elicited.

Our eyes met and for an instant, we were one. Reality slammed into both of us forcing us to step outside to what would have been a spectacular summer's day in Wisconsin. Spring and fall in Atlanta are when the weather's best - not too hot and not too cold - void of the oppressive summer humidity as the fall foliage had begun its stunning arrival with vibrant colors transforming the city's landscape as well as a respite from vacationing crowds, thereby allowing me to surmise there were no threats of hurricanes or tornadoes, anyway not weather-wise this day.

Life was good as the bright blue sky and soft breeze welcomed me to Megan's world! We walked out to the North short-term lot and my mouth dropped open. Megan was driving a midnight black Lexus LC 500 Convertible. Simply gorgeous... both the car and Megan!

I opened the passenger door and slid into the seat as Megan walked around and got behind the wheel. I tried not to stare but couldn't help but glance at her long, tan legs as her skirt rode slightly above mid-thigh. If she was attempting to entice me, she was doing a fantastic job.

Megan smiled and offered. "Great day. Want to go topless?" The double entendre could have been accidental or intentional, I didn't know and really didn't care.

"This is when I love my car," Megan offered as she leaned across, brushed against my left shoulder, pulled down the visor, unlocked the windshield hook, pressed the button and exposed the two of us to glorious sunshine.

"I could have done that," I offered, referring to unlocking the passenger side lever.

"I know," Megan offered with a smile, leaving me wondering what she meant while filling me with all sorts of expectations.

With the visor down, I glanced at her now exposed vehicle registration that read 'Mary Ann Egan'. I thought for a moment that it was odd until I realized she'd simply taken the first letter of Mary and her last name to create 'Megan', the name I'd known since the very first time we met. In our contemporary world it's sad when names become obsolete only to have them recycle in another generation. Such was the case with Mary where the only less-popular name was George. My mind quickly did the gymnastics. Perhaps George Terrill could become Gerrill, but that sounded really stupid and so I put the thought in my mental wastebasket to simply be tossed like so many other innocuous thoughts.

As we pulled out of Hartsfield and headed north, I glanced at Megan's tousled hair that made her even that much more desirous. As she drove Megan steered the conversation away from my mess and filled me in on her world and all that was transpiring at the clinic. When it was my turn I extended the conversation regarding Melia and 'V', avoiding any more exchange regarding Amy, with no mention of Derrick. I don't know if it was obvious but was intentionally there.

"What's new with you?" I asked, simply trying to generalize our conversation.

"Well, I've been going to school."

"You have?" I replied somewhat surprised as if she didn't have enough to do.

"Yes, I've taken classes regarding the psychology of medicine."

"Really?"

"Yes. I wanted to better understand the provider and patient dynamics that led me into all sorts of different subjects that I found incredibly interesting."

"Like what?"

"My goal is moving our clinic towards a more holistic approach by considering the patient's entire well-being— physical, mental, and social. To do this, psychology plays a vital role in achieving this by addressing the emotional and social aspects of health to which we've joined with a team pf psychologists to create a program of measurement and assistance."

"Traditionally, medicine focused heavily on the physical aspects of illness. Now, in order to provide total care we have begun to recognize the strong link between the mind and body and how thoughts, emotions, and behaviors can influence health and recovery. Today, I believe psychology is no longer separate from medicine. It's an integrated field that helps us understand the whole person, to promote healing and improve overall well-being."

Megan passed a quick glance my way and then, with eyes on the growing traffic in front of us added. "Believe it or not, a patient's outlook can significantly impact the success of the procedure or treatment. While our team used to simply recommend the prescribed physical treatment. Today, we're expanding our follow-up to make sure our patients are following through with therapy recommendations. In order to do this we're looking at the factors that influence their adherence to postoperative rehabilitation, such as their beliefs about medication and a patient's support system. In order to do that, I've been studying a lot of the social issues facing our world and how they're affecting attitudes and beliefs as well as social dynamics."

"Social dynamics, what's that?" I asked.

Megan glanced at me again and then back at the highway as she offered. "Social dynamics is all about the ever-changing patterns of behavior and interactions within a social group and looking at the relationship between people in a group and how they influence each other to create a complex social environment. These include all sorts of relationships and how individuals behave like spouses, families, friends, work teams, or even entire societies and how people's actions affect each other and the group as a whole.

"Can you give me some examples."

Megan glanced my way again and then back at the slowing traffic as she offered. "Every group has its own set of unspoken rules and expectations. Social dynamics examines how people take on different roles within the group, like leader, follower, mediator, or comedian. Understanding these roles helps people navigate interactions effectively and, in our case, allows our clinic's members to better function as a team."

Looking straight ahead, Megan smiled and added, "We've established what we call "norms", which are the accepted ways of behaving and values, that represent the core beliefs that guide the group. Part of my job is to understand how these norms and values influence communication, decision-making and overall group behavior. By minimizing the social stratification that traditionally happens between doctors, physician assistants, nurse practitioners, clinical nurse associates and the support staff we've been able to increase the depth of communication and provide a more comprehensive and consistent pattern of patient care while also unifying our team without the political aspects normally found in a clinical environment."

"What about your physical therapy?" I asked remembering how Megan and I first met.

"It's part of the team. However, today my roles and responsibilities are to integrate all of the different aspects of medical care into one cohesive unit who's only goal is the proper and successful treatment of our patients in a just and humane way."

I was now beginning to realize that Megan's job was much more, make that much, much more than one can initially perceive and why there was so much pressure on her on a daily basis as I asked. "Are you doing all that, plus the classes?"

Megan shook her head no as she replied. "I'm only involved in the classes when there's a change in the curriculum, like today. After we get all the kinks out, I have an incredible Nurse Practitioner named Sarah who handles the meetings on a bi-weekly basis."

"So I get the A-Team?" I replied with a smirk on my face.

"George, you've set the standard and that's why I wanted you back. Like everything else in life we needed a refresher and you certainly have that innate ability to do just that."

I was honored as the topic finally got around to the day's class, agenda and all the new prostate cancer treatments. Megan went through the list of new drugs and noted "there have been several promising new medications," upon which she provided a litany designed to improve the odds for those affected by what had already affected me.

I didn't have a clue what she was referring to but really didn't care. Every time her eyes shifted from me to the road, mine shifted from her smile to her thighs...God she had gorgeous thighs... lithe, tan and defined is such a way that every nuance meant a reincarnation of form from smooth when her foot was pressed on the gas, to sinewy when her foot tapped the brake.

Megan looked at me and smiled again making me sincerely feel welcomed and she added. "In addition to the new drugs, there have also been advances in other areas of determination and treatment, such as a new urine test for changes in PSA, along with radiation therapy and surgical procedures that are more effective and have fewer side effects, as well as new techniques that allow for more precise removal of prostate cancer cells."

With her eyes still on the road and mine on her thighs, Megan replied, "The overall goal for today's session remains developing a positive attitude and giving the spouses hope that everything will turn out all right like it has for you, while showing them it's not the end of their physical world as well. In doing over twenty classes, we've obtained a great deal of response data where the members had questions and wanted further explanations or demonstrations. Some of the initial hesitations we had concerning content matter have been debunked and so we've changed the presentation a bit and added more post-op information. Nothing major! Beyond that, one of the things the members requested was more time with a person who's gone through the process which is why you're here."

"We? Who's we?"

Megan paused for a moment and then replied. "The entire syllabus is discussed and the content approved by the staff including the Doctors, PA's and nurses. They all know what's included and have approved the syllabus. After each session they're given a written summary of the responses we receive. You didn't think I did this without their knowledge and approval, did you?"

For some reason, knowing involvement of the staff made it all seem less prurient and more medical. This wasn't being critical of Megan but there's something to say about safety in numbers, especially when it transcended both genders and all medical personnel.

Surprises:

We arrived at the clinic parking lot and pulled into Megan's reserved spot. We got out of the car and Megan smiled as we entered through the side door and it was like putting on an old pair of shoes as nothing had changed. We made our way through the labyrinth of exam rooms and offices until we reached the front of the clinic where Megan punched in the code for the classroom. It was like I was home again. Situated in a plastic tub was a neatly folded, navy-blue scrub outfit. Megan excused herself and I quickly got into the scrubs.

Megan returned and placed the release form in front of me and excused herself, leaving me alone in the classroom, feeling somewhat like a prostitute, imagining how they justify what they do for a living and quite honestly no longer seeming to care. I was here. I needed money and all that was about to transpire was transitory in nature. No photos. Only memories. No friends. Only strangers. In three hours, I'd be nothing more than a recollection.

I quickly signed the release without reading it as Megan returned noting that it was ten-minutes to 'show time and offering, "George, you've never been too bashful, is it all right if we show the class what this is all about?"

"Ok" I replied, no longer concerned and devoid of any reticence.

Megan smiled and detailed. "Like last time, I'll be the moderator and we can have show-and-tell through the basics, procedures, results and consequences. You know, anatomy and physiology, practices and procedures. All the attendees have signed the same affidavit outlining the presentation and what's included and accepted the content matter. As you read in your release form, the document is very specific and no one has ever appeared to be surprised or offended by what they've seen or heard. When we start, I'll outline what we're going to discuss and then offer a five-minute break in case someone doesn't feel comfortable and wants to discretely leave."

I took a deep breath as the reality of what was about to transpire took hold and wondered if the five-minute hiatus was also intended for me. Once again, I took a moment to justify it to myself. I'd agreed to the meeting, flew to Atlanta to have a group of ladies, whose spouses were about to go through what I did, who'd signed the document that outlined the contents of the meeting be exposed to me physically and emotionally. Once again, I justified what was about to transpire with the rationale … 'I need the money if I'm going to pay the bills'.

The ladies finished their tour and entered the room at precisely three. The classes had grown to eight and all of the women were in their fifties or sixties and casually dressed just like the last time. Once again, I was introduced as simply 'George' who was previously one of Megan's patients, willing to share all that's transpired to help them better understand what to expect. For some reason, this put me at ease. I was just another body and so what if they saw all of it.

Megan paused for a moment, looked at her audience and then at me. I could tell she was deep in thought. After what seemed like an extended period, Megan offered. "This session deals not only with the consequences your spouse is facing but also how it will affect you from physical, emotional and intimate perspectives and that means a focus on sex. Historically, women have found it difficult to talk about the subject simply because we've grown up in a society that sexualizes women only from a male gaze, where women are to be sexual but only from a man's perspective. To that end, women are often uncomfortable to discuss the subject because we're punished for it. It's not hard to find examples of people shaming women for the number of partners they've had or what we enjoy. We all know that owning our sexuality frequently comes with a price, not to mention sexual encounters that, for some women, are often traumatic or violent, exacerbated by a media that rarely show accurate examples of female pleasure."

"Today we're going to review the physical, social and emotional consequences of prostate cancer and how it may affect your spouse and also you and what you can do to minimize the negative consequences and return to an altered, but physically satisfying life."

"First, I want to assure you that prostate cancer is very treatable when caught early enough. Still men's reluctance to share their health issues makes treating more difficult. This is because family history impacts one's prostate cancer risk and many men don't know if they have a family history of the illness because their relatives didn't, won't or don't want to talk about it.

"Needless to say, prostate cancer and the associated procedures are obviously, deeply personal. Psychologists say cultural attitudes and pressures regarding masculinity play a role in any man's hesitancy to reveal his diagnosis. These expectations include that men remain sexually vigorous and self-sufficient throughout their lives. Prostate cancer may cause erectile dysfunction and urinary incontinence, resulting in a deep level shame for some men. Our goal today is to open the door and give you an understanding of what's happening, how it's happening and what you can do to minimize the negative effects on both you and your spouse."

I nodded as my mind curved inward realizing I was a living example of what Megan was saying... depressed, dejected, alone and defeated.

Megan continued as my mind returned from self-pity to the dialogue. I looked at the ladies and realized I was in the profound minority... a man willing to not only talk about the malady but share not only his thoughts but himself, as my attention turned back to the attractive lady at the podium who continued. "The only way doctors can help a patient is if they talk about it. While there's no self-check for prostate cancer, it'd be great if it was something men were willing to talk about and ask their friends, 'Hey, did you get your prostate checked? Have you talked to your doctor about this?' That would be an ideal world."

Megan turned to me and added. "I look at George and see a hero. He's taken his experience and is willing to talk about it, share it and help others. For some men, they feel it's a sign of weakness. To me, there's a special strength when a man willingly displays and shares his vulnerabilities, especially for the good of others."

The ladies gazed at me and I saw a glimpse of admiration. It felt good to have someone look up at me for a change instead of down. It had been a long time and just that look, if only for an instant, made the entire trip worthwhile. In their eyes I could see a sense of gratitude. Instead of some deep dark secret, instead of third-party references, the ladies had someone in front of them who had something in common with their spouses... someone who'd 'been there' and experienced what their spouses were about to experience and feel what their spouses were about to feel. Simply believing this made me feel good, proud to be a man again, not some eunuch dragged through life's physical, mental and social agonies.

I nodded to indicate I agreed, as the attention shifted back to Megan who went through the prostate cancer statistics. "Prostate cancer is estimated to be the second most diagnosed and the fifth leading cause of cancer mortality among men with an estimated 1.4 million new cases and 375,000 deaths globally last year. It's a disease of public health importance due to its burden on not only those directly affected but society in general."

Megan paused for a moment as if to indicate a change in direction and depth of consequence. "Beyond the treatment itself, the diagnosis has a significant impact on the sexuality of prostate cancer patients and their partners, with a subsequent impact on their quality of life. Thus, the management of prostate cancer should include sex therapy and rehabilitation in couples from the point of initial diagnosis through the surgical procedure to post-operative options whose goal it is to maintain intimate function and an improved post-operative quality of life."

Once again, there was a pause and I knew what was coming as Megan orated. "There are significant changes in sexual activities and the quality of life associated with the diagnosis and treatment of prostate cancer. There are five critical consequences we're going to address in great detail concerning their cause, treatment and alternatives. They include, sterilization, ED or erectile dysfunction, UI or urinary incontinence, PLS or penile length shortening and depression which can, if not addressed, lead to PTSD or post-traumatic stress disorder."

"Now that you're here, if you're offended by the subject matter and frank discussions, don't feel embarrassed or reticent about departing before we begin. This class aims to highlight the characteristics of prostate cancer patients and the altered sexuality that might require intervention by our healthcare providers, while also examining ways to regain some, if not all, the critical aspects of intimacy, not only for your spouse but you, as well."

This last sentence threw me a loop. The first session was all about the patient. What Megan was detailing was the fact that the discussion now included information pertaining to the women themselves.

Megan paused and then announced. "Before we begin, I'd like to take a short break to allow anyone who thinks they'll feel uncomfortable with the topics to have the opportunity to discretely depart. What we're about to present is quite frank and forthright and will deal with several subjects you're probably not used to examining. I want to make absolutely certain you understand we're not here to recommend, suggest or infer that you partake in what we're about to offer. Our only goal is to inform and provide insight into the challenges in front of you and discuss some of the solutions you may consider. We have water and soft drinks in the hallway, if you'd like them and then we will begin."

At first none of the ladies moved. However, after more coaxing by Megan, each went to select a beverage. I watched to see if any of the ladies would depart of which none did.

When we reconvened Megan began again. "In order to understand what's about to happen and what you can do about it, I want to spend the first segment of today's session going over anatomy and physiology and all the basics".

Megan looked at me to indicate it was 'showtime'. As had been the case in the first session, graphic images appeared on the screen that Megan used to point out where everything was located and how it all worked. At first, I found myself profoundly embarrassed... not for being nearly naked but feeling like an object. I took a deep breath and began my silent mantra...'Three-thousand, three-thousand, three-thousand,' realizing somewhere in the world someone was probably spending that on a dinner that included the Terrill steaks, bourbon and wine we produced.

As I acclimated, I resumed my thought process from the airport and morphed to a level of indifference, simply justifying the objectivization as nothing more than a clinical study with strangers who would walk out the door and never be seen again for which I was getting more than what I was paid before. For Megan, it was just another day at the office as 'three-thousand, three-thousand, three-thousand' reverberated within my brain.

As Megan continued, she noted. "All of your spouses have been prescribed to incorporate the DaVinci Robot. There are several advantages to using a robot for a nerve-sparing radical prostatectomy compared to traditional open surgery. Here are some of the key benefits."

Megan projected an image of the robot on the screen and announced. "The robotic arms provide enhanced precision and dexterity compared to the surgeon's own hands which allows for more meticulous dissection of the nerves and surrounding tissues, potentially leading to a higher chance of preserving nerve function and maintaining continence and erectile function after surgery. It offers magnified 3D high-resolution and visualization of the surgical field which allows the surgeon to see the nerves and other structures in greater detail, which can improve surgical decision-making and minimize the risk of unintended damage."

Megan nodded at me as if to infer she was ready to draw the incision points on my torso. I stepped in front of the ladies, took off the top and raised my arms above my head as Megan noted. "Procedurally, a robotic nerve-sparing radical prostatectomy typically involves only a few incision points, usually between four and six, which are much smaller compared to a traditional open retropubic prostatectomy."

Taking a black medical Sharpie, Megan began putting the incision marks on my torso as she noted. "Here's a breakdown of the incision points. There are typically four or five main laparoscopic ports used for the robotic instruments and camera. These incisions are usually around half an inch each. In some cases, an additional small incision might be needed for additional instruments or for specimen removal."

With that, Megan pulled on my scrub bottom strings and the pants fell to the floor to a slight raising of eyebrows by the ladies present, as she continued by drawing a black line from just beneath my navel to the top of my penis and added. "Even though most procedures incorporate the minimally invasive laser, standard surgical protocol requires necessary steps for all possible situations which means being prepared for any and all complications. The planned robotic procedure has been done over two-thousand times by our surgeons such that it includes the VERY slight chance there will need to be a full incision called a radical retropubic prostectomy. I want to emphasize that the preparation is a standard *just in case* procedure and doesn't represent anything more than that. To do so, and so you and your spouse are aware, there will be removal of the pubic hair as a precaution."

Standing there, I acclimated and what would have previously been a mortifying experience was relegated to nothing more than an event that no longer mattered. I was neither aroused, nor embarrassed, simply a showroom dummy in a world no longer governed by any sense of modesty, propriety or decorum, all done in the name of science, all done for one reason...need. I'd relinquished my soul for the sake of a dollar. Sadly, realistically, undeniably, I was indifferent, unconcerned and apathetic regarding standing in front of nine women, totally exposed, as if I was nothing, absolutely nothing. 'Three-thousand, three-thousand, three-thousand' churned through my brain as my artificial indifference masqueraded the true feelings of degradation inside.

I was less than three feet away from the gaggle of gawkers as my mind wandered first to my Tuxedo and the Nobel Peace Prize and how uncomfortable I was and then to St. Martin and how the lexicon of Orient Beach and all the naked people that once titillated me became mundane and how, through the years, I'd adapted and overcome my reticence to being likewise with Amy at the Lighthouse. While this was different and I was the proverbial center of attention, my logical-self overcame my social self and all the reservations evaporated as I justified it first in the name of science and second in the name of commerce.   When the cookie jar is full you think nothing of taking one cookie. When the cookie jar is empty and you need sustenance you simply lick your fingers of pride and slide them deep within the jar looking for any last crumb that will satisfy your craving.

As I stood there with the rapt attention from the audience, I wondered, "Is this what strippers think as they bump and grind upon a stage? Is this how they justify doing what they do in front of those who pay to see them? The prurient thoughts dissipated as I justified my role from a clinical perspective and not some way to sway the libido of those ogling my body as 'Three-thousand, three-thousand, three-thousand!' ricocheted within my mind.

I'd never know how the ladies actually felt but began to sense I was just a pawn...a simple molded plastic piece on the chessboard of life who'd been moved front and-center to be examined, controlled and then, in some way, eventually sacrificed... trashed, along with my dignity, in the name of science but in reality, the name of financial gain. 'Three-thousand, three-thousand, three-thousand!'

I hoped my role was important in helping others. I hoped my face would quickly morph into nothing more than a memory of some man who stood exposed with the tacit objective of helping others such that they would understand what I never knew, cope better than I ever did and adjust in a way that is still unfathomable to me. 'Three-thousand, three-thousand, three-thousand!'

Megan then went through the post-surgical process and finally the five consequences of a nerve sparing prostatectomy - sterilization, erectile dysfunction, penile length shortening, urinary incontinence and post-surgical depression. With each one, Megan outlined what would be done by the surgeons to minimize the magnitude of the consequence and the post-op timetable for physical therapy which included the attempt to increase blood flow to the penile region and why.

Upon completion of the post-surgical summary, I thought we'd be done. However, it was only four o'clock and that's when I realized the session would now include the compensatory intimate activities that needed to be reviewed and the timeline for each one.

Megan began by sharing the seven components of a successful marriage offered in the first session.... attraction, association, communication, understanding, trust, compromise and forgiveness - which put a satisfaction smile on my face.

Megan then noted that beyond the physical recovery of the patient, were the mental and emotional aspects as she added. "Imagine your spouse's mind as a computer where mental health is like the hardware in terms of its processing power, memory, and overall functioning while emotional health is like the software - the programs that run on the hardware and influences how it operates. You and your spouse, and all of us, need both the mental and emotional health simply because our thoughts can trigger emotions, and emotions which can cloud our thinking."

Megan pointed at the ladies and then herself and added. "If we... you and I... do our job, your spouse will think about all that's happening and from those thoughts deduce feelings. If we fail, his feelings will cloud reality and may end up causing profound levels of depression. The question then becomes, how do we - you and I - make sure he uses his thought processes to minimize the negative emotional consequences that come with the procedure. It's not easy! Yet, it's something that can help speed recovery and return to post-surgical normal life. To this end, we need to break the recovery process down into three phases...post-operative, transitional and ongoing," from which she proceeded to review all that was going to happen and what the standard recovery timetable was as I stood there, totally indifferent to the now-infrequent glances.

It was Q&A time and I thought I was supposed to get dressed when Megan caught my glance and shook her head 'no'. Standing naked in front of eight ladies for an extended period of time was not what I'd expected and yet, it was truly was like Club Orient, the thrill was long gone, replaced, once again, by a concept of acclimation as three-thousand, three-thousand, three-thousand roiled within my brain.

Lady number four raised her hand, looked at me and inquired. "What was it like for you?"

"How do you mean?" I inquired.

Lady number four clarified. "I mean, were there phases? What was your journey like from finding out you had cancer to today? How has it been emotionally?"

I paused for a moment and then began. "When I was a little boy, one of my favorite toys was an old metal toy car that had been my grandpa's. It must have been from the 1940's or 50's and was red with a blue top and a yellow accent stripe. What was neat was the fact that it had a turnkey sticking out of the roof that you carefully wound, which would tighten the spring inside. When it was as tight as it would go, you'd set the car on the ground, press the release and watch the car scoot along the floor."

"If you wanted a cheap thrill, you simply held the old car up off the ground, pressed the button, watched the wheels spin and listened for a few seconds to the buzzing sound of the spring uncoiling as the vibration evolved from one that was initially quite intense to one that quickly softened and then disappeared. Having cancer and then surgery is like that old toy car. With each revelation, you turn the key and tighten the spring."

I took my left palm and opened it so the ladies could see it, then I took my right hand positioned and cupped it as if I was twisting a knob. With each sentence, I would turn my hand as if winding the invisible key and sound out the word click to represent the spring being wound tighter.

"First, it's learning you have cancer - *Click*!"

"Then it's the DRE or digital rectal exam, where they go through your colon and take a snip of your prostate to find out the cancer's veracity - *Click*!"

"Then, it's finding out the stage of your cancer where stage one means some cancer cells that can be treated chemically. Stage two means more cancer cells. Stage three means the cancer has reached the outside walls of the prostate and Stage Four means the cancer has gone through the prostate wall and invaded other parts of your body - *Click*!"

"Then it's preparing for surgery - *Click*!"

"Then it's the pre-op preparation and, in my case the preliminary surprise, followed by the realization that in a few hours things will be different - *Click*!"

"Then it's waiting for the post-op results - *Click*!"

"Then, it's going home and waiting to regain some form of bladder control - Click!"

"Then it's the post-surgical review where you learn what the aggression of the cancer was that's measured in what are called Gleason's - *Click*!"

"Then it's the ninety-day post-surgical exam as the spring just keeps getting wound tighter and tighter! - *Click*!"

I paused for a moment and looked at the ladies who were now deeply involved in the litany of emotional pressures as I began again. "Now it's time for your six-month review - *Click*!"

"Now it's time for another blood test and your PSA and the dreaded phone call where you don't sleep for a week before the results - *Click*!"

I stopped again, looked at the ladies and then continued. "I can remember being in our kitchen when the phone rang. I was afraid to answer but did. The nurse on the other end was polite and pleasant as she said...'George, good news, your PSA is negligible'.

For the audience, in a demonstrative way, my hands fell to my sides as I exclaimed *"Buzzzzz!* as the coiled emotional spring quickly unwinds. Deep breaths of reprieve filled my lungs. Tears trickled down my cheeks and there was liberation.... profound... almost indescribable... relief."

All the ladies' mouths were agape as I continued. "Every anniversary means another visit, another set of tests with the spring being wound again but not nearly as tight as that first year. Each year, you wait for the phone call. Each year, in my case, it's been the same news as the spring unwinds.... *Buzzzz* and you're relieved, grateful and aware your time has not yet come."

The mood in the room was shifting. Slight smiles crossed the ladies' faces as I imagined they were thinking of their spouses and giving themselves hope. I continued. "Year five comes and you've gone from a period of trepidation to one of expectation as the caller announces you're now classified as 'cancer clear'. Once again the spring winds but not nearly as tight and then unwinds.... *Buzz!"*

I paused and then interjected in a lower, almost self-effacing tone, "It's been nearly ten years and soon I'll be called a Cancer Survivor. The spring no longer winds. There's no more tension, nor relief. I am what I am, no longer able to do things I always thought were so important."

I glanced at the ladies and then continued in a somewhat peaceful tone. "What I endured has slid back into my subconsciousness until I hear about this man or that who's entering what I call 'the tunnel', imagining that he too is hoping, praying, believing there's a light at the other end and it's not a hearse. It's then that I remember the little metal car with the spring inside and realize that each man who enters the tunnel doesn't go alone. He has a little metal car with him with a spring inside that will be wound and hopefully released time-after-time-after-time until he too is called a Cancer Survivor."

I hesitated, looked at the ladies and added. "This isn't just about men with prostate cancer, it's about all men and women who endure the physical, mental and emotional challenges of cancer. If, for just a moment, I can relieve some of the fear, the stress and in the case of prostate cancer, the self-depravation, then what little I do, what little I say and what little I show is more than worthwhile."

There was total silence in the room as Megan allowed my soliloquy to sink in and then quietly announced another five-minute break. I glanced at her and saw a small tear in her right eye that she casually wiped away. It seems that, even after all the years and all the men, there was still a soft spot in her heart that reaped the bounty of emotion.

Truth or Consequences:

During the break, the ladies selected some snacks that had been placed on a hallway table as Megan took me by the side and whispered. "You did fine. Thank you! Can you run the Power Point for me so that I can be more involved with the audience?"

I nodded in the affirmative as we reconvened and I sat next to the laptop as Megan began. "The reason you're here is because you care for your spouse and want them to be happy and satisfied with life. When we delve into the subject and the consequence of what's about to transpire, we need to look at the underlying factor, which is the type of relationship you have with your spouse."

"What your relationship is remains a personal and private matter. The reason you're here is because you care for the man about to go through a radical change in their lives. At the same time, you need to understand, not only the physical but emotional consequences as well."

Megan held up her right hand and emphasized by raising a finger for each physical consequence..."Sterilization, ED, UI, PLS which may, and I emphasize may, affect the dynamics of your relationship."

Megan stepped away from the podium and noted. "We've talked about the physical changes and what you can do to minimize their consequence. Now we need to discuss the mental and emotional aspects of depression which can lead to PTSD and how you can regain or sustain the relationship with the man you love including your needs, as well."

Results:

Megan paused to indicate a change and then began. "I'd like to read an article written by a man suffering from ED that details the emotions your spouse is highly likely to go through."

There was a pause as Megan picked up a piece of paper and recited.

"Everything is on track for a fulfilling sexual connection. I feel impassioned. My partner does too, not that she shows it as obviously as I usually do but there are subtle signals between us as a 40-year couple. Our bodies speak: A microsecond longer in a kiss, a brush of a hand against the hip, a warmer shade of approval in an apparently unrelated conversation. I feel tingling. The essence of promise. For me as a man sex and orgasm are the most exciting things I can do with my body."

"Then, we are in bed loving, cuddling and stroking. The sense of anticipation mingles with love and connectedness to perfume the air. Next thing I am sliding into heaven. We are melding in the most primal way we know. It is too deeply fulfilling to describe, except with a roar of joy, love, lust and passion. Our bodies undulate together in timeless existential bliss."

"We are both connecting with our own and each other's essence, with our love and joy, and with the origin of our species. Then I notice that the actual physical sensation of this joyful connection has faded. The joy has vanished and the gap it leaves is palpable. I am softening and shrinking even more. Our love and deep connection are still precious but their manifestation is in danger of literally slipping out."

"My emotions are going crazy. She stays calm. We both tell ourselves and each other that it's Ok. But there is an immense hollowness for me, like a wasteland after a fire. Sexually, the most thrilling way I can find physical joy is out of reach. It's taunting me from behind an invisible curtain that feels more like a wall. Connectedness with my wife is deeply challenged. If this disappointment is how it's going to end, then maybe I don't want to even start getting close to my wife. Anger starts to boil up. My confidence is shattered. Sexual potency is imprinted in me as a core of my identity and now I know it's simply not there.

My hope fades as the sense of sexual possibility always buoyed me—throughout the day, not only in sexual situations but life itself is gone. Now it is like somebody has sucked the warmth and color out of my entire life. I realize how that hope was a deep part of my now-cracked Foundation."

"I can sense myself pulling away not just in bed but all the time. I am not angry with her but the look in her eyes shows that I'm behaving like an angry man. I'm angry about what I have lost. Outside the blankness of this wasteland, of course, I love my wife. I'm committed. I know we can still make love somehow. But right now, I don't want to get close. Because I know it will end in tears. I'm hurt, angry, frightened and sad all at the same time. It's hard to imagine how anyone, including me, can be positive. The disappointment hangs like a stench in the air, a sourness in the pit of my stomach. It's a reek that only I can smell, a sourness only I can taste in full. My wife certainly gets the bad air that goes with it. And millions and millions of other men and couples are battling the same beast."

There was a long pause to allow images to sink in and the emotional whitecaps to calm as Megan commenced in a softer, more gentle tone. "Relationships can vary where the potential change and a goal of minimizing the negative aspects concerns what we're going to discuss next. First, you must accept that things will initially be different. You must also accept that only time will allow your spouse to adjust. Third, how he adjusts will partially depend on how you interact with him to ensure that his self-concept regains its current place within your platonic/romantic relationship that seems to best define long term situations. Sadly, we've seen that depression can result in the creation of toxic relations which is what we're trying to help you avoid."

Megan examined the audience and asked. "You're here because you care. How many of you informed your husband you were coming today?"

I looked at the ladies and saw three hands go up. This meant five of the ladies were reluctant to let their husbands know they were going to try and help.

Megan nodded with a doleful look on her face. Reality had struck. Instead of commenting, she continued. "While there's a myriad of things you can do to assist in the mental aspect of recovery, what we're about to share deals only with the physical aspect. Once again, I must state, it includes topics I'm not recommending, suggesting or inferring and please feel free to disregard any suggestion if it goes against your own sense of propriety. My only goal is to outline the options and provide a professional discussion of what they are and how they can or cannot be implemented. My objective is to inform in a clinical manner so that you don't go on the internet and seek out what might be answers that are more prurient in nature than you desire."

I could see the demeanor within the room shifting as Megan announced. "All of you are in a situation where your life is about to change. For some the change might be quite small. For others the physical and emotional challenges can be quite immense. Right now, you and your spouses are in a very critical period. For you its concern about your spouses' overall well-being both physically and mentally. For your spouse it's a combination of fear, followed by belief that, after the procedure, he won't be able to function that can motivate him to incorrectly conclude he's no longer a man nor intimate."

"Called the 'post-prostatectomy intimacy void', the phase refers to the emotional and physical challenges men may face after surgery regarding intimacy. If that's not enough, there are also the social factors. For some it's the stigma where he no longer perceives of himself as a man, thereby making it difficult for him to seek help and support. Even though he has you he may feel isolated and alone in his struggles, which can exacerbate feelings of depression." I thought about Amy and my relationship and realized Megan was spot on. What was once healthy had become non-existent. Was my wife reluctant for fear it would be indirectly inferred as demeaning by simply reminding me of what had slipped into my subconscious mind?

For effect, Megan paused and then offered. "Intimacy is significantly important to a healthy and thriving marriage. It's the glue that binds partners together, creating a deep connection that transcends the day-to-day routine. While the exact balance and expression of intimacy can vary greatly between couples, its overall significance remains undeniable."

"Intimacy goes beyond physical closeness. It encompasses emotional, intellectual, and spiritual sharing. This vulnerability allows couples to truly understand each other, fostering open and honest communication that strengthens the bonds and builds trust and security simply because, knowing that your partner accepts and understands you, even in your most vulnerable moments, builds the confidence and wellbeing that create a safe haven where you can let down your guard and be your authentic self. In so doing, intimacy increases contentment and happiness."

"Sadly, in men with prostate cancer, a study found that only half of the men interested in seeking treatment for ED actually took steps to find it. Of men who seek help, compliance is poor. It's estimated that somewhere between fifty-to-eighty percent of men discontinue their use of ED treatments within a year. This applies to men with and without prostate cancer. Considering the importance of penile rehabilitation following surgery, the difficulty starting and sustaining treatment could have a negative impact on men's recovery following surgery"

"Even more problematic, this psychological burden can lead to problems between the patients and their partners and poor marital adjustment after surgery. Loss of intimacy can occur and lead to relationship distress, conflict and frustration. Couples often avoid the issue and put off seeking help. This avoidance may seem useful at the time to circumvent dealing with the stressful problems of cancer and sexual dysfunction. However, as healthy spousal communication has been associated with greater marital adjustment in dealing with prostate cancer, seeking help and developing healthy communication would be the optimal strategy."

Megan paused, looked up from her notes and added "As you can see the psychological aspects are not only going to affect your spouse but you, as well, simply because witnessing your partner struggle can be emotionally draining when the focus is simply on him and not the two of you which may result in you feeling neglected, insecure or unsure about how to initiate intimacy differently."

"Discussing sensitive topics might be difficult for both of you. However, if you don't, it can lead to communication breakdowns and unresolved feelings while adapting to a new reality in your relationship. You may need time and support to adjust expectations, explore alternative forms of intimacy and rediscover closeness."

"Just like your spouse, you, too, might experience a dip in self-esteem due to changes in your intimate life and role within the relationship. We offer this class to help you not only better understand what's going to happen but to minimize your psychological burden. We know that you're experiencing anxiety and depression as you witness your partner's struggles in navigating their own emotional turmoil. As is the case in any caregiver situation, there will be stress as you support your partner's recovery while dealing with changes in their emotional well-being. We also recognize the potential social isolation you're probably feeling, thinking things are different or misunderstood, especially if you hesitate to share your experiences openly. Finally, we also understand and respect that you have your own intimacy wants that need to be recognized and addressed."

Megan paused as much for effect as to allow the previous thoughts to sink in, took a sip of water and offered. "Depending on where your level of intimacy is now, the sexual side effects will add varying degrees of pressure to any relationship as many men find themselves getting increasingly agitated over the most trivial and stupid things." Megan hesitated and offered. "I want to give you a couple of warning signs regarding post-prostatectomy depression. First, will be the reticence of interest in intimacy we discussed. If it goes untended, when his depression hits rock bottom, it will be when he suggests a solution that involves you seeking intimacy outside the relationship. Don't do it! To do so will exploit his vulnerability and manipulate his emotional state."

"The suggestion itself constitutes a significant betrayal of trust, potentially shattering the foundation of the relationship while causing immense emotional pain to the partner. Seeking intimacy outside the relationship often backfires, leading to increased feelings of guilt, shame and jealousy for both partners, ultimately worsening the depression and potentially pushing the relationship towards irreparable damage. The focus should be on supporting the man through his depression and exploring alternative solutions to rebuild intimacy within the relationship."

The room was completely silent as Megan allowed the ladies and me to digest a very critical consequence. I thought for a moment and wondered how the depression number could be so low. You're sterilized, suffering from erectile dysfunction, urinary incontinence and penile length shortening as my mind wandered to Amy while I realized Megan was spot on.

After an extended period of silence, Megan continued. "I'm going to outline several options for you. However, before I do, I want to be perfectly clear I'm not suggesting, recommending or inferring you experiment with different forms of intimacy unless you truly want to.

Lady number seven raised her hand and inquired, "You mean, be the initiator?"

Megan nodded in the affirmative and continued. "When it's Ok to begin physical interaction, there will normally be reticence on the part of your spouse to begin expressing themselves physically. This is normal! It's also normal they're afraid to make the first move and this is where you need to step in."

Lady number six asked, "But, how?"

Megan smiled as the ladies were leading her down the descriptive path she wanted to go. "You don't want to be too obvious and there's a good chance he's not going to initially be receptive. Remember, he's going through a lot of physical and emotional challenges. Yet, by doing a few things that are probably different from the past, you can motivate even the greatest curmudgeon to be the lover you once knew."

Megan waited to let it all sink in and then continued, "After all these years, if you're still wondering what turns men on, the very first thing is to love yourself. There's nothing sexier than a woman who's confident about herself and her body. As women, we're taught to believe that we shouldn't let a guy know we're interested in them. This is simply wrong when you've got a man who is scared, depressed and feeling all alone while asking himself...'Why me?' Both men and women want to feel desired. There's nothing wrong with having intimate feelings towards someone. It's okay for him to know you love him; it's okay for him to know you want him. It will also make him more confident because he isn't going to be scared of rejection."

There was another vocal gap as Megan moved away from the podium and looked directly at her audience and noted. "Contrary to current attempts to control or deny our fundamental sexual nature, we are living in incredibly sexually liberated times. We've moved light years beyond the sexual mores of our parents and grandparents that provide refreshing possibilities when we step away from shame."

"When it comes to intimacy, whether you're a man or woman, it all starts in the mind. If you're not mentally aroused by each other, and open to moving the bar, potential sex will be less than impressive. I'm not suggesting anything extreme, just an open mind and the realization that things are different and different things mean different circumstances that might require different actions and activities."

Megan looked at the ladies and then me and continued. "While we were all conditioned to be uncomfortable about discussing sex, women owning their own sexuality often has come with a price. Whether it's humiliation, rejection or just simply shaming. It's something buried deep within you that you now need to overcome simply because you need to recognize and accept it might take your initiative to get things rolling again."

"To this end, you need to be verbal and express what feels good, what you like, and what you want him to do. It'll get his imagination rolling, and that's exactly what you need if you want to learn about turn-ons for guys. However, if you're not comfortable doing something, don't do it. Being open-minded has nothing to do with following orders. If he's into something that you don't really like, don't judge him for it. Everyone is into different things. If you're open to trying new things, make sure you have a safe word."

Once again, my mind drifted back to Amy as I felt profoundly stupid realizing she'd been sending me messages and I simply didn't get the drift. Would it be possible to make it up to her? Could I simply compensate someway for all the times she was sending dispatches to deaf ears?

There was a pause in the conversation until Megan thought she had the white caps of reaction calm themselves as she began again. "Remember it's just you and him and no one else and you want to send the message that he's a man and you want him."

I reflected on Amy and the way she dressed in Saint Martin in her short shorts and tank tops and surmised it wasn't just for her, it was for me and I'd missed it, never once getting the hint, never responding in the way Amy wanted me to. God, I'd been a dolt! So many overtures that went right by me. No wonder why she was so frustrated!

Looking at me, Megan nodded and I pressed the button. As was always the case and I'm certain some Atlanta lawyer told Megan she needed to recite, she offered. "Let's talk about kinky sex." I watched as eyebrows went up and mouths dropped open as Megan added the disclaimer. "Once again, this is simply a reference and nothing I'm suggesting, inferring, recommending or endorsing"

With that, Megan read off an entire list of things that were kinky to say the least. Talk dirty. Get icy. Send a racy text. Tie them up. Use a blindfold, nibble and bite. Give them a naked massage. Dress up. Spank them. Pull their hair. Get loud, Leave the windows open. Experiment with role play. Play with sex toys. Try new positions. Get steamy in the shower. Have some strap-on fun. Get a sex pillow. Make a home movie. Have anal sex. Watch porn together. Get down in public. Forgo panties. Lounge in lingerie. Find pleasure in the fridge. Did someone say 'threesome? 40% of America women fantasize about them and 10% join in. The most popular trio is call F/M/F."

There were deep breaths, muted smiles and a lot of gulps as Megan added. "Now let's look at the best places simply because they open up a whole new world when it comes to great alternatives!" as she noted. The Car. Deserted Parks or Beaches. Hotel Windows. Private Bathrooms. A Movie Theater. Empty College Classrooms or Libraries. A Private Roof Deck. At your pool. In your backyard. "

Megan smiled and added. "Of course, this is just a few that I picked out. Some of them might be unlawful so I recommend you fantasize about a few of them instead of trying them out, unless, of course... well...... let's just leave it at that."

Megan paused for the snickers to stop before leveling the playing field with "Once again, this is simply a list and nothing I'm suggesting, inferring, recommending or endorsing."

Woman number four, who'd been quiet all day, reluctantly raised her hand and asked. "You mean people really have sex in these places?"

Megan looked at her, smiled and said, "Sure why not? There's an old adage from basketball, 'no harm, no foul' which seems apropos. The goal is to put a little spice in your life and if any of these do it, go for it. If not, don't force it."

The next slide was entitled *'Sexual Appliances'*. Even I knew she wasn't referring to refrigerators and freezers as Megan went through the entire litany of options and detailed the form, function and quality of the different devices while outlining which ones were best and why. I had no idea!

I thought the ladies would be as squeamish only to see they were keenly interested in the subject matter and what each product did and why one was better than the next.

OMG:

Between the kinky summary and the toy story, Megan had the ladies nervously smiling. For some it was out of embarrassment, for others it was because Megan lit the fuse on their imagination and they were seeing themselves in locations or with the devices or even both that made them accept there was nothing dirty, wrong or sinful with any of them as she noted, "Sex should be fun. Now and even after what's about to transpire."

I thought back to Megan's statement that all the medical staff had approved the meeting content and, for some reason, it eradicated any obscene or indecent tone that might have existed in my mind as there was a very intentional pause until Megan inquired. "What about you? What about your needs? What about your level of depression? What can you do?"

All the ladies' heads dropped for a moment as I could sense their remorse as Megan continued. "You love your spouse or you wouldn't be here. It's normal that you're also worried. What if you try and well...nothing transpires? How do you satisfy your own needs? There's a conundrum, isn't there? It's called spontaneous desire which most men have but few women experience."

"'Spontaneous desire' can be thought of as the feeling that you get when you randomly, out of the blue, want to be intimate. It's what most of us traditionally view as being horny or whatever you want to call it. Seventy-five percent of men primarily experience desire this way. However, most women are different. For most women, physical arousal actually precedes the feeling of sexual desire; women's desire is primarily "responsive desire," meaning sexual desire that occurs in response to arousal or stimuli. With this being the case, you need to realize this is natural and, if you want to 're-light the fire', you're probably going to overcome your natural reticence and take the lead."

The facial expressions I witnessed indicated Megan had hit a tender spot. Were the ladies willing to give up their own physical needs or reservations because their husbands no longer felt like a man? The question was hitting home, not only with the ladies but with me.

Megan took a deep breath, lowered her voice for a moment and offered in a very clinical tone. "If you need to be... uhh... satisfied, what do you do? Perhaps it's the appliances we outlined. For some men, they'll offer to allow you to find a surrogate."

Megan paused and then offered. "They might say 'go ahead' but most really don't believe it and to do so may create a marital calamity as it can exacerbate his depression and sense of worthlessness. Granted, you have needs and that might result in infidelity. If you do have those needs and are willing, infidelity with a same-sex partner is considerably less harmful to the mental fitness of men than infidelity involving the opposite-sex."

I glanced at the audience and there wasn't a single non-expression. Every woman had some sort of look from shock to lecherous grin.

Megan lingered, looked at me and then continued as a slight shudder of self-doubt slid through my veins. "Once again, I'm not suggesting, recommending or inferring you participate. However, if your needs are such you require something you can't get at home, you might want to consider a relationship outside your current one. However, I recommend it's done with another woman."

I heard a gasp as Megan offered. "Just don't do it on the sly and don't do it without your spouse's knowledge and approval. Be aware the subject matter will take you into extremely dangerous territory. There are emotional risks and you need to be sensitive they are there and you need to evaluate whether your needs are greater than the potential risks involved."

One woman put her hands to her mouth as if in total shock. Megan caught her gist and offered. "With today's increased acceptance of expanded forms of physical interaction, the question arises... 'If an individual is involved with a third person in their hitherto straight sex life, does this mean they or their partner are bisexual?' The answer! Not really! Many individuals who have experienced the same-sex relationships identify themselves as straight because they can't imagine themselves having a long-term relationship with another person of the same sex. It more about the moment to them and not a lifetime."

I thought about Amy and our relationship. I thought of how I felt when I found out that before we were married, she'd been with Sydney. I then thought about her tryst with Karen, her assistant, and the realization that my anger wasn't about what she did but the risk to our family and business. Finally, I thought about my feelings after my surgery and the fact that deep down, if she needed it, she should go for it. Perhaps she had. I don't know and, with our relationship dwindling, I don't think, other than a bruised ego, I cared if and only if, it would make her happy again."

Lady number three yet again. "How would we broach the subject and why do you think men are so...so turned on by same-sex situations?"

Looking at the ladies, Megan asked. "Why is this pertinent to you? Simply because you probably have no idea how your spouse would respond if the subject comes up. What's important is happiness and satisfaction for both of you and not just for one of you. Once again, I must note you're skating on thin ice but the subject still needs to be one you're aware of."

I observed the ladies and saw wide open eyes. I don't think they were expecting a discourse on their sexual satisfaction and yet, as the disclaimer noted, when I finally got around to reading it, there were no holds barred.

Lady number two raised her hand and inquired "So, you're detailing a threesome?"

Megan stopped for a moment and then offered. "As our society has changed so has the appeal of two women together and there's almost nothing that turns a guy on more than watching two girls enjoying each other physically. A threesome might be all right when things are 'normal' but to take a man who has questions about his own... uhh... abilities and put him in a stressful situation where's he's expected to perform, you're simply inviting disaster."

My eyes bulged out...a threesome. Jesus! Megan never addressed that subject the last time. My thoughts went back to Saint Martin and the night in the hot tub wIth Amy and Michelle as I realized, it was my conservative nature that superseded what Amy wanted. Oh my God! Was I really that blind?

I could sense that Megan felt she was getting in too deep and was relieved when she offered. "I'm only broaching the subject with the goal of providing information simply because some of those who've taken the class before you asked for more information regarding the matter. Once again, I'm neither suggesting, recommending or inferring that you participate. However, I would be remiss if in our discussion the subject wasn't addressed."

"For most, or perhaps all of you, the subject lies beyond your realm of acceptance which is both normal and acceptable. For some of you it might be something you considered. For others it might be something you've already tried. All I'm suggesting is that consenting adults should free themselves of the social and cultural restraints and do what they want to, when they want and with whom they want without fear, reservation and/or the emotional baggage that was formerly attached to even thoughts and fantasies hidden within our minds."

Megan was near the end and it was time for her closing remarks. "Today, we are free! Free to expand our own bounds! Free to reach out beyond here and now and touch things we've only thought about, dreamt about or wondered about. To journey beyond your own or your spouse' borders to seek out 'more' should only lead to a better, richer, fuller life and, as long as another's feelings aren't destroyed, we are legally and socially emancipated to have a relationship with *whomever* we want, *however* we want, *whenever* we want, with the only limitation being *wherever* we want. In so doing, we have the right to label ourselves anyway we desire as long as that classification represents our true feelings and not something contrived because it's what we THINK other people want us to be."

"The ultimate key that determines right and wrong, good and bad is the simple caveat...what is right is what makes you happy without making someone else unhappy where happiness is the combination of sincerely feeling wanted, needed and loved ... not only by others but of oneself, where 'happy' is the richest and most rewarding label of all."

Q and A:

The entire subject of satisfaction had been the grand finale to Megan's recommendations concerning what women could do to inspire their partners. By now, I was no longer uncomfortable with the eight ladies and totally ambivalent as one lady raised her hand nodded towards me and inquired. "Have you always been so...so open?"

"Hardly!" I replied. "I was, and remain, quite conservative until I realized, in a clinical setting, I needed to check my modesty at the door. My only goal is to help you understand so that you can help your spouse recover both physically and emotionally. I never intended on making my... ahh... situation public. I've seen what prostate cancer can do to a man and how, through education and counseling we...you and I...can help others go 'through the tunnel' as I call it."

The next lady asked, "How has your experienced changed your perspective on life?"

I waited for a moment as I felt the need to assure the ladies this was intended as a serious medical presentation. I sat on the edge of the table and noted. "I didn't come here to thrill you, embarrass or even titillate you. I came here to help you better understand what your spouse is about to go through. Would I have done this before meeting with Megan? Absolutely not!"

I looked at lady number six who was fidgeting with her pen as she offered. I can't speak for the other ladies, but I'm glad I came."

I nodded as if to accept the compliment and replied. "I commend all of you for being concerned and open enough to enroll in this program. When I had my surgery there was nothing like this. My wife and I went in blind and came out scared, scarred and despondent. With this program you have an idea of what's going to happen and how you can help."

"At first I thought this would be couples but now realize that would be a mistake. Because of her compassion Megan developed this program for women to allow for more in-depth discussions without all the reservations if we were in mixed company. We all know most men are a lot more... uhh... inhibited than women and so the topics and questions wouldn't have been as open."

I glanced at all the ladies again and added. "My only goal has been to help minimize confusion and, most importantly, help you reduce the depression that's going to follow. Trust me, the depression will be there. Sadly, most men are too reticent to talk about what's going on. Depression and PTSD are real and oft-times debilitating circumstances. It's only through compassion and support that men can recover and begin to relive their lives."

"You're here because you love your spouses and want to help them. You need to be aware of the symptoms that may include disturbing thoughts, feelings or dreams related to the events, mental or physical distress, alterations in the way they think and feel and an increase in the fight-or-flight response. These symptoms can last a month or more after the procedure and will remain somewhat latent for a longer period of time."

Megan turned off the computer as she proposed. "Remember, all of us have our own preferences and needs when it comes to life's satisfaction. The reason you came today was to learn and expand your information horizon and learn ways to help the one you love. Our goal was to inform you and expand your thoughts and alternatives."

"I hope we've accomplished this. The next few months are NOT going to be easy. There will be days. There will be instances. There will be episodes that will challenge you, your spouse and your relationship. We hope the information we've provided will assist in making you aware of the road you're about to travel. I thank you for coming. I thank you for your attention and for your compassion."

The ladies all smiled as I could sense a level of relief as well as one of gratitude. The subjects covered and the methodology were such they could have resulted in a real mess. Instead, the ladies were provided critical information that would assist them. As the meeting ended there was a round of applause. For many, it was an exceptional experience that informed them of what lie ahead. My mind went to my Theory of Acclimation and I realized it was in effect. The subjects that had been uncomfortable for me the first time were now commonplace. Those that were new, piqued my senses, made me pause and accept the fact that, for Megan, it was simply a typical day at the clinic and nothing more.

The topics, the questions, the openness had become her standard based on what she'd experienced previously. There was no eroticism. It was just her job and she did it very well.

As the ladies filed out I hoped they realized what they'd been given was incredibly valuable where my only wish was I'd known before my procedure what they knew and then the trauma of the entire experience wouldn't have been as deep. In three hours I felt I'd personified the malady and given hope, while potentially minimizing both concern and confusion.

Megan offered to lead the ladies out the door, providing them with a goodie bag that included written materials covering the topics presented. She returned and smiled, offering, "George, you were great! Funny when needed, sincere when required and sensitive when necessary. I can't thank you enough. Now, let's get those marker lines off you."

I was somewhat reticent after my last visit to have Megan proceed with removing the markers, but was now so indifferent I no longer cared. Unlike the first time, Megan left out the emotional response and simply took the alcohol wipe and erased the lines in a clinical way as nothing more than what needed to be done. I stood waiting for more, simultaneously hoping she would, while also fearing that she'd do so. I guess the $2,000 difference in my fee and my requisite need for money had taken my form of payment from dollars and senses to simply dollars all the way around.

The Thighs the Limit:

I looked at the clock and it was nearly five and was about to call for the Uber driver when I checked my watch concerning my flight, whispered "damn" as Megan returned and inquired, "What time's your flight?"

"It was supposed to be at eight but it was cancelled and they've got me on the ten" I replied.

"Tell you what, our house is only a few minutes from here, why not have a glass of wine and then I'll take you to the airport?"

That sounded great to me. Anything was better than an Uber driver and sitting at Hartsfield. Megan locked up, turned on the alarm system and we got in the car. Once again, as she slipped into the driver's seat I glanced down and saw that her skirt had ridden up a little higher on her thighs. If she was trying to seduce me, entice me or arouse me she was certainly doing a fantastic job as she drove to Habersham Road in Buckhead.

As we slowly made our way down the tree-lined street I admired a variety of architectural styles, from charming bungalows to stately mansions all with manicured lawns and blooming flowers until we pulled in the driveway of a gorgeous cream-colored brick ranch with black shutters. Megan pressed a button on the windshield support and the garage door opened to a spotless environ as she shut off the car and offered, "Welcome home."

"It's gorgeous," I proposed.

"Thank you, we really love it."

We? We? I guess I didn't understand and it showed.

Megan stopped and offered. "Rick and I had a condo and were friendly with our neighbors, Elli and Charlie. When Rick left I had too many memories and wanted to move. I'd mentioned it to Elli one day and she said they were looking for houses in Buckhead but couldn't afford what they liked because this is an expensive neighborhood."

I could tell it cost a bundle to live on Habersham just by the houses and the cars as Megan continued "One day, Elli called and wanted to know if I'd like to go with her to look at houses. I thought, 'anything to get away,' and we came over, saw the house and fell in love with it.

That night Elli and Charlie were over and asked me if we could buy it together as it was out of both of our price ranges. I asked if she meant as partners and it was agreed they'd put up two-thirds and I'd put up one-third and we'd split the expenses the same way."

My mind was whirling as Megan continued. "We both knew it was the only way we could afford to live here and so I thought, 'Why not?' We drew up papers, formed an LLC, put our condos up for sale and they both sold in a week because the Atlanta real estate market is hot, especially for upscale condos, and most couples can't afford luxury homes, or even nice houses in this area."

Explanation given! Explanation accepted, as we entered through the kitchen with its high-end appliances and all-white cupboards with brass handles and granite countertops, Megan put her purse on the breakfast island.

"Do you mind if I change?" Megan inquired.

"Not at all," I replied.

As Megan was gone, I perused the kitchen and the great room with its fieldstone fireplace and incredible, and I mean incredible, pictures on the walls. Above the fireplace in metal script, was Einstein's mass-energy equivalence $E=MC^2$ which I found quite perplexing. Why would someone put a theory of relativity above their fireplace?

I remembered the theory of Special Relativity deals with physics in the absence of gravity where Einstein noted that the laws of physics are the same and the speed of light in a vacuum remains constant regardless of the motion of the light source.

I also remembered that the word 'relativity' was a synonym for dependence such that all the components were dependent on and/or inter-related to each other to the point where the aggregate was greater than the net sum. I had no idea the significance of why it was above the fireplace or even why I remembered it from Mr. Coleman's high school physics class. Was this a scientific or social statement and why was it above the fireplace?

There's an old adage, 'you are what you wear'. In Megan's case, I'd only seen her in scrubs when she was my physical therapist and her 'business clothes' which were very sophisticated and professional and that was my opinion of her. Gone only a few minutes, she returned barefoot with her hair in a pony tail, wearing the type of shorts found normally on younger girls that literally have no legs... the shorts that is, not the girls.

On most women, the short, short, short-shorts would probably have looked somewhat out of place. However, the other adage... *'if you got it flaunt it and if you don't, then hide it'* certainly seemed apropos as the shorts on Megan underscored her long legs, while her white, button-front, sleeveless top was quite appealing, reminding me of Amy in St. Martin that, perhaps took, fifteen years off Megan's perceived age, while taking my mind off the day.

Without sitting, Megan asked. "Care for that glass of wine?"

"Sounds great!" I replied.

"Red, if I remember correctly."

"Yes." I nodded with a smile, impressed and yet somewhat embarrassed she remembered.

"Cabernet Sauvignon?"

Again, I nodded in the affirmative as Megan turned, went to what looked like a kitchen cabinet, pulled open the doors and exposed an entire rack of wine.

Opening the wine she offered. "Let's sit on the couch and go over all that happened today."

I motioned to the pictures that included some of scenery and some of people and noted their beauty. Megan noted that Elli was a professional photographer and had taken all the photos to which I offered. "She's got a real talent."

"Wait until you meet her. She's fantastic!" Megan offered with an enthusiastic smile.

Feeling relieved I could relax, I nodded in the affirmative as we made our way to the family room while peeking into the dining room and observing the place was simply impeccable.

Megan made her way back to the family room couch, offered me my wine and proceeded to the opposite end. After my initial visit I was still filled with trepidation and I think she felt the same way.

"Here's to a great day!" Megan offered as she slid back into the couch cushions and lifted her glass.

"Agreed." I replied, with a smile of satisfaction realizing the 'show' was over and it was time to unwind.

"Care for a snack?"

"That would be nice," I replied.

"Cheese and crackers?"

"Sounds great," not letting on that I really didn't like cheese. Something about being raised on it had taken the allure away.

I sat and gawked as Megan was once again, up and into the kitchen before returning and placing the cheese on the coffee table. The two of us sat adjacent to each other so that we could share the cheese and talked about the ladies and how it all seemed to go so well. Megan reiterated some of the events of other meetings that hadn't gone quite as planned. I noted that I was, at first, skeptical about the sessions but totally blown away by the clinical nature and how so much information was presented that made the classmates feel comfortable to the point they were willing to open up and ask questions.

Soon our glasses were empty and Megan offered more. I thought *'What the heck?"* I hadn't had any wine in months as Megan made her way to the kitchen and returned with two full glasses.

As Megan bent over to hand me glass number two, instead of watching the wine glass slide into my hand, I was staring at Megan's cleavage - as any man would do - and the full glass of Cabernet Sauvignon slipped into my lap.

"Shit!" I exclaimed in a sudden burst of frustration and embarrassment.

Megan jumped into action, went to the kitchen and returned with a roll of paper towels and quickly began dabbing up the spilled wine. I felt like some type of clumsy dolt before inquiring, "Can I help?"

Before another word was spoken, I quickly realized 90% of what was spilled was on me. Megan looked, laughed and offered, "Leather couch, wood floor, no problem. Let me get some leather cleaner and Windex and we should be good as new."

Megan returned to the scene of the spill and began wiping up the wine as I patted the purple stains on my shirt and pants and tried to absorb as much as possible realizing I had nothing else to wear.

"You need to get out of those clothes before the stains set in. I'll wash them."

For the first time in I don't know how long, I was laughing as Megan looked at my soaked shirt and pants and announced, *"Chateau Laffite George, 2024! A new and vibrant Cabernet Sauvignon personally soaked in the clothes of the Vigneron to provide a fuller body."*

Reality struck! I'd assumed this would be an in-and-out day and didn't bring a thing with me and the thought of wearing sticky wine-stained clothes on the airplane actually grossed me out."

"There's a bathroom there." Megan directed, pointing to a door off the kitchen. "I'll get a towel for you."

Megan had seen all of me and yet I appreciated the fact she was offering a little modesty as a sense of propriety as she offered. "Why don't you hand me your clothes and I'll get them started?"

I entered the bathroom, undressed and handed my clothes to Megan. The biggest problem consisted of a way to wash the wine off my skin. I remembered back to Tommie and my Vintner days and the fact that wine can be sticky because of the tannins that can clump together and form gels. Of all the red wines, the one with the highest level of tannins is Cabernet Sauvignon.

Here I was, standing naked in Megan's half-bath with Cabernet Sauvignon sticking to my body. As a half-bath, all there was consisted of one of those pump dispensers for soap and a white hand-towel. There was no way of washing the wine off without water all over the floor and I didn't want to stain her white towel. Instead, I opened the bathroom door and called, "Megan!"

No answer!

"Megan!"

Still no answer.

I surmised Megan had to be washing my clothes or cleaning up after my accident. Naked, and somewhat reluctant, I walked out into the kitchen and peeked in the laundry room and Megan wasn't there. I checked the family room and, again, no Megan. I walked down the hall to the primary bedroom and glanced inside. Above the bed was a large photo of Megan wearing a smile and little else.

Megan came in from the garage with a container of Tide as I stood gazing at her photo in my birthday suit. "Sorry!" was all I could offer in a very embarrassed way. "I called out to you but you didn't answer. I checked the laundry and family room and you weren't there."

"Well, you got to see a lot of me, didn't you?" Megan giggled. "And now we're even."

"Sure did." I said, somewhat sheepishly.

"And?" Megan asked.

"Well, I... uhh... I guess I was surprised but also realized it's very tastefully done."

"So, you like it?" Megan inquired.

I shrugged again and politely offered, "Sure, it's really nice."

"It's my motivator," Megan said with a smile. "I was at Elli's studio one day and she convinced me to take it. When the proof came back, I really liked it and thought 'what the heck?'

"Motivator?" I inquired.

"Sure, to stay in shape. I wake up in the morning, look at the photo and make it my goal to do my exercises."

"You're in great shape," I offered.

"I try," Megan replied with a slight and somewhat shy smile on her face.

I was beginning to realize Megan's outlook on life was more contemporary than I first thought. Perhaps I was the one in the minority. As we stood there, Megan's taciturn side was revealed as she elicited an expose' on why the photo existed and how she was impressed by what she thought was my similar attitude as exhibited by my lack of inhibition during the session. Little did she know!

Here I was, standing naked in Megan's bedroom and she simply didn't seem to care. She looked at me and tried to appease my discomfort by stating. "I don't know why Americans are so hung up. I was that way once. However, my education and career changed all of that. Today I look at the body as nothing more than the superstructure for our mind and, therefore, our soul."

My God, I could be listening to Amy. We could be in Saint Martin. It could be 30 years ago as I simply nodded and allowed Megan to provide her rationale.

Megan smiled and nodded in agreement as if I'd validated her comment and my uhh... lack of attire as she inquired. "You have a house in France, correct?

"We did." I replied.

"You also have a house in Saint Martin."
"We did."

"In both France and Saint Martin public nudity is allowed and no one thinks anything of it, correct?"
"Only the tourists. Especially those on cruises, who come to the beach to gawk and bring their cameras." I offered.

"You have your Theory of Acclimation where what was once special, erotic or unique, through repetition, becomes commonplace. What was once commonplace, through repetition, becomes mundane. What was once mundane, through repetition, becomes moribund or insignificant. Don't you think that's applicable to nudity as well?"

"I guess so," realizing I was neither aroused, nor embarrassed standing there.

"Sure," I proposed in agreement.

Megan continued. "It's the same thing with sex. If it's repetitious, it too can morph from special to commonplace, then to moribund and insignificant. It's only through variety it can remain special."

We were getting into the subject that caused my initial trepidation about coming to Megan's house. I knew she was liberal in many ways but also knew I didn't want to, or at least didn't think I wanted to do anything to violate the sanctity of my marriage, even if there were so many challenges going on at home.

Wanting to change subjects, I inquired. "You don't happen to have a different wash cloth, do you? The wine is sticky and I didn't want to stain the one in the bathroom."

"How about a shower or slipping into the pool?" Megan offered.

"The pool would be nice."

Megan walked me to the sliders, pulled back the drapes and I saw the in-ground pool. As was the case for all the houses on the block, the backyard was a private enclave with a high, brick wall encasing a group of Magnolia trees and flowering shrubs. In the center of the yard was the pool, glistening in the early evening light.

Feeling a bit awkward, I walked naked out onto the patio and was struck by the two headless statues on pedestals on each side of the pool stairs. The first statue was that of a woman. As I got closer, I realized the torso's features resembled Megan's bedroom photo, while the second statue was of some headless man who had to be some sort of body builder. Needless to say, it wasn't what I was expecting.

As I made my way into the water, the pool lights came on as I realized the timer was already set for late fall making my envious of the ability to extend the summer season while not realizing that summer in Atlanta can be brutal.

Carrying two white terrycloth bath towels, Megan placed them on the patio table and made her way to the pool stairs where the subject of what I thought of the presentation at the clinic began. I'd had time to think about a response and simply told her I thought it was fine. She knew I had something on my mind. Little did I realize she knew exactly what I wanted to know but was afraid to ask.

Megan smiled and noted. "George, your Theory of Acclimation is really spot on and I believe it's apropos to a lot of different things in life including individual... uhh... personal experiences. I've seen it in your face and wondered if you were upset, offended or simply embarrassed by the subject matters and what transpired today."

I sort of shrugged my shoulders in response, not wanting to embarrass myself by admitting the only reason I was there was for the money. Megan paused and then added. "When we did the first session none of the last hour was included simply because we didn't think it was pertinent. As we did more sessions and got the surveys, we learned women were interested as much in the post-op situation, practices and limitations, as they were in what their spouses were going to endure. It opened a lot of eyes in the clinic as we came to the realization we were addressing only half the topic instead of giving the participants a full course of what they wanted and needed to know. While I'm certain the subject matter probably made some of the class uneasy, when it's put in a clinical, non-prurient perspective with the caveats included, we haven't received a single negative comment."

As my hand slowly made waves in the pool, Megan sat down on the top stair of the pool with elbows on her knees and feet in the water and inquired, "what topics of today's session if any, do you think we need to change or improve?"

I paused for a moment to arrange my response before adding, "While your kinky list was actually funny and the discussion of all the different appliances sort of uncomfortable, the thing I was somewhat mortified by was the discussion on cheating."

"Really?"

"Yes. I guess I'm old fashioned."

"George, there were eight women in the class and statistically nearly one-in-eight women in America have cheated and the number has increased by forty percent in the past 25 years. This means, statistically, one of the ladies in that room cheated on her spouse."

"Holy shit! What about men?" I asked.

"One-in-five." Megan replied.

I thought to myself. 'God, I really am blind."

Megan continued. "In grad school, I took a clinical psychology class and one of the subjects dealt with patient guilt complexes where my professor didn't call it cheating or infidelity. Instead, he outlined *'Outside Marital Encounters'* or 'OME's', which represent men and women who were having a non-committed sexual relationships outside of marriage without establishing blame by associating the activity with negative terms like infidelity or cheating.

"That's logical, I guess."

Megan continued. "His premise was, when you don't know the cause regarding why someone is going outside the traditional bounds of marriage, is it right to categorize the participant with derogatory terms? If you look at it, infidelity is a violation of trust in a romantic relationship that happens when someone breaks the expectation of emotional and/or physical exclusivity with their partner. Religiously, a marriage vow is traditionally considered a covenant of physical, emotional and social commitment between two parties. The professor posed the question 'what happens if one side breaks the covenant in an emotional or social manner, is the other side still required to maintain the agreement? If not, are they infidel or cheating?"

I sort of cringed simply because no one knew about Amy's experiences except me and it was something I'd thought about but was reticent to bring up while the term 'OME' settled into my psyche.

Megan continued "George, first you need to realize both ends of the Baby Boomer Generation are different than my Millennials, who are then different than today's Gen Z's. It could be because your generation broke ground on so many things that became commonplace for us and are now mundane for the Z's. Whatever, I hope you realize your generation's values and outlook are different from mine and neither one of them is wrong. Just think of your concept of acclimation."

Megan lingered, smiled, nodded and offered. "Regarding the kinky stuff. We added that to not only broaden horizons but add a little levity to the meeting."

"So, in other words, people really don't do what you suggested?"

Megan looked at me as if I was some sort of dolt and noted. "George, people do those things all the time. We actually culled the list to make it less...uhh, adventuresome than what's going on out there."

"Really?"

"Uhh huh!"

Megan leaned back and continued. "As for the appliances, the industry grosses nearly ten billion dollars a year in sales in the United States and it's what's already happening in a lot of homes. Once again, it was reported as 'missing' in previous sessions from the anonymous surveys we received. As such, my goal was simply trying to legitimize it in case it's needed to help rebuild intimacy after surgery."

Megan paused, looked at the water and then at me and added. "While there were some women who were probably shocked or offended, there were also those who realize there are things they could do to help their spouses and themselves be a lot more physically satisfied. By making the attendees more aware of the subject matter, I hope I softened the blow, while trying to address the products and activities in a clinical way."

I nodded, catalogued the double-entendre, whether it was intended or not, while realizing why they'd been added and doing my best to justify their inclusion. While Amy had been more liberal than me when it came to doing things, I was beginning to realize we were actually behind the curve regarding what some people were participating in. I also realized that the acceptance of products and activities that were once considered taboo was now so widespread they were no longer considered deviant, thereby breaking the cultural reins that had limited their application.

"What about the nudity?" I asked.

"Well, how do we describe things without showing examples?"

I sort of shrugged as Megan continued. "What's really crazy is the fact that, as our society has allowed pornography to reach virtually everyone, the attitudes towards nudity or even topless sunbathing, have gone in the opposite direction with bathing attire for women has gotten smaller and smaller and smaller while men's more conservative."

I thought about Saint Martin and how It had transcended. When we first went there, half the women were topless but their rear-ends were fully covered. The last time I was there, only a few women were topless but the idea of full coverage in back was a thing of the past with thongs and what I think they called Brazilians the style and from what I'd heard it was a trend sweeping America as well."

Megan added. "Clothes enhance sexual mystery and the potential for unhealthy sexual fantasies and actually focus attention on sexuality, not away from it, to the point it often enhances immature forms of sexuality rather than promoting healthy body acceptance. If I was here in a minuscule bikini that barely covered anything, it would be more sexually stimulating, in often unhealthy ways, than full nudity."

Boy, she had that right. A great looking woman in a sleeveless top and short, short, short shorts! Hello! Enough to spill a full glass of wine in my lap.

There was a pause as if Megan was measuring what she wanted to say and then began. "George, I've been involved with male patients for almost twenty years. At first, I guess I was a little squeamish then, through your 'acclimation', I got used to it in a clinical setting. As for the ladies, I'm certain some of them were titillated, some of them concerned and some ambivalent. In the end, I believe the clinical setting set the tone that this wasn't a strip club, but a medical discussion that required more anatomical review."

I looked at Megan and countered. "I'm just glad there wasn't one of the brass poles."

Megan giggled as her voice slipped into my mental background while I did the math on her comment of 'almost twenty years'. I figured, college graduate at 22. Four years to earn her PHD in physical therapy which would make her 26 when she began her practice. Now add 'almost twenty years' and she had to be in her mid-forties and not thirties, unless, of course, she was including her post graduate work in the twenties, which still made her in her early forties. Now I was really impressed by how good she looked and just seventeen years younger than me.

My attention returned Megan as she professed. "We really live in a mixed-up society where modesty - especially enforced modesty - only adds to sexual interest and desire such that the enforced modesty further eroticizes human anatomy by tagging it shameful to expose it. It's so upside down that the element of being forbidden merely perpetuates increased reaction the lack of exposure allegedly inspires."

Wow! My mind ambled to the spilled wine and Megan's cleavage and realized, she was right. I mean, what was I really looking at? Cleavage? A split or division and therefore a space. As I ogled, I was simply looking at nothing as I had so many times before and in looking at nothing, I spilled my wine.

Megan paused and then inquired. "How about you? How did you feel today?"

I paused, ran my hand through the water to make tiny ripples and then noted. "At first, somewhat reticent. Then, I simply realized there was nothing I could do about it. I'd made a commitment and was living up to my side of the bargain. Finally, I got to the point of acclimation and became indifferent as I told myself I was doing this for a good cause and there was no permanence."

"How do you think you would feel next time?"

"The Theory of Acclimation," was all I offered which we both subconsciously realized was a metaphorical way to say that the trepidation, reservation and consternation was dissipating.

"And what if we used you as the live anatomy model instead of the structural images?"

Gulp! I didn't know if she was for real or simply pulling my chain and really didn't want to find out.

With the long pause, our conversation had reached a logical stopping point as Megan noted the first batch of my clothes were probably washed and needed to go in the dryer. With that, Megan stood up and I realized the back of her shorts were soaked. Oops! I guess my pool ripples were a bit too much or she was a lot more excited having a naked man in her pool than she let on.

"How about a salad?" Megan asked as she wiped her hands on the back of her shorts.

"Sounds good to me."

Truth Be Told:

A few minutes later Megan made her way back from the dryer and saw I'd dried myself off and was sitting at the patio table with the towel around my waist as she continued her discourse. "We have a real cultural collision in America. Your parent's generation's women banned the bra as a matter of protest. Yet today, they've morphed back to a very conservative mindset. At the same time, Millennial women are more likely to have more liberal attitudes towards sex as a recreational activity and not just for procreation and today's new adults are even more liberal and casual. The net result is that my generation and those following mine are more comfortable with non-traditional relationships and sexual identities."

"Why has this happened?" I asked.

Megan replied. "Because we've been exposed to nudity, sexual content and variation through the internet and media over and over and over resulting in your Theory of Acclimation! Add to that the profound expansion of tolerant practices and relationships and things have changed. Everything from mixed marriages racially and sexually are no longer taboo. Even admissions to same-sex experiences has dramatically increased. While there's still some reservation, today the social stigma involved is fading as tolerance levels increase."

Whew! I'd asked Megan what time it was and she explained how and why she built watches as she added. "While the racial and orientation biases have somewhat diminished, it hasn't happened nearly as fast, or as broad-based as the biases facing American women, where the biggest challenge is probably best summarized in what's called the *Objectivization Theory* where a woman is seen as a sexual object and their physical appearance and sexual characteristics are emphasized, while their other qualities and abilities are ignored. This can be done through explicit means, such as catcalling or unwanted sexual advances, or through implicit means, such as the portrayal of women in advertising or media as primarily being attractive and sexually available."

Megan shook her head as if in disdain and added. "The real tragedy is how it affects a woman's body image and their subsequent thoughts, feelings and perception regarding the aesthetics of their own physique and how they view themselves respective to their height, shape, and weight. Sadly, the expectations aren't created by a woman's self-concept but by air-brushed photos of half-starved models that help create prevalent social and cultural ideals."

Megan glanced at a bug about to land on the table, looked me in the eyes and added. "A woman with a negative body image may feel self-conscious or ashamed that others are more attractive. In a time where social media holds a very important place and is used frequently in our daily lives, people of different ages are, in different ways, affected emotionally and mentally by the appearance and body size/shape ideals set by the society we live in. These standards were created by and changed by society in a world filled with body shaming comments and acts of humiliating an individual by mocking or making critical comments about a person's appearance."

"What about men?" I inquired.

"What do you mean?" Megan countered.

"Aren't we held up to some appearance standard and when we don't meet it, aren't we also denigrated?"

Megan looked at me and replied. Physical appearance does play a role in how women perceive men, especially initially. Studies suggest women are more likely to be drawn to men they find physically attractive for evolutionary reasons where attractiveness is often seen as a sign of good genes and health. However, it's not the whole story. Women place greater value on personality, intelligence, humor, and shared interests. What a woman finds attractive can vary based on her age, life stage, and individual preferences. Above all of these, confidence and self-assuredness can be very attractive, regardless of conventional attractiveness."

"So, it exists both ways?"

Megan nodded 'yes' and then added, "Women are more often objectified based on their physical appearance and sexuality, while men tend to be objectified for their physique or status. Women are typically objectified in a way that reinforces a power imbalance, while male objectification often emphasizes strength and dominance while studies suggest women are objectified more frequently and intensely than men."

"What's the power imbalance you noted?" I asked wondering if I fit into that category.

Megan paused and then offered. First, it's economic. Women often earn less than men for equal work and may also face challenges, like lack of access to credit or ownership rights. Second, it's political simply because men are generally overrepresented in positions of power like government, leadership roles and corporate boards which limits women's influence on policies and decision-making. Third, the imbalance is social, because gender norms and stereotypes can limit opportunities for women due to the fact they may face social pressure to prioritize childcare and domestic work that restricts career advancement or participation in public life. Finally in the threat of violence, women are disproportionately affected including intimate partner violence, sexual assault, and harassment which can create fear and vulnerability that can further limit their power and freedom."

"Do you feel this imbalance?" I asked, sensing how strong Megan was.

"Yes, of course. It's the little things...the tone of voice, the egregious smile, the 'look' that I get that I find demeaning.

"What about your friend out there?" I asked, nodding at the male statue.

Instead of answering Megan posed the question "How does he affect you?"

"He makes me feel somewhat inadequate." I replied.

"Really?"

"Well yes. I mean he's got a great physique and uhh....."

Megan smiled and noted. "There's no one-size-fits-all answer to what women think of men. Whether physical attractiveness plays a role where some women might find a man appealing, while others might not. We all have to accept that the male body, in a respectful and romantic context, can be perceived differently. Some women might appreciate seeing a man's body to get to know him better, while others might find it impersonal and prefer to focus on personality."

"Do you think attitudes have changed?" I asked, somewhat leaning forward as a sign of my increased level of interest.

Megan shrugged as if it was a somewhat naive question and responded. "I think there's been a shift in women's attitudes towards men over the past 50 years, reflecting broader cultural changes around sexuality and body image. Fifty years ago, we wouldn't have the statue by the pool and if we did, especially here in Georgia, there could have been legal issues. Back then, there wouldn't have been a way to have you do what you did at the clinic. It just wouldn't have happened."

Megan looked at me, slightly smiled and noted. "You were naked in the classroom. You were naked in the house.

You were naked in the pool. You're sitting now with nothing but a towel wrapped around your waist. If you want to take the towel off, it's fine with me."

"And if I do?" I replied in a somewhat challenging tone.

"Fine."

"And if I don't?"

"That's Ok too."

"What about you?" I countered.

"You mean removing my clothes?"

"Yes."

"If you want me to, I will."

I got a wry grin on my face as the thought made its way through my mind and into my body without stopping at my conscience along the way. With that, Megan put her fork down and noted. "If you do want me to, then perhaps...and just perhaps, you're sending a different message but I don't think so." Megan paused, bit her lower lip and added. "George, we're, or at least I'm, beyond that realm and arriving at what I call the comfort phase in our relationship."

"The what?" I asked, not having a clue what Megan meant.

Megan looked down as if to reflect on what to say and then at me as she detailed. "The comfort phase is when two people begin to understand, accept and, above all else, respect each other. When two people are in that phase, physical touch transcends to the point it becomes a way to express affection and feel secure that's not just driven by sexual desire. It's that point when physical intimacy becomes about enjoying one another's presence and feeling a sense of connection and less about individual pleasure and more about creating a shared experience."

Megan paused and then noted. "It's also when there's reduced sexual pressure, which is where I believe we're at right now, built on a foundation of trust and emotional, not physical intimacy, where you feel comfortable being vulnerable with your partner and expressing your needs openly with me as I am willing to do with you."

"I know that when we first see each other, there's a physical rush on both sides. I also know that, as the day wears on and we interact, those physical urges somewhat dissipate and, like tonight, we begin to look at intercourse not as a physical entity but a mental, emotional and philosophical interaction where there's a natural fluctuation simply because relationships go through cycles, where the level of passion and intensity can fluctuate simply because the comfort phase doesn't mean a lack of desire but rather a shift in focus.

My mind was going crazy. My heart was pounding so hard I felt it in my brain as I inquired in a somewhat serious tone, "And what do you want me to do?"

Megan stopped, looked at me as her tone of voice changed as she added. "I want you to be comfortable with yourself. I want you to feel free. I want you to accept that we are becoming friends. If the towel represents the last vestiges of reservation and you want to be totally open, go for it. If, it serves as a protective wrapper, leave it on."

I didn't know how to take Megan's response.

I was both humbled and intrigued and simply asked, "why me?"

Megan looked at me and smiled. Then pausing, she offered. "From the first time I met you, I saw a man I could respect who didn't have ulterior motives. A man who is kind, generous and above all else, humble. Beyond the physical you, I also see someone I admire and hope will become a dear friend. Someone I can share things with. Someone that will allow me to take down the facade and be myself. Someone I can trust... I mean really trust... who will listen to my secrets, provide a shoulder to cry on and a tear to shed. In return, I offer the same to you if you so desire."

There was another extended gap as if Megan was providing time for me to mentally evaluate her offer and then she added. "If times were different. If circumstances were different. Then things might be different. What's really crazy is that I believe the physical aspect between us has, for some reason, already been broached and we're in a phase of mutual emotional discovery where few people ever journey. From this, I think we're creating the foundation of understanding from which we...you and I... can move beyond the superfluous and lean on each other in a way where we both have someone we can trust with our feelings and more importantly, our emotions, proclivities and fears."

I nodded in confirmation. This wasn't about a man and a woman. This wasn't about anything carnal. This was about sharing each other in an emotional way that I was realizing we both profoundly needed being built on trust and respect, two things I greatly desired and now profoundly missed in my life.

Generations:

We continued eating on our salads where the quiet time seemed to serve as a natural break. Finally, I looked at Megan and asked, "What about men and sex?"

"What do you mean?" Megan inquired, as I realized the question could have multiple meanings.

I gulped, not wanting to have her think I was prying into her personal life as I clarified. "In America today."

Megan paused and then replied. "Men's eagerness to mate is highlighted by the sex industries of pornography and prostitution that cater principally to guys. Whereas men are generally more interested in casual sex, women look for greater emotional commitment in a relationship. This sensibility is reflected in successful romance novels written and read mainly by women."

Megan continued. "When you were young, advertising created Macho America with this mythical male persona that depicted a white, working-class male, often married with children, living in the suburbs, and holding a blue-collar job, who was stoic, practical and unexpressive that emphasized self-reliance and independence, had a pioneering spirit and was portrayed as being strong, adventurous and even aggressive."

"In other words, the Marlboro man," I offered.

Megan smiled and nodded in the affirmative before adding, "And what did it get him? Bad breath, lung cancer and an early death. Now let's look at Baby Boomer women. First, boomer women had limited career options as they faced significant barriers in many professions. The focus was on family life, where the 'ideal' for many was marriage and motherhood, simply due to societal pressure to prioritize domesticity."

"Then what happened?" I asked, while already knowing the answer as Megan elucidated. "We need to go back and look at the consequence of World War II which was a catalyst for significant changes in the role of women in society that dramatically transformed their role in the workforce where many women experienced financial independence for the first time that led to a shift in societal attitudes about women's roles and challenged traditional norms."

"Unfortunately, despite their wartime achievements, many women were pressured to return to domestic roles after the war where the "baby boom" further reinforced traditional gender expectations. This stress contributed to the feminist movement of the 1960s that continues today regarding women's entry into the workforce as the second-wave of feminism reared it's oppressed head generating significant activism for women's rights which impacted Boomers' later lives and consciousness. Gone was the concept that the only 'right' thing was for the wife to be a homemaker who stood home to support her all-knowing husband and resolve 'family matters'."

"Father's Know Best!" I offered referring to the 1950's television show.

"Yes, until dad came home one day and found his wife in bed with the pool boy or perhaps, the woman next door."

I sort of grinned and chagrinned at the association as Megan continued. "In my generation the typical man became the 'Wall Street Bro' - the young, urban, wealthy male obsessed with money, success and material possessions who was often stereotyped as being arrogant, materialistic, and entitled. We Millennials, are often characterized as being more adventurous and less religious than previous generations where many of us are more open to questioning traditional norms and experimenting with different forms of physical expression."

Megan paused and then added. "Women of the early part of your generation realized the importance of education as a way to social freedom and sent their daughters to school to the point Millennials are the most educated generation ever. With women of my age achieving more professional success than previous generations, we're more likely to prioritize careers and personal goals before starting families and consider intimacy from a recreational perspective and not a procreational one."

Megan looked at me and posed the question. "Do you think thirty years ago a woman would be managing the largest medical clinic in the South? The changes have been enhanced by technology and social media. Today, online platforms have empowered women to connect, share experiences and challenge traditional norms including spearheading movements while addressing diversity and inclusion that includes not only gender Identities but sexual orientation and racial dynamics as well. All of these have, and continue to influence, Millennial women's perspectives and experiences."

"What about today's generation?"

Megan got a somewhat sardonic grin on her face and replied. "Generation Z? Their persona is reflected as the 'Tech Bro' who depicts a young, tech-savvy male working in the technology industry who's introverted, socially awkward and obsessed with gadgets, whose social circles and support systems accept individuals and encourage positive and healthy sexual exploration."

I paused to realize that, because of Amy, my opinions and values had changed and I fit somewhere in between all the generations which was both good and bad, as it created a level of tolerance, acceptance and trepidation while, also creating in some ways, guilt.

Megan continued. "I once read that the difference between your generation and today is the fact that kids get older younger and stay younger older."

I must have had a frowned expression as Megan explained. "Today's fourteen-year-olds know and want to experience what your generation did at twenty-one. In the late 1960's, the median age for women marrying for the first time was twenty-years-old while today it's twenty-eight. Today, the average age for men getting married the first time is thirty-two and a lot of them need to be that old to finally mature. That eight-year difference for women is what I call the 'exploratory' or 'tween' years where the number of women find themselves in an over-supplied situation."

"Huh?"

"While you're probably wondering why I have so much social information, you need to realize that urology is not just about eliminating bodily waste, it's about reproduction. Because of this, even here in Georgia, we need to keep up on what's going on *out there* as the world is rapidly changing and those changes affect the challenges and changes our patients are experiencing not only in terms of their bodily functions, but mental health as well."

I never thought of it that way but could see Megan's point as she continued. "If you remember back to basic economics and the law of supply-and-demand as it affects price and therefore value, in a social market we have exactly the same thing. Today's market imbalance between women and men in the same socio-economic strata results in the fact that, in order to compete, the over-supplied, twenty-something females elect to enter into the spirit of men's penchant for recreational sex simply to have the opportunity to socialize and hopefully find someone in their strata to settle down with."

"I don't know what you mean," I offered.

Megan continued. "When there's an over-abundance of supply versus demand, one's bargaining power declines and with it the value. In the case of young, educated females, they begin to behave more like men in order to remain active in the romantic sphere to the point they've become more physically adventurous as they adopt the penchant for sex without strings and a more masculine sensibility regarding issues concerning the number of sexual partners, variety and the satisfaction they derive."

Megan put her fork down and added. "At first it was the women's magazines who kept pushing the envelope when it came to sexual practices with each year finding a new once-forbidden topic that became mainstream. Today, literally anything and everything goes resulting in all the items I showed the ladies this afternoon."

Megan paused, looked down at the table and somewhat forlornly added. "Women have certainly gained sexual freedom compared to their grandmothers. However, they've lost out in the emotional commitment that was previously there. This psychology is at an extreme point on U.S. college campuses where there are only about seventy-five men for every one-hundred women. The net result is called 'hooking up'... which is some level of physical intimacy that lasts for just one night that has largely replaced dating."

I stopped and simply thought, 'Oh my God!' as Megan got somewhat pensive and continued. "The uhhh...freedom they experience in college or those 'tween' years doesn't stop, it just widens the parameters of acceptability, to the point their sexual liberation means more sex outside marriage in terms of both pre-marital and extramarital experiences. Today, most young women are not only sexually active before marriage, ten-to-fifteen percent, continue to be active outside their marriage as well."

"Why do you think more women are cheating today?"

Megan looked at me and realized she was talking to a very conservative, very traditional totally naive individual as she noted, "Some of the reasons include shifting social norms while studies suggest that, while men tend to be driven by physical attraction and sexual desire for someone outside their marriage, women, report seeking an emotional connection because they say they're feeling a lack of intimacy or expressive support in their primary relationship."

"Emotional connection?"

"George, American men are experiencing a profound identity crises today and it appears to be affecting marital relationships."

"We are?" I said totally incredulous to the statement.

Megan looked at me and offered. "It's never been easy for either gender. For men, job insecurity and income inequality can make it difficult to live up to the traditional 'provider' role while the pressure to portray a perfect life can contribute to feelings of inadequacy. Today, it's tough to live the American dream simply because the dream expectation has risen so high it's virtually impossible to afford. There are sixty...that's right sixty more things today that people consider necessary that didn't exist in 1965. Sixty things people need to purchase, maintain and replace. All of which cost money which means the basket of goods requires a higher percentage of disposable income than ever before as well as all the non-discretionary goods and services you must have to simply exist."

"Do you mean, essential goods and services? I inquired.

"Yes George. The things you must have to live...food, housing, transportation, healthcare, insurance, clothing, personal Care, childcare, education, technology products like computers and cellphones and entertainment. There not wants, but needs simply to exist in our society. Then add in all the other things you want but can't afford and you quickly see why we're such a frustrated society where the thought of women not working has become almost incomprehensible simply because of the financial strain a single income family endures."

I nodded, never realizing what it took simply to live as Megan added. "While some men embrace change, others struggle to adjust to a world where traditional gender roles are less rigid. All of these 'pressures' can cause huge relationship issues at home which may result in a threatened or challenged covenant to the point that either side may begin to believe the grass is greener on the other side of the fence only to learn it's because that's where all the bull shit is."

"What about men and fidelity?" I asked, remembering men were always considered the culprits.

Megan looked at me, swallowed and replied. "While still a higher percentage than women, studies show that over the past 50 years, there's been a slight decrease In the percent of out-of-marriage experiences for men, to the point that, in terms of probability, two of the classes' wives' husbands have probably done so. What's interesting is that today younger men are reporting the greatest decline in extra-marital experiences which is being compensated by a surge in older age groups."

"Huh?" I responded, again totally surprised.

Megan looked at me and noted. "Studies point to men in their 50s, 60s, and even 70s becoming more deleterious, with some studies indicating out-of-marriage experiences increases to one-in-four men in their age group."

I was incredulous and simply shook my head as Megan continued. "Experts suggest several factors for this trend that includes the infamous midlife crises, decreased partner interest, increased opportunities, as well as the belief they were left out of the sexual revolution when they were young. Add to this. all the medical advancements that continue to take place that are compensating for natural changes that allow men to be sexually active at a much greater age. You need to remember that, just because the age is increasing, it doesn't mean the libido is decreasing."

Somewhat changing the subject I asked Megan. "How many of the ladies today won't really be... uhh... disappointed if their husbands can no longer be intimate?"

Megan paused, thought about the audience and added. "I think two or three will probably be relieved. As a woman gets older, things don't work as well as they did for either partner, many women are happy without any form of physical interaction and the surgical results will mean less pressure which they will welcome."

"Do you think the out-of-marriage percentages between men and women will continue to get closer to being the same?" I asked.

Megan hesitated, looked at me and then replied. "I think the number for men will probably decline a little more to the point the numbers might be closer to that of women simply because of the societal changes regarding gender roles and expectations. Today, women are feeling freer in seeking fulfillment outside their marriages. Another reason is their growing financial independence that allows them to risk leaving a dissatisfying marriage to pursue affairs without fearing economic hardship. Finally, and probably the biggest reason is the increased opportunities to meet people through social media that's making it easier for people to connect and potentially cheat."

"So it's mainly the internet?" I asked needing to blame someone or something.

Megan shook her head in the affirmative and noted. "A recent survey found 53% of women do it with a close friend. Another 29% become intimate with a neighbor, person from work or long-term acquaintance. These numbers have remained somewhat constant. The growth area has been in random sex where 21% report it being on a casual date or hookup while 8% report doing it with a total stranger, which rarely happened in the past. However, in all instances there seems to be a deterioration in both the quantitative and qualitative responses to the internet experience. "

"Why do think there's been the deterioration?" I inquired.

"Because people who go there believe it's going to be nirvana and then they find out it's, in many ways, a huge wasteland."

"Wasteland?"

Megan lingered, pondered the inquiry and replied. "Today, there are fifty million people or nearly 20% of all those over the age of 18 using the internet's dating apps that present a seemingly endless pool of potential partners. With so much supply, once again, you see a decreasing value on both ends. Imagine having tens of thousands of people to look at. You visit their site and make a decision based solely on their image. You have no interaction and no consequence and so you casually flip to the next person and then the next and then the next to the point called 'swiping fatigue' which is a sense of objectification, contrary to real-life interactions."

"Swiping fatigue?" I inquired, once again feeling totally out of it.

Megan glanced at me and realized, I was from a different time zone and probably even a different planet as she outlined. "Swiping fatigue refers to the feeling of exhaustion, frustration and burnout that can accompany prolonged use of dating apps. It's often characterized by a loss of interest and motivation simply because spending time swiping through profiles loses its initial excitement and becomes tedious. Compound this by the reality people are doing the same thing to you where there's a constant need to make quick decisions about potential matches which can become overwhelming, making it difficult to focus and invest energy."

"I had no idea."

"What causes the fatigue?" I asked.

"First, is the abundance of choices. Second, is the pressure to swipe quickly. App designs often encourage speedy decisions, leaving little time for thoughtful evaluation. Third, is the focus on appearance. Profiles often rely heavily on photos, leading to superficial judgments and neglecting deeper compatibility. Fourth, is the lack of genuine interaction. Initial interactions on dating apps tend to be brief and lack meaningful conversations. Finally, are all the unsuccessful matches. Repeated unsuccessful matches can lead to feelings of discouragement and low self-esteem."

Megan continued. "Beyond the magnitude and speed of the entire venue there are the emotional aspects. There's the feeling of it all being superficial simply because focusing on quick judgments, based on limited information, can make you feel shallow and unsatisfying. Swiping through literally hundreds of profiles without finding genuine connections can be discouraging."

"Let's say you surf the site and find someone and begin a dialogue. Normally, depending on the type of site, you begin by seeing what you have in common. As it progresses, you may reach a point where one side wants to stop and then you risk what is called ghosting."

"Ghosting?"

"Simply the act of suddenly ending all communication with someone without any explanation or warning as well as unresponsive matches, all of which can contribute to frustration and negativity. Now, all the excitement of finding someone turns into a real sad situation where all the hopes, dreams and effort can lead to a point where the lost and lonely feel rejected, dejected and sometimes humiliated when all they initially sought was someone to make them feel wanted, needed and loved."

God! I was getting a social tutorial that was opening my eyes to not only America but specifically my own kids. Had I really been this naive? I was interested from a personal level and so I inquired. "How long do these uhh... internet relationships last and once a person participates; do they keep doing so?"

Megan looked at me and I think she realized something had or was happening at home and so she answered. "In the case of women, short-term situations that are fueled by excitement or revenge, might fizzle out quickly. Emotional relationships, where the woman is seeking connection and intimacy, can last longer. The duration depends on factors like opportunity, as well as secrecy and finally if or how soon it's discovered."

"A woman or even a man, seeking validation might end the relationship once their needs are met. Someone unhappy in their marriage might be more likely to continue or repeat the experience. However, each person is different and the need can be based on several factors including their overall relationship satisfaction, personality traits and coping mechanisms. Someone with a history of multiple experiences, who hasn't addressed the underlying issues or has a low tolerance for frustration is probably at higher risk."

My mind wandered to Amy and wondered if this was the reason for her indiscretions. Once again, a sense of guilt permeated my mind as I looked inward and thought it was my fault as I inquired. "Is the increase in female extra-marital experiences because of women's lib.?"

Megan politely shook her head 'no' and added. "Women's liberation strikes me as semantically troubling. It implies that females are finally getting what they have long wanted. The big question is who's been more liberated men or women? The reason for having sex has changed for women. Who's having sex with whom changed for men. It's crucial to remember that labels like 'sexually liberated' can be both subjective and limiting simply because what one person considers 'liberated' might differ greatly for another. I sincerely believe every individual has the right to express their sexuality in a way that feels safe, respectful and fulfilling for them and not for everyone. Sexual liberation is a journey, not a destination. People's experiences and perspectives can evolve throughout their lives."

"Why do you think the divorce rate is so high?" I asked.

"Surveys indicate that lack of commitment is the most common reason for divorce in the United States which seems to also be a problem in the workplace and society as well. Sadly, the fervent passion for 'what's good' has been replaced by 'what's good for me'. This egocentric propensity can manifest in various ways within a relationship but ultimately signifies a breakdown in the couple's willingness to work on the marriage."

"Do you mind if I ask, is this what happened to you?"

"Not at all." Megan replied before responding. "Our problems started in Milwaukee where both sides refused to compromise. Moving to Atlanta was my idea. I thought it would give us a fresh start in terms of friends and commitments to each other. Instead, my work load was incredible, the hours invested beyond what either of us expected and Rick felt as if he was being left out. Then, because of what I'm involved with I think Rick really felt insignificant, all wrapped up in the fact that he was homesick for his family and buddies."

Megan hesitated as if to contemplate what to say next, looked at her hands and then at me before continuing. "It was a Saturday, which didn't mean much as I was working twelve hours almost every day. I said I'd be home for dinner. When I arrived around eight, his parking spot was empty and a chill went through me as I realized it was bad."

"I went in the house and found a piece of paper on the kitchen table with one word written on it...'Goodbye'. It was like someone stuck an ice pick in me. I didn't know the severity until I went into our bedroom to change clothes, opened the closet and found his side empty. It was then I realized what 'goodbye' meant. I tried calling his cellphone but got no answer. I attempted to text him but it was blocked. I knew then that 'goodbye' meant forever."

Megan's hands were trembling as she was reliving the day as she continued, "I remember going back into the kitchen and picking up the piece of paper and realizing it was finally over. All the anger! All the pain! All the threats had come to fruition."

I looked at Megan and saw the sadness. It was then that it struck home, as Megan added. "For the first time in my life, I was all alone. My family was in Wisconsin. In college, I'd had roommates and then Rick and then, for the first time ever, it was just me who had no life beyond the walls of the clinic. I went into our living room and sat on the couch and was deafened by the profound sounds of silence. Nothing! Absolutely nothing! No noise! No sounds! Just the thump, thump, thump of my broken heart."

Megan had a sad look in her eyes as she confessed. "I realized I'd been so immersed in my job, I failed in my marriage. I vowed that night I'd get better, but the insatiable hunger of the job kept eating away at me, clawing, clamoring, demanding more and more and more. Days turned into weeks, which turned into months. Day upon day, they all blended together, only segmented by sleepless nights, alone in an empty house, where silence was my only companion."

Jesus! I felt I could write a tragedy on what I'd heard as Megan added. "When you're all alone you have the innate ability to talk yourself into or out of anything. You can justify actions and reactions. You can legitimize change and even modify or validate your own rules, your own values, and even your own perspectives on right and wrong."

I just sat, mouth agape, shaking my head from side-to-side in unison with each emotion as Megan continued. "One Wednesday night I'd had enough of being alone and decided to go out for dinner. When I'd come for my job interview, they'd put me up at the Waldorf Astoria in Buckhead. I remembered they had great food and, being alone, felt I wouldn't feel out of place as most people would think I was a solo traveler staying there on business."

"I got somewhat dressed up and went to the hotel. The restaurant was full and so I decided to have a drink in the bar. While there, I met a guy and we started talking and he made me laugh. It felt so good! I watched as he glanced at my left hand and saw there was no ring. I looked at his and realized it didn't matter."

"One thing led to another and well, it all began - my trip down the rabbit hole into a version of Wonderland where I encountered my own set of characters who made me challenge my own rules and expectations and do so in an attempt to quash the one thing I wanted removed... simply not to be alone anymore... no longer buried in the sounds of silence."

There was a long pause to allow both of us to regain some semblance of composure. In the hiatus, my mind wandered back to Madison and the realization you can be all alone even when someone else is there as you listen to the sounds of silence and the thump, thump, thump of a broken heart.

Within You, Without You:

Megan went into the laundry room to check on my clothes, which she found out were still tumbling. I realized later that this respite also provided time for Megan to collect her thoughts and establish what she wanted to share. When she returned we went to the table and, as we sat looking at each other, the conversation began plunging to a level that was much deeper and more intimate than I'd ever anticipated.

While somewhat cautious, I was honored that Megan realized that the depth of our conversation was to the point it was becoming philosophical as she rendered. "You're so much more than I thought. I mean I haven't had a conversation like this since... since college and even then, not so... so free."

"Me too." I replied.

Megan took a deep breath as if to expel some of the sadness that was accumulating from reliving some of her past as she admitted. "So far, I've given you the 'official' version of what transpired. Do you mind if I share more of my journey?"

"Please do," I replied, wondering where the conversation was going.

"Do you mind if we go over by the pool?"

"Not at all," as we stood and walked over so that the shimmering pool lights reflected off our faces allowing both of us to experience the emotional consequences of our conversation.

Megan paused as if to choose her words carefully and then began. What was about to transpire was much weightier than what she initially told me, punctuated by a long pause that allowed Megan's index finger to slowly make its way around the rim of her wine glass until she finally spoke. "When Rick left I really didn't like myself. Instead of self-pity,

I began trying to justify my dislike in many, many ways. In so doing, my basic instincts became virtually self-destructive that overrode my internalized scruples, permitting me to objectivize myself as I became willing to demean the person within me in many, many ways. In so doing, I reached a point where I had no respect for myself and none from those who equated me as nothing more than an object to be used to satisfy their own carnal pleasures where sadly, I didn't care."

After a gasp, as if what was said had a bitter taste that needed to be spit out, Megan continued. "George, your Theory of Acclimation is so adroit. As I began... uhh... trying things, I went through the phases you laid out. With each... uhh...event there was first the excitement and titillation, then through repetition, commonplace acceptance; then through even more repetition, mundane affirmation and finally, in many instances, profound boredom superseded periodically by my own realization I'd finally gone too far while feeling the depravity it represented."

Now, deep within the chasm of discussion, thought and evocation, Megan added. "In going down my rabbit hole, I simply assimilated my core values and inclinations that can happen when diverse subcultures come in contact with each other where I found myself in the middle trying to traverse both worlds which was probably the core reason for my bewilderment."

Megan looked directly in my eyes and I saw anguish where, for the first time since we'd known each other, I sensed a softer more sensitive soul, grateful simply to have someone to talk to who wouldn't judge, denigrate or chastise her as she looked at me and noted. "In my case, my journey had me ponder a totally different subculture where, instead of racial or ethnic differentiation, mine happened to be more of a corporal exchange that exposed me to world profoundly different than mainstream America and... uhh... certainly more liberal, vile and open to different forms of expression."

"In other words, a different social matrix?" I inquired.

Megan shrugged her shoulders, furrowed her brow and nodded in the affirmative. "Sort of, where the context was similar to our perceived society with greater emphasis on the physical inter-connectedness and web-like structure of relationships and freedoms of physical expression."

I thought I knew what Megan was alluding to but thought it best to not respond for fear I'd misconstrued her message as she continued. "While my personal institutions remained the same reference points, it's how I began to physically interact with others that simply overwhelmed me and basically brought me to my emotional knees. In my journey, I did things, experienced things and felt things that are, in retrospect, beyond me physically, socially and perhaps morally now. Yet, I now justify it simply because it liberated me and allowed me to regain a sense of self so that I could examine my values and beliefs and determine what's important to me and what moral compass guides my actions."

There was a sorrowful expression on Megan's face as she continued. "George, it wasn't one occurrence or one dalliance. It was over and over and over until I found myself deeply involved in a lascivious subculture in which those who participate slither in their own fantasies regardless of how it hurts others that many people fail to even realize exists. Now I simply can't imagine I willingly did all that I did."

Megan took a deep breath, looked at the deep end as it metaphorically represented what she wanted to share, shook her head as if in remorse and continued. "My realizations finally began to show me that I'd gone too far and got in too deep. I needed some sort of justification such that I began to validate all that I did simply by convincing myself that doing so moved me beyond the erotic aspect into a more clinical perspective. This self-justification permitted me to become more detached and dispassionate about the subject matter and its consequence. By expanding my own physical parameters, I was able to remove the emotional aspect. By removing the emotional aspect, I became more comfortable with the subject matter to the point of elocution and practice devoid of any amatory aspect so many others would probably feel."

"In other words, all the 'things' you outlined in the class came from first-hand experience?"

Megan slowly nodded in the affirmative as she added "and a lot more." It was then I realized this conversation was getting really, really deep. However, I could tell Megan needed it... and admitted to myself it was what I needed, as well. Not in the physical or prurient sense but for simply having someone who needed me. What was profound was the fact that Megan's elocution had been emotionless. There had been no anger or sorrow. Simply a statement of fact of what transpired. And yet, her sharing what happened was serving as a form of catharsis that was allowing her to finally move on while providing me with a sense of self-importance that had been rubbed away day-by-day, week-by-week, month-by-month simply because of all that was happening to Amy and me.

Megan looked at the ground and then at me, shook her head and offered. "I shouldn't have said anything."

"It's all right!" I whispered. "It's all right!" I assured her again as she moved beyond an emotional flat line and allowed sadness to erupt again and again and again. All the pain. All the sorrow. All the frustration. All the fear that had been stored within her gushed forth as she simply let go of all that had been hidden...kept within her with no one to share, no one to care and no one who would understand.

It was then that Megan's arm reached out as if I could save her from the depth of her remorse. Slowly, I pulled her in until my hands were around her waist. It was then I heard the soft cries for help that she was emanating. Perhaps it was the touch. Perhaps the support. Perhaps nothing more than to have a shoulder to dry on. For several long minutes I held her and let her cry... deep, dark, damp tears that made her body quiver in sorrow. For the first time in months I held a woman and felt her pressed against my body, not a sensual experience, but the culmination of two people simply needing each other for support, reassurance and compassion.

I leaned back and took my left index finger and wiped away her tears as she pulled me back in as if I was some sort of shield that would protect her from the ravages of reality. This wasn't an amorous gesture. It was simply a sign of oneness as our hearts beat in a syncopated rhythm that's simply called life. I could feel her! I could sense her! The texture of her heartbeat reverberated within my soul as my mind wandered across the peaks and valleys of the woman ensconced within my embrace wondering, imagining what all had transpired.

"It's Ok! It's Ok!" I whispered as I gently brushed the hair away from her face.

"I'm sorry!" Megan offered as she feebly attempted to regain her composure.

"Sorry for what? For being human? For being sad? For being alone?"

Megan curled her head upon my chest as I simply held her and felt her breathing begin to calm while I slowly caressed her.

Like waves after a storm, the emotional breakers that had created whitecaps of remorse slowly diminished as Megan's arms willowed their way between mine while her hands pressed against my back as she pulled me in closer and closer and closer until our bodies were flush from our heads to our knees. My God, it felt good to simply sense the peaks and valleys of another woman. It had been so long...too long as the tactile sensation served as testament to our singularity. My hands rose and pressed against her back, first as an expression of acceptance and then, subconsciously to simply allow our interaction to sustain itself for as long as possible.

Finally, the storm passed as Megan pulled back, looked at me and, biting her lower lip, finally whispered. "Thank you for being my friend."

"That's what real friends are for." I whispered.

Megan looked deep into my eyes and then as a token of gratitude simply kissed me on the cheek. Not an amorous kiss. Simply one that reflected her appreciation.

My mind wandered as my intention was a like response as the space between us grew such that we could look in each other's eyes as Megan added. "One day, I had an epiphany and knew I needed to stop. In order to do that, I had to look inward and began outlining what all happened, what I liked and what really turned me off physically, socially and emotionally. I then detailed my interests and passions to determine the things I enjoy and what sparks my curiosity until I discovered my breadth of imagination in categories I'd never considered before. After my journey where I thought I needed to...uhh...find myself and the realization I went off the deep-end in terms of my... uhh... liberation... until I came to understand and accept that, instead of exploration, I needed to maintain healthy relationships and navigate the world with resilience."

Megan looked at me and there was a completely different expression that had a softer, gentler manner as she noted. "I've held so much inside and for some reason, with you, I feel so... so free... to share what's holding me up and holding me back. At work, I need to maintain a facade of authority built on an image of confidence. Yet underneath, I've been this quivering, quaking somewhat Nervous Nellie, who wonders why it is and why I'm the way I am and why I've been given the opportunity I have."

I gazed at Megan and offered. "Look, we're all that way. Shakespeare had it right...'We just strut and fret our hour upon the stage and then are heard no more.' We're all just facades when you get down to it, producing a fantasy folk who encompasses our true being by creating the protective armor that keeps us from being hurt."

I paused, peered back at the yard and continued. "Sadly, in your case, your armor was pierced and you suffered the pain of the slings and arrows of outrageous misfortune where what you thought was right was apparently engaged in the depths of anger, grief and loneliness."

Megan's head turned to the side as her eyes closed and then her chin dropped to her chest. "I've been so sad," she whispered.

"Because?" I inquired.

"Because, I've been so... so mixed up... so confused... so much in need of answers."

"Have you found what you're looking for? I asked.

"I'm recovering, but not there yet."

"So, you're on your way?"

"I think so. However, I'm aware that, compared to others, I have a level of moral perplexity that continues to cloud my judgment and still leads me to prioritize physical gratification over ethical considerations. I also accept that, while another person or persons can trigger shame in me, simply because my thoughts and actions are different from theirs, I'm still responsible for any self-inflected state of negativity they cause."

I gazed at Megan and offered. "I remember back when I had an epiphany about my life and how it was affecting our marriage and the shame I felt. It was then I realized that shame can be internal where we feel broken or bad for our desires or it can be external when politicians, pastors, teachers and parents tell us we're wrong. Even our peers can shame us based on false narratives they've internalized."

I paused and then inquired. "Don't you agree that when we hide the sting from others we're actually impeding our self-consciousness and vulnerability, while allowing them to become our weaknesses?"

Megan nodded and slightly smiled realizing her conundrum was being understood while her soliloquy was helping heal my wounds as well. After a short pause I responded to affirm what she said while being somewhat self-edifying. "In other words acculturation?"

After several lingering moments the tidal wave of remorse finally washed completely out to the sea of tranquility. With that, Megan's head tilted back and a soft, sad smile caressed her lips as she whispered as much to herself as me. "Thank you again."

My eyes closed and then the moment was gone. Like morning dew, the sunshine of relief dried the tears and took away the whispers, leaving us standing like the two statues wondering what all this meant.

For her, it was as if a ghastly secret had finally been set free. For me it was the catharsis I so desperately needed as, for the first time in a long, long time, I felt needed and appreciated. This had not been a sexual encounter nor even a physical one. It had simply been two people in need, who'd shared something much deeper than themselves. Two people who stood emotionally naked in front of each other, who bared their souls for which both would be forever grateful.

Megan looked at me and then glanced into the family room as if it could reinforce what she was about to admit. While focusing there, she noted. "Everything that happened, happened before we came here. This house, Elli and Charlie probably saved me, simply because it took away the silence and filled my life with the sounds of laughter and times of mirth."

In retrospect, the day, the evening, the night was allowing me to traverse from deep within the valley of sadness in which I'd arrived, back towards the mountain of self-respect where my simple presence had served to set someone free from pain and yearning that had been held inside, while she, in-turn, set me free from my travails of self-depreciation.

Megan was returning from her emotional voyage and simply reached out and took both of my hands in hers and continued, but did so in a matter-of-fact tone. "It took a long time for me to realize that, for a wound to heal it must first be exposed. Time and reflection can heal wounds but the ego responds and with this response comes fear which we call shame."

I paused and gazed at the woman across from me. I thought for a moment and then let my guard down as I offered. "There's a place called the Forest. It's my respite where I go to cleanse my soul. It's where I come in contact with Mother Earth and the souls who have departed. Someday I want you to come with me to the Forest. I want to see how you react. For many it's simply the majesty of the trees. For others, of which I now believe you are a chosen one, the majesty of innocence will flow into you and you will be at peace. I've taken many people to the Forest. I've witnessed how it has challenged them, enlightened them and, in many cases, cured them as it seeps the sadness from their souls and fills them with love and joy."

I simply took my right thumb to wipe the tears from my eyes. It wasn't me talking, it was Little Spirit who'd been buried beneath the rubble of disrespect and was finally coming out, thereby, allowing me to realize a world that I thought was lost, a world full of good, loving people there to assure me that in the end, I would win. Not the bad guys! Not the government! Not those whose greed allows them to destroy goodness and the people whose only purpose is love.

Acclimation:

Dinner was done and it was time to head to Hartsfield. We returned from the pool and went into the kitchen. Megan got my clothes out of the dryer and I changed. It was then I realized that, through acclimation and two hours of some really deep conversation, what had been embarrassing had become commonplace. What had been commonplace had become mundane and what had been mundane had become irrelevant.

I was accepting the soul of the person who stood before me who, in her own way, had stripped away all the vestiges to expose the guilt and pain she'd been holding and literally, emotionally become exposed before my eyes creating a unified bond simply because the two of us had bared our souls and all that came with it and it felt good.

Megan looked at me and inquired, "where did you come up with your Theory of Acclimation?"

I paused, remembered back to Father Pat and how he got me involved in relaxation therapy and how that practice got me studying acclimation. I remembered Pat's comments about stress. I replied to Megan. "It all began with the realization that everything that exists is in some form of change and that Newton's third law of motion states that for every action there is an opposite and equal reaction."

"Ok?"

"Well if everything is changing and affects everything else, you create a form of constant stress. Not just the emotional type but physical as well that can cause an object to change its shape or size which can be temporary or permanent."

"OK." Megan offered with a smile as she realized I was purporting some sort of philosophical treatise.

"The human body is not immune to these forms of stress which are normally called stressors and can literally be anything that changes the immediate state of balance or equilibrium that goes beyond the physical aspect and into the intellectual and emotional balance our body attempts to maintain that can vary greatly from person to person depending on our individual perception of the situation, past experiences, and coping mechanisms.

"Social stressors are challenges or strains that arise from our interactions and relationships with others, or the broader social environment we live in. They can be temporary or chronic, and can have a significant impact on our mental and physical well-being. With repeated exposure to a novel stressor, it can be a signal to the body that adjustments are needed. Through repetition, our body and therefore our brain gathers information about the new environment, situation, circumstance or challenges the stressor presents and allows the brain to begin to initiate appropriate responses."

Megan was nodding in the affirmative as she saw where this was going and I continued. "As we're repeatedly exposed to a stressor, the body's initial adaptation strengthens which can involve increased efficiency of existing mechanisms or developing of entirely new ones. Repetition then helps our brain create a memory of the new environment which allows us to anticipate the demands it will face and potentially adjust its responses accordingly."

"And so, we adapt?"

"Yes and no." I replied. "There are limitations depending on the nature of the stressor and our social, cultural and genetic make-up which is why people respond differently to the same stimuli. What's important is to accept that repetition is a crucial element in acclimation but not the sole factor. The effectiveness of acclimation depends on the interplay between repetition, the nature of the stressor, and our social, cultural and biological makeup."

"How does it work?" Megan asked, now totally intrigued by my soliloquy.

I smiled, looked at the light coming from the pool in the kitchen window and replied. There's a famous saying "neurons that fire together wire together" which aptly describes the impact of repetition on the brain. When we experience something repeatedly, the involved neurons communicate more frequently. This strengthens the connections or synapses between them, creating a more efficient pathway for the information to travel. In so doing, repetition helps consolidate information into long-term memory such that, as we repeatedly encounter something, the brain strengthens the neural pathways associated with it which allows for easier retrieval of the information later on. Through repeated exposure, the brain becomes more efficient at processing information and requires less effort to recognize and understand familiar stimuli. Remember when you first saw this house?"
Megan nodded in the affirmative.

"Remember how excited you were and how special you thought it was?"
"Yes"
"Now that you've lived here, the house remains the same. However, because of repetition and therefore familiarity, the special feeling is diminished. The same thing can be said about all material possessions, experiences and relationships. Repetition plays a key role in habit formation. When a behavior is repeated consistently, the brain creates a strong neural association between the cues and the behavior itself, and rewards associated with it. This paves the way for automatic behavior patterns, or acclimation, which can definitely affect the impact of special people, events, things, or places."

Megan had one of those "gotcha!" expressions as I continued. "With repetition you begin to experience a sense of diminishing returns. Repeated exposure to something special can lead to a sense of familiarity and comfort. While still enjoyable, the initial excitement or intensity of the experience might diminish simply because, with repeated enjoyment, the impact weakens.

"Similar to the brain's response to stimuli, constant exposure to a special or unique person or place, thing, event or circumstance can lead to a "desensitization" effect. We may take them for granted and appreciate them less readily which why it's important to cherish special moments and create novelty to reignite the spark. Acclimation can have a paradoxical effect on the positive impact of people, places, events, or things."

I looked at Megan and inquired. "Remember the thrill when you got your Lexus and that first ride with the top down? It's called the "new car" thrill. Over time and, because of repetition, you still enjoy your car but the thrill is gone."

Megan nodded in the affirmative as I added. "Acclimation's effect on special things depends on the nature of the experience and our conscious approach. While repetition can sometimes lessen the initial intensity, it can also lead to deeper appreciation, growth, and lasting memories. It's about finding the balance between cherishing the familiar and seeking new experiences to keep the spark alive.

"It's really important to realize that acclimation doesn't negate the response, it simply reduces the impact. In so doing, it doesn't erase the inherent value of people, places, events or things."

"Early experiences, especially those we repeatedly encounter, can leave a lasting impact and can continue to hold significance even after years of familiarity simply because the foundation they provide shapes us and becomes a reference point throughout life.

"So, everything eventually becomes commonplace?" Megan asked.

I shook my head "no" and offered. "The key is to find a balance between acclimation's desensitizing effect and cherishing the familiar by introducing new experiences or visiting old favorites in a fresh way to reignite the spark. The one thing I learned and cherish is that I now take time to appreciate the positive aspects in my life and try to invest quality time in connecting with those that are meaningful."

Megan nodded as if in agreement as I took a breath and concluded. "While acclimation can fade the colors of the rainbow, it doesn't have to blend them all into white. By understanding repetition's role in acclimation and its potential effects, I try to approach my experiences with intentionality, thereby fostering a deeper appreciation for the special things in my life."

"Coming here, I really did so with mixed feelings... fear of potential embarrassment, regret that I needed to come for the money and trepidation that things wouldn't work out. Instead, because of the clinical setting and your sharing the fact the syllabus had been outlined and detailed by your entire medical staff, along with it being my second time around, I didn't feel the embarrassment I feared."

"I must readily admit things right now at home are not great. The challenge of so many different elements has affected my outlook on life and my belief in tomorrow. Finally, by coming here, to your house, and having time to meet and therefore begin understand you, I see a person who is so much more than what I'd perceived."

Megan had a somewhat laconic look on her face as I concluded. "Megan, you are a kind, sensitive, compassionate person. You're someone who has taken something that's really difficult to discuss and made it palatable for those ladies and provided the tools needed to help their spouses and themselves in a way few others, including me, ever had the chance of receiving."

I glanced and saw an expression of gratitude forming in Megan's eyes as I continued. "I know that in your life, there are sacrifices you've made to be able to give what you have. I sense that the happiness you desire is not there. I accept that what has happened is not all you hoped for, dreamed about or would want for others to experience. Yet, I also know there's goodness in your heart and joy in your soul that will someday be rewarded for all you've given of yourself to others."

Reality:

I glanced at the clock and began to get a little nervous about time. Megan caught my drift and noted that it was only eighteen miles to the airport and as long as we left by 8:30 we'd be fine. We went out to the garage, got in the car and headed for Hartsfield. As we passed under a streetlight, I caught a glimpse of Megan's famous thighs. While the skirt had been tantalizing, her short, short, short-shorts exposed literally the entire tops of her legs. The view was incredibly distracting to the point I began anticipating the next street light to catch another peek. I know, dirty old man! Tee hee!

With three glasses - make that four - of wine in me, along with the one on me, and so many unexpected subjects broached I finally got around to asking. "Where did you get the statues?"

Megan replied, "Elli is an incredible photographer but a lousy businessperson. She had this idea but no money. I had the money but no idea and so we became partners in this part of her business. These are the first statues she created. We thought we needed some conversation pieces and with her being a photographer and what I do for a living they made sense. She needed representations and so Charlie and I became her models."

"So that's Charlie?"

"Somewhat. Elli was having fun playing around with the computer that allowed her to literally take a basic form and use Photo Shop to enhance it."

"And he doesn't mind being so...uhh...exposed?"

"Again, it's an interpretation and not really him."

"What do people think when they see the statues?"

Megan paused for a moment to gather her thoughts and then responded. "Just like with any artwork or representation, the emotional responses of women viewing nude women are diverse and depend on a multitude of factors. First and foremast, we need to accept that every woman's background, experiences and perspectives will shape their reactions. Someone who values body positivity might feel empowered, while another who has faced objectification might feel uncomfortable."

"The second element is the context in which the woman is seeing the statues as the depiction greatly influences interpretations. A medical illustration differs vastly from a sensual painting both visually and emotionally. Some women simply appreciate the beauty and artistry of the human form, regardless of gender. Others might find certain portrayals less aesthetically pleasing. The artwork might evoke diverse emotions depending on individual experiences and interpretations. A nude self-portrait could resonate with themes of self-acceptance, while a classical sculpture might spark curiosity about historical representations of femininity."

"But what about the Charlie statue?" I asked.

Megan considered my question and then answered. "There are three factors that go into the type of response women have. First, are the individual differences based on personal values and experiences. Someone who values body positivity and artistic expression might feel empowered or intrigued by a statue of a nude man, while another who has faced objectification or discomfort might feel neutral or even unsettled."

"The second component is just like what we saw this afternoon where the response is based on cultural background and upbringing. Societal attitudes and the human body can vary greatly across cultures and communities that influence how individuals interpret and respond to such depictions."

"The third aspect is what I call context and intent. A classical Greek statue in a museum setting evokes different emotions and interpretations than a contemporary art installation or a casual image online or in my backyard. The artist's intent and the overall message of the piece also plays a role. Here all Elli and I were trying to communicate was a sense of liberation... freedom from the hang-ups so many people have. If you're a guest at our house, we want you to feel free and uninhibited without adding sexual content to it and that was what we attempted to communicate. Some of our guests might simply appreciate the beauty and artistry of the human form regardless of gender. Others might find certain portrayals less aesthetically pleasing or even jarring depending on their personal preferences and cultural background."

Megan added. "Finally, are the personal connections and interpretations. Artwork might trigger diverse emotions depending on individual experiences and interpretations. A statue of a muscular athlete in action could resonate with themes of strength and determination, while a sculpture of a reclining figure might spark curiosity about vulnerability and introspection. Our only goal was allowing the person to find meaning and symbolism while connecting it to their own lives, experiences or cultural understanding of the human body."

There was a long interval before Megan seriously inquired. "Does it bother you, George?"

"What?

"That the statues are totally nude?"

I looked at her and replied. "I was just surprised and then, like most guys, think the Charlie statue made me feel a little inadequate."

"Have you ever seen Michelangelo's 'David'?

"Yes"

"And?"

"And, it's incredible."

"Did you feel inadequate with him?"

"Just incredibly short!" I joked, adding, "If he was alive, at seventeen feet tall, he could play in the NBA."

Megan shook her head and giggled, resulting in precisely what we both needed as she noted "I asked Elli to put my statue there to remind me what's paying my share of this house, car, clothes and everything else. By having one that's...uhh...the way it is, it's a reminder what the ultimate goal at work is."

After a few more light shows, I didn't want to pry but had to ask "Can you tell me how this house deal works?"

"Sure, the three of us shared the down payment and now share the costs and any work that needs to be done. There's no way I could afford this house on my own."

"What about Charlie?"

"He's a pilot for Delta and so he's gone a lot and it's just Elli and me most of the time."

I dldn't want to broach the subject but I think Megan knew what I wanted to learn as she added. " Elli and I are wonderful friends who keep each other company."

There was a pause as if Megan was measuring her words and then added. "There are some elements to our relationship. First there's friendship. We obviously know each other, share common interests, care about and respect each other and enjoy spending time together. Because Charlie is a captain, we get to go on vacations with his employee discounts and do all kinds of things together."

There was a distinct pause and then Megan added. "Our relationship is about enjoying each other's company without any commitment or expectations. The last thing any of us want is to hurt each other or jeopardize our friendship. In order to ensure we don't, we sat down and explicitly agreed to the terms of the relationship. We've been open and honest and made certain the communication paths between us remain accessible allowing us to navigate jealousy, manage boundaries and address concerns."

"And it works?"

Megan sort of laughed as if it were a dumb question and replied. "Sure! Elli and I are committed to each other as friends. At the same time, I know she loves Charlie and I wouldn't do anything to jeopardize that."

"Does anyone else know about this...this relationship?"

"George, it's a financial relationship, not physical. Our real friends who come to visit normally have an initial misunderstanding and some degree of titillation. Then when we explain the partnership like I did with you, they understand and appreciate our situation. When the subject comes up, which rarely happens, we simply express how societal views on relationships are archaic and ask them to challenge their own norms to see how, in some ways, we affect their own relationships when we're simply roommates."

Megan looked my way and reassured me. "I love Elli to the point I'd never do anything to jeopardize her marriage. I'm aware that when two people are already together and a third person enters the equation, there's almost always a power imbalance, with the two longer-term people having a stronger coalition than either of them with the new person. This can contribute to a two-against-one dynamic, where the established couple has more united power than the new person. I knew and accepted this going in and yet it felt like the right thing to do at the time and still do. Without them, I'd be alone and miserable. Where the big difference comes into play is the fact that when Charlie travels and Elli and I are together, we have each other. With this dynamic it changes the relative ratio and equalizes the relationship."

"What about you?" I inquired.

"I've tried dating other people, which I do every now and then."

"And now?"

"Right now, no one special's come along. However, if someone does, and it's someone I want to be with, then we'll probably split up.

"What's the future?"

"I don't know. A lot of situations like ours are short-lived. We've been together for nearly three years and so far it's working out."

"What does Elli think?"

"She's like me. We're both satisfied with the arrangement. You have to realize, in order for it to work, you need to be open and upfront about what you want. Because you've doubled the deck, you need to be loud about your yes's and just as loud about your no's so that you establish boundaries up front."

"What happens if you decide to split?"

"We have it in our agreement that they could buy me out for one-third the appraised value of the house or I could buy them out for two-thirds. If we all decide to move on, we would split the net revenue in the same percentage."

All of a sudden, Atlanta's famous downtown traffic became a reality as our speed slowed to a crawl. I sensed I'd dug too deep and felt Megan was getting uneasy and it was time to change the subject anyway. As we sat in silence with Megan's total attention on traffic, my mind wandered and I thought of the similarities and differences between Amy and Megan. When I learned about Amy's inclinations, she was filled with guilt and remorse as if it was a curse. With Megan, she was matter of fact.   I wondered why there could be such a difference. Was it because of the thirty-year spread between the two conversations? Was it because of the difference in generations and what was now acceptable? Was it their backgrounds? I had no idea. What I did know was the fact that I had been attracted to the same type of people with the same perspectives and that made me wonder if it was me. What was really crazy was the fact that in both instances, it really didn't bother me.

Suddenly, the mysterious Atlanta downtown slowdown was over as I asked, "What time is it?" Now concerned about missing my flight.

"Don't worry, it's only 8:50 and we're less than ten minutes away."

"Thanks. I hope I didn't intrude tonight."

"You needed that George and, quite honestly, so did I. It must be horrible what you're going through."

I really didn't know what to say as Megan glanced at me and smiled before offering. "You're a good man George Terrill. You've got a level of dignity and decency about you that shows through. I hope my...uhh...liberation was taken as an expression of compassion and gratitude for what you're willing to do for the class. I know we both let our hair down and I hope it isn't misconstrued as anything more than what it was, a way to allow me to help you regain the majesty and dignity that's bottled up inside you right now, while also sharing some of myself that I also truly needed."

She added. "It's tough having to wear a mask every day and never having anyone to open up to. I don't know why, but for some reason, I feel comfortable with you and trust you to the point I was able to show you the real me and not the corporate person most people see. It's been a long time since I've been so... so open with anyone and I want to thank you for that."

I was touched by the comments and the subsequent feelings that I wasn't the loser I thought I was as I abruptly asked. "Why me?

Megan took a quick glance at me and then back at the road as she noted. "First, George, is your demeanor and outward behavior and the impression it creates. The way you carry yourself simply makes a warm statement that you care. Then it's your facial expressions. I mean, when you smile you simply light up a room and the way you frown or curl your upper lip replaces a thousand words as it tells the world what you're really thinking. Then, when you speak it's the tone of your voice... you speak with authority and compassion that makes people want to listen. Finally, it's how you interact with others and how much better you communicate your feelings."

Megan paused and then added. "I've met very few people as sincere and believable as you. None of the other volunteers have connected with the audience the way you do or moved me as much. Your stature is such that you represent yourself as more honorable than others. Some of the men thought it was a peep show and that's not what this is all about.

I was both esteemed and discouraged by the statement. I was flattered by the words majesty and dignity and, yet, like any guy, also keenly affected by the words 'anything more than what it was,' that stabbed me right in the libido. Had I been nothing more than a plaything? I hoped not but then I also hoped that's all it was. All of a sudden, I was feeling profoundly guilty, vowing to never do it again. Well, maybe...No! Never...Well, perhaps.

As we were nearing the airport exit ramp I interjected. "I have one more question."

"What?" Megan replied.

"Why $E=MC^2$?"

"'E' for Ellie, 'M' for Megan, 'C' for Charlie. If you understand Einstein's formula, you realize that 'E' and M' can be interchanged and even connected such that it represents our relationship with each other where we are equals and yet can also interact individually. The reason for the square is because we believe our relationship produces an incredible amount of positive energy."

"So, in other words...."

Megan's voice became very matter-of-fact as she replied. "George, nothing has happened. There's no way I'd do anything with Charlie if it meant jeopardizing he and Elli."

Megan continued carefully monitoring the slowing traffic and, while simply shrugging her shoulders and speaking directly into the windshield offered, "With Elli, if Charlie wasn't in the picture?... Perhaps?... Why not?"

As we entered the Hartsfield exit ramp Megan's tone got somewhat serious as she offered. "George, there's a lot of progress being made in terms of post-operative parasympathetic therapy that's allowing a percentage of men to regain function that includes a combination of tantric, chemical and procedural practices. We don't bring it up in the class as we feel it would create a false sense of hope. In your case, if you'd like and can come back, we could implement the program to see if we couldn't regain some of your function."

With that my heart skipped a beat. One can live with the dribbles and drips. One can accept the fact that procreation is impossible. The deepest, darkest chasm is the subconscious realization that, even though the desire is there, you can't really do anything about it.

Megan added. "There's no promise and no guarantees and probably no regaining 100% but I believe we could garner some level of improvement if you're up for it."

While I needed to get home, I wanted a few more minutes simply to learn more. Unfortunately, time was of the essence. As we stopped in front of the departure area doors, Megan leaned across the seat, gave me a polite kiss on the cheek and said, "Thanks, George. I hope everything works out OK."

"Thanks." I replied.

Megan paused, checked the dash clock, looked in the rearview mirror and elected to enter the Northern hourly parking area instead. As we slid into a parking spot, Megan pulled me in to give me another hug and then a romantic embrace as our lips met for a period neither of us wanted to stop as she whispered. "Come again?"

I replied, "Next time you want to re-do the program, count me in."

"Kinky stuff?" Megan giggled.

"Oh, my God!" I exclaimed as an embarrassed expression sprinted across my face.

"Georgie, we could really have some fun!"

Georgie? Georgie? No one had called me that in years and it sounded good.

"You can bring Amy if you want to."

"Perhaps!" I offered, wondering what she meant by that, while knowing there was no way in hell that would ever happen. Or then, perhaps it was just what Amy needed as a weak wave of prurient reality sashayed through my entire body and into my soul.

One glance at the Lexus dash clock indicated it was nearing the very last instant to make my flight. Even though I wanted the episode to last, I took in a deep breath, turned back and slid my arm across the console and gently grasped Megan's chin turning her head so that we faced each other. Our eyes met and, without speaking, so did our lips again. I then took my left hand and placed my fingers within Megan's right-hand fingers. For what seemed like an eternity, our mouths continued enmeshed in each other's passion as we felt each other's heartbeats.

As our breathing went deeper, we both knew we had to stop or we wouldn't or couldn't. I listened to the passionate huffing as Megan whispered. "Next time, I'll try to wear shorter shorts," as her hand slid between my thighs and her tongue slid across the inner ridges of my ear.

A shiver went up my spine as I wondered how that would be possible as I slowly brushed the hair from Megan's face and lamented..."Or perhaps none at all".

Megan paused while her tone changed as she then implored, "I don't want you to leave."

The temptation was so great and yet I knew I had to go for more than one reason. My nerves were rattled and then reality struck as I glanced at the clock and it read 9:20. I now had forty minutes to traverse Hartsfield terminal. After another quick kiss and then another, I reluctantly opened the passenger door and got out of the car. I looked in and saw Megan smiling as her tongue slowly caressed her upper lip as if something delectable had been encountered. I smiled in acceptance and also glee, realizing for the first time in a long, long time, I was being seduced.

I kissed my hand and waved it at her and then focused on traffic, while making my way to the terminal entrance door. I scurried and just, and I mean just, made my way through security and into Terminal T as they were calling my name and threatening to close the jetway door.

Whew, I made it! As the very last person to board and time for push-back, I was told to take any seat in coach of which there were plenty available. I'd heard that flying used to be special and people even got dressed up and felt important. I also remember Greyhound buses at the other end of the spectrum. Somewhere, somehow, airplanes morphed into Greyhounds in more ways than one. Instead, I sat down until after take-off and then made my way back to the bathrooms and the last row where I sat alone, sequestered in my thoughts with my eyes closed, enveloped in the rush of solitary existence as I reflected on the day where I'd started out so far down the rabbit hole, I really didn't know if I'd ever crawl out.

The pain I was enduring was like being slowly crushed by some heavy weight upon my chest making it hard to breathe. For some reason, the slogan 'No pain. No gain' became prevalent in my thought pattern as I realized that, during my life, I'd mumbled that mantra more than once and surmised it was currently apropos where my pain vibrated along a wide spectrum of things that should have been easy to ignore.

I admitted to myself that my world could revolve around the physical pain like a splinter in my finger or the accident with Jeepers Creepers that smashed my teeth. They were all curable and replaceable that soon became faded and somewhat forgotten. It was the pain in my heart that mattered the most. The pain of regret! The pain of fear! The pain of feeling insignificant all rolled up into one immense agony I was dealing with in a time called 'now'.

The one thing about the physical pain is that when it happens, it gets all the attention and requirement of immediate remedy. I accept that it's hard to forget physical pain. Sadly, it's even harder to remember everyday sweetness... the little things we take for granted... a pleasant smile, an accommodation, a little concern! We have no bruises, marks or scars to show for happiness. We learn so little from harmony simply because happiness doesn't leave a visible stain.

I do have lasting good memories. Sadly, it's easier to point to painful moments than the bits of happiness that made me smile or feel good each day. Forlornly, I think I lean too often towards the negative, when being more positive would make me and those around me feel much better. Pain, of course, has purpose. It teaches us how to avoid the touch physically and emotionally. It's only when pain and joy embrace that there's so much to gain and perhaps that's what today was all about.

It had been an 'interesting' day to say the least. I knew I had another chapter or two for my unwritten book. The flight home was just that... a flight home, long enough to allow my nerves to calm, only to be replaced by a sense of depredation simply because I felt no guilt for all that happened.

The wheels were down and we were at Truax. We taxied to the gate and the few sleepy-eyed fellow passengers disembarked on a flight no one wanted to take but was necessary simply for the airline to reset tomorrow. I slowly rose from my seat and made my way to the front of the plane. I got a somewhat stiff thank you from the flight attendant who I could tell was tired and only wanted one thing and that was for me to leave. I nodded and made my way up the Jetway realizing it was a different person who'd walked down the same steel tunnel that morning where the only thing that changed was my attitude. I no longer felt like the humiliated victim and was ready for the war that seemed to be on the horizon.

While there were things I probably shouldn't have done, in the end, there was nothing I was ashamed of and nothing I'd regret and that's what made the trip worthwhile, along with the check for $3,000 in my wallet. Poverty and loneliness have ways of doing that to you, making you justify things you shouldn't do, but do anyway, sacrificing your values and scruples simply to move the doomsday clock one tick further back from reality.

The Letter:

When I got home, I stopped at our mailbox. Inside was a formal letter from the US Department of Justice addressed to me. I thought 'Now what?' as I held the letter tight until within the confines of our apartment. I opened the letter, felt my mouth drop open, grabbed for a kitchen chair, sat down and tried to re-read the contents with trembling hands. I'd been named an unindicted co-conspirator or a person who, according to the indictment, 'may have participated in a criminal conspiracy but was not being formally charged with a crime themselves.' I was essentially named in the indictment as having played a role in the crime but for various reasons was not actively being prosecuted. I'd made a vow to relinquish certain words from my vocabulary but, in total isolation, I expelled one very long expression..."F-------k!"

The letter not only called out my name and the charges but the reasons why, *at that time,* I was not being indicted with the warning I still could be. The first reason given was the prosecution didn't have enough evidence *at that time* to bring a separate case against me. It then noted that I *might* be granted immunity from prosecution in exchange for my testimony against other defendants. How in hell could I do that if I didn't know what was going on? The third caveat was somewhat of a relief in that they felt my role in the crime *might* have been minimal and not worth the resources to prosecute me.

To my knowledge, the letter said it all and it wasn't public knowledge. I also understood that being named as a co-conspirator could still damage my reputation, even though I hadn't been convicted of a crime. What really scared me was the indication that unindicted co-conspirators have limited legal recourse to defend themselves against the accusations in the indictment.

How can one defend themselves if first, all their assets are frozen and they can't afford a lawyer and second, they, don't know what in hell is going on? The last sentence sent chills up my spine when it stated 'there remained potential future prosecution if new evidence emerged,' and I could be prosecuted at that time.

Sleep did not come to me that night. Anger! Fear! Frustration rattled around in my brain. Finally at 6:30 I got up and went into the kitchen just as Amy's bedroom door opened. "Good morning!" I tersely announced as Amy walked out into the kitchen.

I stared at her in total silence. I was angry! I was petrified! I was profoundly confused! Never having been a good poker player, she could read my emotions and proceeded towards me with caution.

"How was Atlanta?" Amy inquired.

"Ok,"" I offered, almost biting my lip from exploding.

"What's going on?" was Amy's second question.

I looked down at the table, focused on the letter and then up at her before offering, "I just received a letter from the government."

"And?"

"And, I've been named an unindicted co-conspirator in the bullshit you and your son got involved in."

"You mean our son." Amy retorted with an emphasis on the word "our" as her eyes narrowed to a stiletto-like slit reflecting her anger, frustration and antagonism with my allegation.

"Ok," our son but my ass," I countered.

Before Amy could answer, I looked out at Lake Monona and then back at her. "I don't know what in hell is going on but now it looks like I could go to prison for something I wasn't involved in and had no knowledge of."

"Calm down, George. It's just a scare letter. They're fishing."

"Fishing for what?"

"They send letters like this to scare people so they can collect more information before the trial?"

"What trial?" Now I was no longer angry as my emotions morphed to the point I was distraught.

"There's going to be a trail," Amy retorted.

"For what?"

"Sedition."

"Sedition? What in hell is going on?"

"It's a trumped-up charge, that's all. The did it to scare us and try to get us to negotiate with them."

"Sedition?"

"Yes, George...sedition!" Amy reiterated in a manner that reflected her impatience with my concern.

"What's sedition?"

Amy looked down as if in thought and replied like she would to a six-year-old. "Sedition is a complex legal term but it essentially refers to overt conduct that aims to incite resistance or rebellion against the established government or lawful authority that often involves subversion of the Constitution or existing laws by encouraging or advocating the overthrow or undermining of the existing legal framework of the government. It can also mean incitement of discontent or hatred towards the government by stirring up public anger or hostility towards the authorities with the intention of provoking unrest or rebellion and finally it means advocating the violent overthrow of our government by calling, for or actively planning the use of force to remove the government from power."

"You mean like January Sixth?"

"Yes."

"Jesus!"

"George, they're all erroneous charges simply because that wasn't our intent. We didn't do anything like they're charging and it appears they're throwing the net out to put pressure on all those who might have benefitted from our actions. Don't worry about it. You didn't do anything wrong."

"And when did right and wrong matter in a court of law?" I rebutted as my anger level rose and the color in my face turned red.

"Calm down, we're taking care of it!"

"I get a letter that accuses me of trying to destroy our government and you tell me to calm down? I don't think so!"

"Well, what are you going to do about it?" Amy retorted with a tone of sarcasm in her voice. "You've got no money. You've done nothing wrong. Don't worry about it. Tomorrow put on your little orange apron and go sell screws or whatever it is you do all day"

Scared...demeaned...and insulted! So much for getting my pride back. Welcome home, George.

Depression:

The following morning Amy was gone again. I had no idea where and sadly, no longer seemed to care preferring the peace and quiet of the hum of the refrigerator to her periodic tirades.

With Amy gone, I felt secure enough to go to my email account and saw a message from $E=MC^2$. I opened it and smiled. Megan was simply thanking me for helping with the presentation and reiterating her belief that the recuperative methodology she'd outlined was something that could help while offering, once again, to 'test drive' as she called them, some of the appliances she'd detailed for the ladies. Yet again, a bolt of excitement roared through my mind while I reflected on our night together and her partaking of sharing who she really was.

As I sat there, I reflected on all she'd expressed and was actually envious of her freedom. Perhaps, just perhaps, it was because it moved so far beyond my realm, even the liberal domain Amy and I had created. My mind floated back to the statues and I smiled a somewhat mischievous smile as I remembered my initial shock and intrigue. When your emotional sky is dark and there's a beam of light, it always seems brighter. I quickly responded expressing my gratitude for her hospitality, apologies for my inebriation and confirmation that I certainly would like to come again, hoping the double entendre was recognized before realizing it hadn't happened in the first place.

As I was shutting down the computer, I picked up my cellphone and realized I'd had a call. It was from James, one of my dearest friends. Sadly, time has a way to take close friends and make them distant. Such was the case with Dr. James Johnson. His background included a Bachelor's Degree in psychology from the University of Wisconsin with a Master's Degree from Johns Hopkins and a PHD from

Princeton University. He had recently retired from the University of Wisconsin – Milwaukee where he served as head of the psychology department to work with Milwaukee County Social Services Division concerning troubled youth and had also donated his time to serve as a board member on the bio-ethics team headed up by Luke Arnold.

James' association with the Derrick Williams Foundation came about because he wanted to go fishing with a bunch of his buddies. He'd chartered the boat owned by Wilco. Whereas, it conflicted with my personal schedule, the easiest thing for Wilco to do would have been to say the boat had mechanical problems. Instead, I took it upon myself to make the arrangements to ensure that all parties would have a great time, including me.

As we evolved at the Foundation my most trusted advisors consisted of Peter, James and Luke where Peter was my 'brains' who knew more about what was going on than anyone else in terms of the technology and where we came close to the edge in terms of patent infringement. Luke was the ethicist, telling us right from wrong, good from bad and making certain that what we did was the right thing to do. James and I had grown so close that, in many ways, he'd replaced Rodney as my most trusted friend. This wasn't because of anything that had happened between Rodney and me but simply because James and I were working together on a daily basis, while my interaction with Rodney had become more social and infrequent.

I was never one to share my problems with others and yet, deep down, I knew I needed someone to talk to as I was literally being torn apart emotionally. When you're deep in the valley there are times when you need a hand to help climb back out as you seek the mountain top. I waited and finally called Milwaukee and heard a pleasant voice who noted. "I was wondering when you were going to call. Did you get one of those cheap phones with no buttons on it so that you couldn't call me?"

There was a chuckle on the other end and then a serious inquiry. "How can I help?"

"I need is some guidance."

"I'm all yours."

"You probably know what's going on."

"The whole world knows. You and Amy are getting screwed."

Tears stirred in my eyes as embarrassment of the obvious came to light as I answered. "Is it that obvious?"

"To those who care it is. How is it affecting you and Amy?"

"It's a real disaster," I replied.

"You? Amy? Both?"

"Both, I think. I don't know. All I know is that it's not good."

"Depression?"

"Profound!"

"Need a shoulder?"

"Yes!"

"Let's see if I can help" as James put on his professional hat and detailed. "Deep depression can cast a long shadow on a marriage, affecting both partners in different ways. First, there can be emotional withdrawal where a depressed partner may lose interest in activities they used to enjoy together leading to a sense of emotional distance. This can be due to a symptom called anhedonia, where someone loses the ability to experience pleasure."

I'd just come from Atlanta where, for the first time in months, I laughed and had been so tempted.

I came home and had a scathing argument with the woman I love. James had that one right as he continued. "Next, there can be communication breakdowns. Depression can make it difficult to concentrate, remember things or feel motivated to talk. This can lead to misunderstandings and arguments."

My God, he had us pegged as the deafening silence filled our condo with the murkiness of misery as he added. "There they can be a loss of loss of intimacy. Fatigue, low energy and a general lack of interest in sex are common depression symptoms, which can make the healthy partner feel rejected and unwanted."

We were sleeping in separate bedrooms and hadn't kissed in months as James added. "This can result in an increased burden where the other partner might take on more household chores and responsibilities, leading to resentment and exhaustion."

I was shaking my head up-and-down. Over the phone, James was detailing all that was happening as he added. "In the end, there's a feeling of being unheard and friendless simply because both partners feel alone and unsupported and bearing a burden and feeling unheard and helpless."

Tears slid down my cheeks. My nose was filling with remorse and he could tell by the staccato syllables that I evoked as James asked. "How bad is it?"

"Pretty bad." I replied.

"Do you want to save it?"

"Yes!" I vehemently replied.

"Ok," restarting your marriage takes dedication and effort from both of you but it can be a rewarding journey."

"Ok"

"First, you're going to need to have open, honest and heartfelt conversations which are crucial where you talk about how you're feeling, what's missing in the relationship, and what you both want for the future. Be prepared to listen openly to Amy's perspective without interrupting or getting defensive."

"Ok"

"Second, you need to reconnect and rebuild by looking for ways to rediscover the association you once shared. Schedule regular date nights, plan activities you both enjoy, or simply spend quality time talking and listening to each other."

"But there's so much that's bad going on."

"I know, but you need to talk through them as a team then you need to renew your appreciation for each other by stop taking each other for granted. This means making a conscious effort to appreciate each other by expressing gratitude for the positive things Amy does while acknowledging her efforts. Finally, and most important George practice forgiveness. Stop holding onto anger and resentment. It will only hinder the progress. Forgive Amy for past mistakes and focus on moving forward together."

"What about her?" I asked.

"George, that's up to you. If you begin and give her the benefit of doubt, you'll quickly see if she's ready to begin healing. I've known you two for over twenty years. I've seen greatness and I've seen sadness and I know, in my heart, Amy loves you. I've seen it. I've felt it and I know it's true. If there's anything, and I mean anything, I can do to help I will."

"Thanks for being my friend. Thank you, James."

"I'm serious. Anything!"

"I know and thank God for the day we went fishing."

"Too bad I caught all the big fish!" James joked.

It was time to get my orange apron and go to work. My spirits were lifted and I vowed that today would be better than yesterday, but not as good as tomorrow.

The Bent Shaft:

At 10:40 I headed for work with my orange apron and a paper bag with my PB&J dinner accompanied by an apple and two bottles of water. When you're used to driving a Mercedes-Maybach as your day-to-day car riding the city bus out to East Towne Mall was, at first, quite demeaning until I started seeing the same people every day who actually smiled at me and made me feel welcome.

I got to work and went to the front desk for my assignments. When you're a rookie, without a trades background, you're never trusted with a section. You're a wild card who fills in here, there and everywhere. One day, I'd be stocking shelves and the next day cutting lumber and the third out in the garden area. I never knew where I was going to end up which was fine with me.

As I reached the front counter, I witnessed what had become common, an irate customer blaming us for something he did. I guess you should get used to it and the company policy was not to offend a customer for fear they'd never return but it still rankled me when I knew the score.

Angela was working the front desk. A somewhat portly woman in her forties, probably trying to raise her kids alone on $15.00 an hour and few benefits, she always had a pleasant smile and made me feel like I was part of the team. As I neared the counter I could hear the man verbally abusing her and it wasn't pleasant. Complaints are one thing. Threats another. Abuse, well it crossed the line, as I went up to the guy and said, "Excuse me sir, is there a problem?"

The tirade I got was full of f-bombs and threats about lawsuits and court and then personal when I learned he was upset because the vertical engine shaft on the lawnmower he purchased was bent and he wanted his money back.

"God damn piece of shit! I'll never buying another f---ing thing here again."

I looked at the man and offered to inspect the mower.

"For what? I told you, the f---ing piece of shit ain't no good."

"I understand sir, and I'm trying to be of assistance so we can refund your money, but I need to examine the mower."

I looked at the guy and asked, "Did you register your warranty?"

"F" no! Why in the f---ing world would I do that? You gotta give me my money back. You say satisfaction guaranteed and I ain't satisfied."

"Do you happen to have the receipt?"

"Are you f----ing kidding me? Who the "F' keeps receipts?"

"Did you happen to charge the product?"

"What the "F" difference does that make?"

"So that Angela can look it up in the computer and make sure you get a full refund."

"Jesus Christ! I came in here to get my f---ing money back on this piece of shit and all you do is hassle me. I want to see the manager or I'm calling your home office and filing a complaint against you."

"Sir, my name is George. My employee number is T-104-638. Angela can you please write that on a sheet of paper along with the 800 number to our customer relations department?"

Angela looked at me and for the first time there was a different expression on her face. Gone was the irrelevance shown to just another employee. Instead, there was an indication of respect.

"Sir, do you mind if I look at the mower?"

The clown was calming down and nodded in the affirmative as we walked over to the product returns area. As I knelt down and turned the mower on its side, a piece of bark dropped out from beneath the deck. The idiot had either tried to use it as a stump grinder or ran over a piece of wood.

I picked up the bark and showed it to the guy and noted, "Looks like you've got some really thick grass you were trying to mow."

The clown knew I had him and all of the braggadocio that had been in his demeanor was gone as he replied. "I don't know where that came from."

Taking my fingers I slid them under the deck again and pulled out some more bark that was impaled in the wet grass along the inner edge of the deck. I stood up with the wood muck on my finger, looked at the guy and offered. "The warranty on the product is for use and care as a lawnmower and not a stump grinder. In situations like this we normally would tell you to go to an authorized service center and pay to have them repair your abuse. Today is your lucky day. We happen to have the vertical drive shafts in stock and if you can give me about ten minutes I can have the bent shaft replaced. I'll need a 3/8ths inch socket with an extender so give me a couple minutes and I'll be right back."

I nodded to the guy and went and got the tools from the tool area as well as the shaft before returning. Kneeling on the floor, I simply removed the flywheel, then the keyway which is a small piece of metal that aligns the shaft with the flywheel, then the bearing and finally pulled out the shaft. Reversing the process, I had the engine back in place in less than ten minutes and stood before noting. "The price for a new drive shaft is ten dollars. If you'd gone to the service center, the minimum labor cost would have been $50.00 more. Tell you what, you go back to Angela and apologize and I'll call us even. However, the next time you come in here and verbally abuse that lady I'll throw your ass out of here so fast it will made your head spin."

The guy nodded realizing he'd been way, and I mean way out of line.

I extended my hand and noted. "Sir, you might want to try planting a little thinner grass next time," to which I simply winked, smiled and went back to the tool department to put the tools back in stock.

In all the hubbub I'd forgotten to punch in. I went to the time clock and realized, I'd lost almost an hour's pay and simply shook my head, feeling good about what had transpired. As I was about to examine my worksheet, another customer came up to me, read my name and said. "Gorge, I watched you with that clown. I've got to tell you, you handled it about as well as anyone I've ever seen. My name is Dave and I just wanted to thank you."

I was humbled and somewhat embarrassed, yet, also happy something positive was done and said about me. It had been a long time since I'd had a compliment in the store and it felt good.

Dave went about his shopping and I went about facing the lightbulb section which simply meant pulling those bulbs not along the edge of the shelf forward so the display looked full. As I was nearing the end of the row, Dave reappeared.

"Is there something I can help you with?" I asked.

"This'll probably sound a little weird and I don't know why I'm doing it. I hope you don't take it the wrong way but I'm wondering if you ever get Saturday's off.

"Every now and then, why?"

"Well, my wife and I have had Badger football tickets for over 30 years and she doesn't go anymore. I was wondering if you'd like to go with me."

I paused for a moment and felt honored. Here was a guy who'd seen me dress down a customer asking me to go to a Badger football game with him. I replied, "I love to, when?"

"A week from Saturday, they're playing Penn State."

"Let me see if I can trade days with someone."

I traded days and Dave and I traded e-mail addresses. Something to look forward to...hooray!

Game On:

Arrangements were made for the Saturday off and via email Dave offered to pick me up. I noted that we lived within walking distance to Camp Randall and I would meet him beneath the statue of Pat Richter on the Southeast corner of the stadium in front of Kelner Hall. He e-mailed my ticket and all systems were go.

Saturday came and it was one of those fantastic early fall days. Bright sunshine, a light breeze and high sixties in temperature. As agreed, Dave and I met with smiles on our faces.

"I really appreciate this," I offered.

"Ever been here before?" Dave inquired.

I didn't want to let on what was going on and so I noted I'd been to 'a few' games and left it at that as we made our way to the southwest corner of the stadium and entered section 'B' with Dave apologizing. "Not the greatest seats but under the deck in case it rains and we don't have to pay that damn loyalty tax like the hoity, toities who sit closer to the fifty do."

We were fifty-one rows up and it reminded me of sitting in the coach's seats in Section X on the other side, virtually on the ten-yard line where you're able to see the game but not most of the action.

As we sat down, Dave pulled out some big binoculars, looked at me and smiled as he noted, "I can almost see the players faces with these. Here give them a try."

Jesus! You could see just about everything as I handed them back to Dave.

We'd arrived early enough for the pre-game warm-ups and spent the next several minutes talking about the Badger's season and how we both thought they were going to do.

"Where you from?" Dave inquired.

"A little town called Waldwick," I replied.

"Never heard of it." Dave responded.

"Most people haven't. It's down by Mineral Point." I offered.

"Heard of that one. Great history in high school wrestling and lately they've been a powerhouse in football, too."

I didn't want to let on that Jack Harris, the football coach, was my son-in-law and so I simply nodded my head in agreement.

"How long have you been working at Home Depot?" Dave asked.

"A few months."

"How'd you get to know so much about engines and people?"

"Engines? From living on a farm. You have to learn to be a mechanic. People? I don't know. I just don't like bullies." It was time for the National Anthem and we all stood as the band played on.

As we sat back down Dave asked. "What did you do before Home Depot?"

"Oh, lots of things. A little here. A little there. Nothing much, I guess."

"You just don't seem to be the type who ends up working at Home Depot."

"There are a lot of really good people working there. Like me, they're there because they need the money and it's actually a good place to work. Other than unruly customers the place fits me to a tee right now."

"You get many customers like the guy with the mower?"

"Some days yes. Other days no. Most folks are pretty good and fair."

"But you handled him so well."

"I just happened to be checking in when I saw what was going on. I don't like bullies and I don't like cheats and all I was trying to do was protect a fellow employee from the onslaught.   "The guy was a jerk."

"What do you think of this place?" Dave asked.

"What do you mean?" I inquired, not knowing what he meant.

"I've had tickets for over 30 years and haven't missed a game. Wouldn't you think I'd get better seats than this?"

"These are good seats," I countered.

"If I'd pay the $800 loyalty tax every year, I could move over. Eight hundred bucks! People pay it and right away they get better seats than me. And how about those skyboxes? Do you think those people are watching the games or are they there to show the world they're better than you and me...just a bunch of rich bastards thumbing their nose at the rest of us?"

I cringed at the thought and realized why he was so bitter. Thirty years and you're sitting in the corner on the goal line sure didn't seem fair to me either.

Kickoff commenced and we started watching the game. Every now and then Dave would put his binoculars to his eyes and scan the players. After numerous times he offered the glasses to me and I accepted. Without being too obvious, I scanned the high school coach's section and saw two empty seats concluding that Melia wasn't there. Next, I panned left to the fifty and Section "T" and up to row 27 and saw four strangers sitting in what were our seats. I zoomed up to our skybox and my eyes were only superseded by my disbelief. Sitting in the Wilco box was our son, Derrick, and with him was Senator Mike Fitzgerald, the son of the son-of-a-bitch Senator who'd shut us down so long ago and then bequeathed his Senate seat to his son by retiring shortly after he was re-elected due to 'health reasons', as well as my brother Tommie.

How could it be?" How could Derrick be sitting in the Wilco box? Why in hell was the Senator and a group of his political wonks with him? Tommie? Why in hell would Tommie be there, as well. I shook my head in disbelief and handed the glasses back to Dave and attempted to focus on the game but it was totally, and I mean totally secondary, to my anger, frustration and hurt at seeing our son and my brother living it up while Amy and I were suffering.

As the game progressed Dave began asking questions until I knew this was a set up. He wasn't 'just' at Home Depot that day. The jerk with the mower didn't 'just' happen to come in right when I was arriving for work.

By the middle of the third quarter I knew this was more than two guys at a football game. By the end I was convinced I'd been snookered as Dave offered. "Why don't I give you a ride back to your condo on Wilson Street? Dave asked.

"I can walk."

"I think it's better if I drive."

We made our way back under Kelner Hall by Bucky's Locker room and then out between the east side of Camp Randall and the Memorial Shell to find a nondescript dark brown Chevy Impala in a reserved parking spot.

For some reason I glanced at the license plate. Perhaps it was because it was the only middle-class American car in the VIP parking spots. In the old days your car Wisconsin plate number was simply a letter and then some numbers, unless you had a vanity plate. I knew from the car business that the alpha-numeric sequence of Wisconsin automobile license plates, also known as the issuance format, depended on several factors, including the plate type and issue date and so, when I saw EOP-812 and the parking dichotomy, it was an easy memory point.

Dave unlocked his door and I watched the passenger lock shaft raise. I got in, turned to Dave and asked, "What's this all about?"

"What do you mean?" Dave inquired.

I outlined the coincidences and asked who Dave really was.

"I'm Secret Service Agent David Langdon."

"What the...?

"George, we're trying to find out what in hell is going on and needed to see where you fit in all of this."

The unindicted co-conspirator letter, the angry man with the mower who let me repair it in the store and the football game with the high-powered binoculars were all set-ups to scare me and then share with me that I was a victim and not a perpetrator. All this I shared with Agent Langdon as he simply nodded in the affirmative as I asked. "What in hell do I do about all this?"

"Well, Mr. Terrill, you're living with an indicted co-conspirator and that's the first thing. We're not sure how deep your wife's in but right now she's probably knee-deep and sinking.

I was incredulous. Amy? Involved? Jesus!

"Your wife and son made some really and I mean really big mistakes."

I retorted. "I'm not an accountant or a lawyer and so I, quite honestly, don't understand what happened. I've been semi-retired from the Foundation and actually working with my brother on our beef and bourbon business."

"Do you remember the Enron scandal?" the Agent asked.

"Yes, I remember hearing about it. Why?"

"Well, it created a whole new set of laws and accounting rules designed to protect investors. What's happened at Wilco is like a miniature Enron."

My eyes opened wide as I knew some of their executives went to prison and spent fourteen years there.

Agent Langdon paused and then detailed what happened. "The CEO and CFO devised and implemented complex schemes to hide the company's true financial condition involving off-balance-sheet partnerships, manipulating trading prices and inflating profits through creative accounting measures which appears to be precisely what has gone on at Wilco."

"Holy shit!"

Langdon continued. "Enron executives made false and misleading statements about the company's performance to investors, analysts and the public and portrayed Enron as a successful and growing company while its finances were actually crumbling."

Based on what Amy had shared I could see that this was also the case at Wilco as Langdon continued. "Some Enron executives attempted to cover up their actions by destroying documents and intimidating witnesses which further compounded their legal troubles and showed a deliberate effort to deceive investigators."

As I was digging into the mess I could see where Derrick would do this. Honesty was not one of his strengths, while intimidation had always been a part of his personality.

"We're investigating how your son, brother and Senator Fitzgerald are involved in this. We know it goes beyond the initial sale. We also know your former Foundation, has been working with them."

"What?"

"I can't share that right now except to say your computer has a lot more power than most people can perceive and they're using it to modify the entire concept of supply and demand in the global financial market."

Agent Langdon continued. "In order to get to the bottom of this we've put the squeeze on you and your wife by freezing your assets while allowing your brother and son the liberty of making more mistakes. We know you're going through hard times and went to Atlanta and was paid $3,000 instead of the $1,000 the other time to be part of the presentation regarding prostate cancer."

Jesus!

"We know what took place during the meeting because one of the women in the group is one of our agents. We also know you spent the evening at the home of Mary Egan owned with another woman named Elli Wallace while her husband, Charles, who was flying Delta Flight Number 200 to Johannesburg that night."

"That's because my flight was cancelled."

"Was it?"

"I got a text from the airline."

"Was it really from the airline?"

"So this was all a set up?"

Langdon looked at me and detailed. "Mr. Terrill. This is a serious matter and we need to make sure our investigational security isn't breached. Right now, you're still a suspect. However, everything we've found so far leads us to believe you're innocent. Nonetheless, we need your help."

Just then Agent Langdon placed an earbud in his left ear, raised his right hand to make sure I didn't speak and said, "Got it."

Langdon looked at me and directed, "Get your head down now. Your brother and son are about to walk by and we can't have him see you."

I followed directions until Langdon raised his right hand, spoke into his left sleeve and noted. "All clear."

As the foot traffic egressing from the stadium diminished Langdon started the Impala and headed for the Monroe Street exit where he turned left, made it to the corner with Randall Avenue, turned right and headed south. When we reached Regent Street, there was a traffic cop signaling 'no left turn'. Langdon, flipped a switch. The officer saw the lights in the grill and immediately waved us to turn left as he stopped the other traffic.

We made our way east Regent until we crossed West Washington Avenue that merged onto Proudfit Street. We drove three blocks until Agent Langdon nodded at the parking area at Brittingham Beach and we pulled in.

"Do you mind if I call you George?"

"Not at all."

"Well, George, we know we've been hard on you. We've frozen your assets and taken your dignity. You're the recipient of a Nobel Peace Prize and started the Derrick Williams Foundation. We're aware that, besides your son, Derrick, you have another son, also named George, who has dedicated his life to the wellbeing of others. We also know that your daughter, Melia and her husband Jack, live outside Mineral Point and he's the football coach in town. We also know that everything from their tax records to phone conversations indicate they're fine, honest people. Six weeks ago you took the Lamer's Bus to Dodgeville and then took an Uber to Mineral Point where you were dropped off in front of the old Hotel Royale."

"How do you know so much?"

"Your bus ticket was paid for in cash as was the Uber driver where the fee was $14.70 which you paid in cash because you don't have any active credit cards."

"The driver was another agent," I offered.

Langdon didn't confirm but continued. "You proceeded to the Farmers Savings Bank where you closed your safety deposit box that contained your purchase agreement with your brother, Thomas as well as a notebook that was written by your great, great grandfather about the family farm."

"You went to the Red Rooster for lunch where by coincidence Tank Kennison walked in and the only available stool was the one next to yours."

"You went to his office and discussed farm ownership and whether it belonged in the freeze. Tank then offered to drive you back to Madison, dropping you off two blocks from your condo. Two weeks later, you had a subsequent meeting with Attorney Kennison in the Capitol Park where the Attorney and you sat facing the Old National Bank and discussed whether the farm was part of or not part of the Wilco situation."

I was getting scared. They knew everything.

"George, we do our homework. We know what's going on. The problem is we don't know how to stop it and this is where you come in. Work with us and the farm will become yours. Don't work with us you'll end up in a very lengthy and incredibly expensive court battle to get what you can have simply by cooperating with us."

Agent Langdon paused, looked out at Monona Bay and then back at me. "I want to apologize for putting you through all that you're going through. I know it has to be horrible to experience the loss of everything. Yet, there are clear and present dangers to investors and citizens throughout the world and right now you're the only one we feel can stop it."

I sat totally deflated. All my emotions were ragged. First, was the anger they knew so much. Next, was the concern I'd couldn't do what they wanted. Last, was the rationale I had no choice. My only question was, could I save Amy or was she in too deep? I looked at Langdon and inquired, "What about the Wilco assets?"

"In other words, your personal wealth?"

I nodded in the affirmative.

"That will be left up to the courts."

I rubbed my temples in thought, looked out at the bay and offered. "I help you stop what's going on. You award the farm to me without all the legal hassles. We determine how deep Amy is in this and I help you prosecute my son and his co-conspirators and if there's anything left of Wilco, all the people who've been hurt or destroyed by what's happening will get a piece of the pie?"

"You got it."

"And if I don't?"

"Then your title will cease being a non-indicated co-conspirator and you can try and find a lawyer to help keep you out of jail."

"What do I need to do to help?"

"Keep doing what you're doing but keep your eyes and ears open. I'm assigned as your contact and we'll meet periodically for de-briefing."

"How will I know where or when?"

"Leave that up to me."

"Is there any timetable?"

"Not really."

"What do I do in the meantime?"

"You want to write a book, don't you?"

My eyes opened wide as I pondered, how in hell did he know that'?

Langdon continued. "Keep working, keep the same schedule and write that book. I know you're suffering and that makes all of us want to resolve this much faster. However, we're not going to rush anything or play our hand until we're absolutely certain we have an air tight case against anyone and everyone involved. By the way Ms. Egan is no way involved in any of this and you should take her up on her offer to come again."

With that, Agent Langdon drove the few blocks to the corner of Bedford and Wilson by the J.H. Findorff and Sons corporate offices and stopped the car. "I think you should walk from here. It's been about as long as it would have been had you walked from Camp Randall. You need to keep this to yourself and particularly away from your wife. Remember she's an indicted co-conspirator and aiding her would add a whole other layer of legal problems on you."

I nodded in the affirmative and appreciated a little time to get my thoughts straight. As I got out, Agent Langdon looked across at me and a soft smile crossed his face. "How about you call me Dave? And you know what, everything everyone says about you seems to be true. You are a good man George Terrill, and when this is over I'd be honored to call you my friend."

I nodded and closed the car door as I watched Dave drive away. In less than three hours my world had changed in some ways but remained a disaster in others. At least now I knew what was going on. All I needed to do is figure out what Amy was up to, how deep she was in and what we could do to make it right. In the meantime, I needed to do what I'd been doing and that meant publish 'Waldwick' and begin writing my first novel. With all that was going on, I began wondering if I could make it a legal thriller...Naah! No one would believe it and I'm certain Uncle Sam wouldn't want me telling tales anyway.

Creative Verve:

It was Monday, my day off, and with nowhere to go and no money to do it, anyway, I opened a Spotted Cow and sat watching the sailboats out on Lake Monona and thought to myself, 'I'm broke and the only thing I know how to do is write. Perhaps, just perhaps I could write a novel. I know it's a long-term project. With over two million titles published every year, what chance would I have'?

Before I started, I needed to confirm who Agent Langdon was and find out all I could about him. Why had he been so nice to me? Why was he tailing me? What didn't he arrange for more information? The only thing I had was the license number on his brown Chevy Impala which was EOP-812.

I went online and got nowhere. I needed to know more about Langdon, as an Idea hit me, at which point I called the Madison Police Department and offered. "Recently, I was in a minor fender bender in the East Towne parking lot when I backed into a car. It was my fault and I put a note on the windshield as there wasn't anyone around. I have the license plate number and was wondering if I could find out the owner's name in case the paper either blew off from beneath the wiper blade or, because it was raining, it could have been wet."

"No problem, sir," the person on the other end replied. "EOP-812!." Uhh, sir, I'm not allowed to divulge the owner of that vehicle. If you provide your name I can contact them for you."

"That's Ok."

Instead I Googled the Wisconsin license plate number and it, too, was unavailable. At least I now knew Langdon was associated with the government and was probably a Secret Service Agent. What I didn't know was what the government was up to. Were they tailing Amy and me, as well as Derrick? Were they intercepting our phone calls and e-mails? The issues just got more complex.

So much for being a sleuth, perhaps being an author would be easier. Wrong! I pressed the button on our computer and Googled the category and learned that, within the general and literary fiction category, seventy-five percent of the top writers are female. The general consensus being that male writers have given up on literary fiction because they see more potential in narrative nonfiction or genre fiction, especially crime and sci-fi, which is less mediated by the culture and less involved in conversations on Twitter or whatever they're calling it this day.

I twisted the cap on another Spotted Cow and concluded that my chances of success at writing fiction were slim, narrow and none. However, with more time than money as we awaited the results of our frozen assets, I concluded I might just as well give it a try. The question then became what could I write about that hasn't already been written?

I've always been a free spirit, even in my most corporate days. After the book on the Hochunk I was simply too busy trying to prove to the world I didn't marry Amy for her money and stopped writing. I poured the last of number two, beer that is, down my throat and went back to searching Google with my mind wandering as the statistics regarding male fiction writers kept sinking in, giving me all the more impetus to see if I couldn't break the mold and write a novel every person would want to read.

Back to Google and the fact that most female writers are better at expressing emotions to the point most of their novels include some level of physical interaction, better known as sex. I'd never been one for the explicit stuff and, yet, if that's what sells I felt I could conjure up something. Needless to say, living with Amy certainly had taught me a lot and then all that happened in Atlanta certainly gave me some ideas. All I needed to do was add the emotion.

More reading, more learning and more beer taught me that sex in fiction, like sex on a beach, ought to be a no-brainer. On the one hand sex, is a source of mystifying pleasure and profundity that, for most people rarely elicits any articulation other than a contented grunt, groan or gasp. On the other hand, there's the novel...an artistic enterprise... devoted to making verbal sense of a mute experience. In theory the setup seems to be the perfect illustration of the Reese's principle where nirvana is achieved when two great tastes are even better together like peanut butter and chocolate.

But theory is not practice and life is not a peanut-butter cup. We all recognize that the boy who develops certain notions about the compatibility of sand and skin from the swimsuit issues hidden under his grandfather's chair cushion must someday discover the rough reality of forty-grit lovemaking. A similar lesson awaits the young litterateur who insists that a good book should move not only the head and heart but the loins, as well.

Once upon a time, of course, even bad fictional sex had a rough-and-ready social purpose where a few leather-bound classics stood prepared, if I may borrow a metaphor, to offer an escape to the lonely, frustrated and those in the throes of desperate inexperience. But today what chance would *Delta of Venus* or *Lady Chatterley's Lover* stand against the influx of graphic expression that's virtually everywhere? Most people don't need words when, with the flick of the wrist and slide of a mouse, they can call up an almost unimaginable plethora of images of every type of sex possible. Yet, it's the words and therefore the reader's imagination that can take those images and sculpt them into emotions nestled in a box of wonders that could make even the most liberal reader blush with modesty.

What's tough would be to use my imagination with the underlying fear that it might be too personal. And yet, I ask myself why shy away from what's natural while creating an intimate scene? That might be the fun part. Three beers and I rationalized one must shelve inhibitions, perhaps drink a glass of wine or two or perhaps even three, and then simply let go.

Beer number four and I began to realize that good sex in a book is not like a good sex scene in the movies. No one enjoys reading about a woman penetrated while standing up against the wall but throw that image in a movie and this exact position is a Hollywood staple. How could I describe genitals without saying vagina and penis? How would my character describe private parts in the throes of passion without sounding clinical while still being a little haughty, naughty and bold?

I started looking at what it takes and realized, like my former Corvette, I'd needed to begin by writing in first gear and then build speed in terms of plot and character development, where a form of psychological foreplay with my readers takes place. To do this, I'd need to describe each character as they strip down, not only physically but their thoughts, perceptions and feelings, until they feel unbridled about their own bodies, their partners, and their carnal thoughts.

Then, and only then, are they ready to hit the bed - floor - shower - beach - lawn - living room carpet - pool... wherever. I'd leave any more options up to Megan. Once there, the real passion would need to kick in with sex being a two-way street unless there are more participants involved, which means I'd need to create the right perspectives from both partners. I shook my head about the number of participants and thanked Megan for planting that seed in my imagination to the point I was getting the heebie jeebies even thinking about it.

I shook my head and concluded. 'If I was going to beat the video beast, I'd need to make certain the reader not only visually imagined what was happening but also felt it, heard it, smelled it, tasted it and knew what was going on aside from the obvious, in order to provide a total experience. If I was going to do this, it's not how I'd perform but how the characters would. This wasn't going to be me performing. This wouldn't be my character's sex drive, it would be the readers. It wouldn't be my inhibitions or inclinations, it would be theirs. It wouldn't be my acts, it would be theirs. I could let my imagination go. All the crazy things I'd thought about and even fantasized could be included and, boy, did I have a point of reference 866 miles away.

The characters wouldn't be me and if I thought this through, I would need to know my characters better than anyone else simply because I'd created them by taking pieces of people I'd known and creating a montage of physical, social and emotional fragments all rolled into one with thoughts, emotions and proclivities intended to grasp the reader and allow their minds and their imaginations to run rampant. I'd need to determine how they'd perform. How they'd touch someone else. How they'd respond to being touched. It's them, not me. I'd just be the conductor, they'd be the ones playing the music.

My mind wound back to my college days when one of my professors noted that good stories are unpredictable, which means my characters would need to be the same by simply showing another side of them. Perhaps sensitive, caring, a giver when making love, in other words, the opposite of what they are is in the rest of the story. If I could do this, I could make the intimacy in the story an exposition to convey depth and present an entirely different side of my character thereby making the physical part less important than who this person really is, once stripped naked physically, emotionally and spiritually. I would need to be able create and describe what are their interests, values, and beliefs as well as where and how they process information and learn such that the challenge posed had real meaning. To give the characters depth, I would need to detail their upbringing, past relationships, successes, and failures as well. If it included interaction with other characters, I would need to explain their social context and how they interacted with those characters and what roles they played in their family, community and work environment. To really give them depth, I would also need to express their motivations and dreams as well as their fears and finally even how they think. Are they analytical, creative, or pragmatic?

I realized I would need to write with detail. I knew it wasn't going to be easy. Being so conservative I needed to imagine what it felt like to have a very erotic unexpected experience with lovers who know exactly what they're doing. Again 13 hours and 866 miles by car.

I know that sex sells the story but it's the character's responses that move it along. I'm going to need to dig deep into fantasy and, perhaps, inhibitions and taboos. So many people know so little, including me. If I dig deep enough and elocute well enough, perhaps, just perhaps, I'll hit pay dirt simply because what I'm writing about is something few people know but a lot of people wonder. If what I write is going to be successful the story must seem real and the intimacy must be magnetic to provide both my readers and characters a deeper experience that results in a close, meaningful connection on the most intimate level of all.

I sat with blurry eyes caused by too many hours at the computer and, quite honestly too many spotted cows. As I stood, I heard the key in the door. Amy was home.

As she walked into the living room, she saw all the spotted cow bottles on the kitchen counter and noted, "looks like someone had a good day."

I turned and looked at her and replied. "That's from eight hours of sitting at the computer. I'm not drunk nor am I legally inebriated. I apologize that on my one day off this week I had some beer. At least, I was here in our house and not wherever it is you go every day."

"Where I go every day? Where I go?" the vitriolic spew that came forth was almost shocking. "Where do you think I go?"

I shook my head and shrugged my shoulders and responded. "I don't know."

"We have no money George! We're broke. We need a lawyer but can't afford one. We have our choice, a public defender or me. I've chosen me. Do you have a problem with that?"

Jesus! I had no idea and, yet, I was offended and replied. "Don't you think you should let me know? Don't you think I have the right to understand what's going on...what you're defending? You leave me sitting, like some dolt, in the dark, without a clue regarding what we're being blamed for and how you expect to keep us...both of us...out of prison."

"You won't understand!"

"You think I'm too stupid? You think I'm that naive? Either you start telling me, in detail, what's going on our I'll start looking for my own lawyer."

Amy smirked at my threat which really pissed me off.

"Let's see, Mrs. Terrill. You and your son sold technology that is threatening the world. You did so to raise money. Your son has buried us and yet he continues to thrive. Gee...I wonder how and why the government would want to look into that."

Amy's mouth dropped open as I let her have it.

"I might be working as a clerk at Home Depot but I'm not dumb. I might have been poor once but I can handle it, can you? Can you live without all the things we both got comfortable with? Can you survive with nothing? Will all your phony friends and social circles still put on those plastic smiles and bullshit stories simply to make you feel important? You see, Amy, I've been at the bottom and know what it's like down here and, quite honestly, there's more reality to it than where we've been these past few years where all that's mattered are material things, disposable things... insignificant things and not those things that brought us together...love and respect... respect for each other, love for each other... elements that have faded into the past."

I stood and directly confronted Amy as I inquired. "When was the last time you looked at me without disdain? When was the last time you didn't take me for granted? When was the last time you made me feel as if I was still important in your life? Instead you've been consumed! Consumed by the need for more...more of what? More money? More perks? More phony friends? You see, I can be happy without them and that's where the differences come in. I don't think you can and that's why we're at the point we're at...strangers living in the same house. Two people so discordant...so different...so obtuse that I wonder if when all of this is over, the pain and agony won't be so great, we won't be able to be in love anymore. I love you Amy! I love you and will until the day I die but I can't keep going on this way. I can't be a stranger! I can't be an adversary! We're either in this together forever or we need to split up now. Not tomorrow! Not when this is all over! Now!"

There was shock. There was disbelief. There was finally the reality check we both needed as Amy finally understood I was aware of what was going on. She had her choice, her husband or her son. We were going to battle and I needed to know which side she was going to be on.

The pause was excruciating. She stood frozen in fear, paralyzed by a chilling situation, unable to react or escape as I watched for any semblance of response. I stiffened as Amy examined every nuance of my face looking for any hint that this was a ploy. Was she trapped in a bygone era, yearning for connection or comprehending the present, unable to escape the fantastical or nightmarish visions roiling in her mind, alone, isolated and now unable to experience our world?

Even after thirty years together she was finally aware we'd reached a juncture and she needed to decide. I scrutinized the vitriol within her as it began to subside. I sensed she was pondering both sides... her husband and her son. She now knew the sides had been drawn. There would be no more complicity between Derrick and me. It was over and she knew it.

Amy took a deep breath, looked out at the lake, realized the time was nigh and responded. "George, I love you more than life itself. You've been the stable force within my life that saved my soul and allowed me to exist. I can sense your fear. I can feel your pain. I can understand and appreciate the sadness I've created. As I look at you I realize I've hurt you...deeply, deeply hurt you and for that I'm so, so sorry for what I've done."

So far all Amy had done was share her regret. I needed to know where she stood. I also knew that the next one to talk would lose and so, even though I desperately wanted to say something, I remained mute, simply staring at my wife, waiting for her decision.

After what seemed like an eternity Amy spoke. "George, not only do I love you, I trust you as well. It's this trust that has always provided a feeling of safety and security that comes from knowing that you, above all others, are reliable and will not harm me and that you have and will always act in my best interest, even when it's difficult or inconvenient for you to do so."

There was a pause as if to allow Amy to collect her thoughts and then she continued. "What's difficult is also loving our son which I do for a myriad of reasons. My love for Derrick is a deep and complex bond and there's no single answer to 'why' I love him and how difficult it is for me to choose sides. Perhaps it's because Derrick grew inside me and that immediate connection with him deepened through nurturing care, shared experiences and emotional exchanges. Things George, you never participated in. I've always been so proud of our kids, seeing them as individuals with limitless potential, while witnessing their achievements that has brought immense joy and pride."

Amy stared at the floor and then out at the lake and, finally glanced back at me as she continued. "Even in these darkest hours I contain a natural instinct to protect my child both physically and emotionally and be a source of comfort, support and guidance. Yet, I know deep down there's something wrong. Something deeply troubling that's like a cancer growing within him where, no matter what he achieves, it's never enough. No matter how much he has, it's never enough. No matter how much someone loves him, it will never, ever be enough. Derrick and I share these traits and personalities. While my dad was of the same ilk, he had a woman powerful enough to rein him in. My mom was the one who controlled his dissatisfaction and Derrick has and will probably never have someone like her."

"And, I'm not?" I inquired, feeling inadequate.

"It's not that. Not at all. What it is, is that you're too good, too kind...too generous. Not that mom wasn't but I don't know...she could control dad and you've always simply allowed me to be me with the same weaknesses and challenges you've accepted out of love. George, I love you. I want to be with you until the day I die. I know we are at a crossroads. I know that I need to choose between my husband and my son. I just don't know if I'm brave enough to make that choice."

"But you must." I countered. "Remember back when we lived with Rodney and Ann and you were my legal counsel as we fought to save the Forest? Remember how we were a team and you, yes, you were the one who saved the land. Sure, Charlie was the official lawyer but it was you who prepared the briefs. It was you who developed the strategy. It was you who put the bullets in the gun that allowed us to win. We can do that again...you and me. Sadly, this time, we're not fighting the same battle and against the same people. We're fighting our own son."

"No! you're fighting our son!" Amy said in a tone so dark, so deep and so intense, it sent shivers up my spine.

I paused for a moment to think about what Agent Langdon had expressed and pondered how far I could go without violating the sanctity of my agreement with him and therefore the US government. I waited and then asked, "What did you specifically do to cause the government to involve you in this and make you risk the rest of your life?"

Amy looked at me with a sorrowful expression and stated, "I simply trusted Derrick. I did what most mothers would do. I supported him and, like a fool, trusted him whenever he asked for my signature on papers I never even read."

"Jesus!"

"I know! I was blinded by the light, unable to see what was going on, fully trusting someone without even thinking that his ultimate goal was putting me at risk."

"Tell me what happened."

"Well, there started to be irregularities in the books. There was always plenty of money and the revenue stream was always there. It's just that expenditures began to exceed income."

"Expenditures on what?"

"Derrick kept investing in other businesses and leveraging everything to build his own personal wealth. By showing the company rapidly growing, he was able to borrow against his equity in the company to increase his personal wealth at the expense of the family."

"Why didn't it get stopped?"

"George, how many meetings do we have to go over our wealth?"

"One each year."

"And so he had 364 days to milk the cow before the next meeting, right?

"God damn it!" I seethed before putting my finger to my mouth and shaking my head left and right to infer that Amy say no more.

Amy looked around and lowered her voice and began again. "As he got going he couldn't stop. He was working on margins to expand his wealth simply by using his stock as equity for bigger and bigger loans. He knew that as long as he could keep the Wilco stock value going up he'd be fine."

"In other words, a Ponzi Scheme."

Amy nodded in the affirmative and detailed what Derrick was doing. "Derrick set up his own equities company that lured investors and paid profits to earlier investors with funds from more recent investors. It was essentially a house of cards, built on a continuous flow of new cash to keep the illusion of returns going."

"Derrick used his connections at dad's Milwaukee Club to get started where he promised unrealistically high returns with little or no risk using a secret investment strategy."

"To entice investors, he initially paid out the promised returns using money from the next investors. As more investors joined, their money wasn't actually used for any legitimate investment activities. Instead, it was used to pay off the earlier investors, creating the illusion of ongoing profits."

I shook my head in disbelief as Amy continued. "The scheme relied on a constant stream of new investors to keep the money flowing. Where Derrick was smart was keeping a low cover and relying on word-of-mouth referrals. There are a lot of greedy people out there and he got to know a lot of them."

"Including Senator Fitzgerald."

"Not including Fitzgerald. Fitzgerald's been involved since the beginning."

"What about my brother?"

Amy looked at me with a shocked expression on her face as she tilted her head down, paused to determine how to best say it and then offered. "You always thought the Tommie issue with Heather was resolved. In fact, Tommie never got over what you did or that you were literally his boss at Terrill B&B. Like Fredo in the 'Godfather', Tommie always felt he could do more and you always acted as if you considered him to be inferior."

"Inferior? I gave him everything and even introduced him to his wife," I countered.

"You gave him everything except the one thing he needed most and that was respect."

"This is crazy. What about Su? Aren't they happy?"

Amy remained quiet and did not respond. I didn't know how to interpret her action. Instead I thought of the Wilco booth and the people in it at the Badger game and realized now who they were and why they were there.

Amy paused for a moment and then returned to Derrick and the scheme. "Eventually, it became impossible to attract enough new investors to keep the system afloat. When this happened the house of cards began to crumble and all the invested money was at risk."

"And this is why the government is after us?"

Again, Amy lowered her voice to just above a whisper and she mouthed..."But there's more!"

Up On The Roof:

I took a piece of paper and wrote..."They might be listening, let's go up on the roof."

Amy's mouth dropped open and was soon covered by her hand as if in disbelief as she nodded in the affirmative.

I then took the paper and ran it through the shredder as we headed for the sliders and made our way to the sun deck stairs as I turned and whispered "I think we're being watched. I believe we need to be very careful about what we say and where we say it."

"Why do you think that, George?"

"I just have this feeling."

We made our way up the steps. With the metal privacy screen on three sides, I knew the only place the government could record us from would be out over the lake. To make sure we were protected I turned on the speaker system and selected 'The Flower Duet' which was some of Amy's favorite opera music. My thought was that the eavesdroppers would think we were making up by making love.

There's an old adage that only about ten percent of an iceberg is above water, with the remaining ninety percent hidden beneath the waves and I was about to find out the Enron accounting aspect was just that, the tip of the iceberg, as Amy continued. "There's more. When the dividends came due and Derrick couldn't pay, he needed a money fix. He'd inflated the Wilco stock value as much as possible and, as the company assets became smaller, he began looking at what we owned that had extreme value."

"If there's nothing left, where could he turn?" I inquired.

Amy's expression quickly morphed to one of concern. I could tell she was realizing I knew more than she'd let on and, yet, what she was about to tell me would freeze my soul in fear. Before she could say another word, I continued. "We're not bankrupt, are we? Someone has done something really bad and now we're paying the price...you and me. I don't know what it is but by God I deserve an answer instead of all the bullshit you've been feeding me."

Amy looked at the deck floor, then at the last vestiges of light flickering off Lake Monona's gentle waves and finally at me before responding. "It's bad George. It's really bad!"

"What? What's so bad?"

"The whole thing," Amy whispered.

"Tell me! God damn it! Tell me!" I said, totally frustrated and now profoundly impatient.

Amy slumped as if she had no energy left as she whispered, "It's complicated."

My Minnie Point badass temper erupted. "So, you think I'm too dumb to understand? Is that it?" in a tone she'd never heard before.

"No! No! No!" she cried.

"Tell me or I'm walking out that door and never coming back!"

"God, no! Please, no! Sit down and I'll explain. Just please don't leave me. Not now. Not ever! Please, George, please!" Amy crumpled onto one of the lounge chairs and literally folded in emotional convulsions as torrents of tears cascaded from her eyes.

"Tell me!" I begged.

"Promise me, George! Promise me please!"

"What?"

"Promise me you won't do anything."

Now I knew this was getting really serious. Amy'd seen my bad-ass Minnie Point temper flare and wanted to make sure I wouldn't react as I demanded in a softer tone, "It IS Derrick but it's more than the Ponzi Scheme, isn't it?"

Amy looked at me with woeful eyes and offered. "Derrick unfortunately ran out of both time and suckers and needed an influx of cash. In addition, the margins were coming due on his investments and the only way out was to sell something to cover his losses."

"And...?"

"And he's...he's been working with people."

"What do you mean, working with people?"

"He's been working with people who can program SIMON."

"The Foundation computer?" I offered incredulously.

Amy nodded in the affirmative.

"What about SIMON and what people?"

"Bad people, George. Really bad people."

I was skeptical as I announced. "I don't know what you're talking about."

"Derrick made arrangements with a group of individuals to sell SIMON's software and data."

"Oh my, God!" My worst nightmare was coming to fruition as I asked..."Everything?"

Amy nodded in the affirmative as the waves of life quickly became huge whitecaps of anger, fear and frustration. I was thunderstruck realizing Derrick had sold the personal information including names, locations, medical conditions, DNA and financial data of over one-billion people on earth. By having the data in the wrong hands the information could result in people being assassinated simply by giving them the wrong prescriptions or stealing all their money from their bank accounts.

"It would cause complete pandemonium. But why?" I asked.

"Why do you think?" Amy retorted.

"Money! They want to ransom the world or at least the United States?" I asked, almost praying it wasn't true.

"It's worse than that." Amy offered.

"What?"

"SIMON has also developed programing to potentially control the country's dams, electric grid, financial network, even our ballistic missiles and air traffic control."

"Jesus!"

"George, it's really bad!"

"Who is 'they' you keep talking about, a group of Central American drug lords?"

"Way beyond that. How could it be worse than drug lords?"

"What about a government?"

"A government?"

"Who is America's biggest global competitor?"

"You mean the Chinese?"

"Yes."

"Oh my, God!"

"SIMON is now self-taught and, due to the Foundation's global network and sophistication, they can't shut him down and he's growing more powerful by the day"

I thought back to the day I visited the Foundation, was met at the front door and not allowed in. "This is why I couldn't get in, isn't it?"

"Yes!"

"But why does the government blame us?"

"The bad guys need more time to finish the programming and felt to blame someone would take the government's focus off the real goal and onto you."

"Why me?"

"Because, you're the one who created the Foundation and Fitzgerald has never forgiven you for what you did to his dad."

"Besides the Chinese, who's they?" I asked, already thinking I knew the answer.

"Some people."

"Some people and I'll bet the big winner on this is one Derrick Terrill."

"He's our son, George! Our son!" Amy pleaded.

"Our son who sold his soul so that he can get even richer? Damn his parents! Damn those who spent their lives building your dad's company! Damn the Foundation! Damn the world! Damn, Damn! Damn! I can understand them coming after me but why you?"

"Because...because I trusted Derrick and simply signed the papers he put in front of me."

Now there were profound cries as the sadness that permeated the deck and darkened the sky drilled a hole in my heart and simply took my lust for life and crushed like a boxelder bug walking across a window pane. I shook my head in disbelief and responded. "I can believe the urgency but I can't believe you just signed some papers. That's not like you. That's not the way you're wired."

Amy had tears streaming down her face. "I had no idea it would lead to this. Honest George, I thought if we could sell the database it would solve all of the financial problems."

"Instead you've created a monster so big and so powerful it could destroy the lives of millions of people. Whatever happens, never and I mean never, admit you signed those papers to anyone. Never again! you understand?"

Amy nodded in the affirmative.

"Were you compensated in any way?"

"No."

"Were you promised anything, even a lunch for doing what you did?"

"No."

"And you did this simply as a consultant and not an executive of the company, correct?

"Yes! Why the questions?"

"Come on Amy, you're the lawyer. You simply signed papers your son asked you to sign for which there was no reward of any kind." I was angry beyond words. I was hurt beyond pain! I was shocked until I wreaked in a tumultuous fury, "How could you do this?"

"I'm sorry!"

"Sorry? That's all you can say? Sorry! We've lost everything! I mean everything...our wealth, our belongings, our future, our family and all you can say is 'I'm sorry'?" I was livid. I wanted to throw Amy off the balcony and watch her smash on the railroad tracks below.

Amy reached for my hand as if I would forgive her and all it did was ratchet up the anger inside of me as I espoused. "I started that Foundation for the good of humanity. I started it to help people not turn it into a weapon of mass destruction. Yet, you and YOUR son used it as a poker chip that sold the soul of the two of you to the devil and for what...for money? For power? For what? I know...greed where never is never enough!"

Amy's effusive tears began to calm me down. It was all beginning to make sense. The government was onto the Ponzi Scheme but didn't know about SIMON. Not, yet, anyway. The Duke taught me there is always strength when you have something the other side wants and even more strength when they don't even know they want it.

"How deep is Derrick in with the Chinese?"

"Deep!"

"How did they learn about SIMON?"

"How do you think?"

"I don't know."

"Do you remember Hongshe out of Changzhou China?" Amy asked.

"Yes, they were the company who wanted to purchase the farm."

"They'd done due diligence and had a very deep memory about how my dad stopped them."

"Jesus," I emanated.

"Then you opened the Foundation and won the Nobel Peace Prize that detailed the technology SIMON incorporated."
A sinking feeling permeated my body, taking with it all the vitriol that built up as Amy inquired, "Who do you know who has family living in China?"

"Su!"

"So, you think Su was the conduit?"

Amy nodded in the affirmative.

"And that's how Tommie got involved?"

Again, affirmation.

"But Su is so…so professional."

"George. Think about it. The Chinese threatened to hold Su's family captive to compel her cooperate through intimidation. I don't think she intentionally did it but was pressured to act against her will simply by using her family members as leverage. You have to realize in their culture, one's family is much closer than in America."

"And they used them to get to Derrick."

"No. To Tommie, who then went to Derrick."

"Jesus!"

Amy continued. "The Chinese were keeping track of all Derrick's financial moves. In some cases, I believe they actually helped inflate the stock values to make them more attractive, only to have them implode and leave Derrick unable to cover his liabilities both personally and through the Ponzi scheme. They knew they had him and the only way he could get out of it was by selling the data. Either sell the data or go to jail. It's simple when you're being backed by one of the largest, most powerful and ruthless Cartels in the world."

"Derrick was playing with a few hundred million dollars and the Chinese have hundreds of billions behind them simply because they only had one goal which wasn't financial but political and that was obtaining data they could use to dominate the world."

Reality was settling in as I exclaimed, "Oh my God!"

Amy continued. "It didn't stop there. As they got their fingers deeper into Derrick and realized the power SIMON had, they recognized they could begin to control a lot of different technologies using SIMON's artificial intelligence. As Derrick got deeper and deeper into the scheme they put pressure on him to find someone who could program SIMON to do what they wanted."

"Who was it?"

"I don't know but I think it has to be one of the Mad-City boys. They're the only one's smart enough and close enough to have access to SIMON and also work their magic to have him do what they want done."

"How did the government find out?"

Amy looked at me and went into an almost tutorial tone and shared. "Whenever there's a transaction above a certain amount on the stock exchange the SEC is informed. When there's a pattern to the transactions, the FBI is informed. When the duration and consequences become great enough the Secret Service is informed. God only knows how long they've been monitoring what's going on. All I know is that they've reached a point where they've got enough of the puzzle pieces in place to come out from behind the curtain and publicly challenge all that Derrick has done financially. At this point in time, I don't think they realize what SIMON has done and that's why the lawsuits have been what they are."

"Financial and not treasonous?"

"Yes, George."

"All because of money. All because of greed."

"All because enough is never enough! Can you ever forgive me, George?"

"I love you, Amy. What's changed is my respect. How can I respect someone who's taken my work and set in motion a way to destroy all that we've built?"

"By having me help you save it," Amy replied.

I had the scenario and felt the commitment of Amy. I needed to figure out what I could do. I couldn't tell her that every move we made was under surveillance. I couldn't share that I had seen Derrick with Fitzgerald at the game. I knew I needed to talk with Agent Langdon and try to find out what he knew, or at least what he was willing to tell me. The question was, how? How did I contact him? How did I know when to stop and when to go?

I Owe I Owe So Off to Work I Go:

It had been several days since Amy's "admission". The net result of our altercation was a resolution that began reuniting us as a team. By allowing it all to spew forth Amy had come to realize we were in deep shit and the enemy was my brother and our own son. The challenge was developing some sort of strategy that would not only focus all the blame on Derrick but expunge Amy of any wrong doing. Yes, she knew what was going on but she hadn't participated or gained any advantage, whatsoever.

I'd studied the situation and learned that whether someone knows about something illegal but doesn't gain from it, is a complex question regarding whether they're guilty of anything. The first caveat is the specific nature of the illegal activity and how serious it was. Amy was aware of the Ponzi scheme yet she had no control of it as it was being done outside Wilco and therefore beyond her domain.

The second aspect was her intent or potential harm. Amy knew about the crime and never intended to do anything about it. When she learned what was happening, it was her belief it wouldn't cause any damage. Because she never intended on covering it up, I believed her culpability would be different than if she intended to help cover it up or supposed it could lead to harm.

Amy and I went over and over and over her role to make certain she didn't take any action to assist the illegal activity, even passively. If she had she'd be charged as an accessory, even if we didn't directly benefit. I also asked her, and she vowed, she never attempted to hinder the investigation or prosecution of the crime and understood that if she did we could face more legal consequences.

Was Amy guilty? From our perspective no but we're not the government. And, yet, it was our son and Amy, who had been working with him but was unaware of what had transpired. My goal was not getting money. My goal was ensuring Amy's freedom. Where I felt the key bargaining, point was the fact the government only knew about the Ponzi Scheme and not the sale of SIMON's data to the Chinese. I hoped that reporting the crime to the authorities could be used to ensure her innocence as those who do are not generally considered culpable, even if they initially knew about it.

Besides doing a lot of legal research that Amy and I would then discuss in our rooftop meetings as I called them, I did as I was directed and began attempting to finalize George the First's 'Waldwick' and getting it ready for print. I knew I needed an ISBN number. I knew I needed a cover designed. I knew I needed to have it proofread. Finally, I knew I needed to find a printer I could afford. In addition, I remained gainfully employed at Home Depot punching in on time, every time, riding the bus and allowing my mind to turn to mush.

Within all retail environments employee turnover is higher than one would expect and it wasn't long before I was 'promoted' from a basic stock boy to head of displays. This meant filling the end caps, keeping the pallet aisle full, ensuring the signage was accurate and up to date. In addition I was responsible for moving slow-moving promotional items to the 'dead end' as it was called, better known as the back wall, which was what we called 'death row' that consisted of a plethora of this and that the vendors wouldn't take back.

One day Arnie, the Assistant Manager, gave me the assignment for one of the prime end caps near the store entry. Arne had to be in his forties, was about thirty-pounds overweight with yellow teeth from too many cigarettes and not enough visits to the dentist. If the teeth weren't bad enough, the somewhat greasy combover gave me the creeps and brought back memories of when Amy and I were young and I called on the ad agency when I was Marketing Manager for the Hochunk. No one, and I mean no one, on the crew liked this guy who'd worked his way up through the system until the Peter Principle rang true. There's a saying, "Give a little man a little power and he thinks he's a big man," which was certainly accurate when it came to this clown.

Arnie informed me that this display was the key location where the idea was to 'break the ice', as he called it, such that, when a customer came in with an empty cart from the double entry vestibule and put one promo item in the cart, it usually resulted in the customer buying more than they came for. This was to be my big test as Arnie had always saved the 'ice breaker' display for himself, such that he could admire it whenever he was at the front counter.

There were two items for the display...one was quite small and the other quite large. Arnie told me to put the small items on the bottom and the large on the top. Knowing a little bit about aesthetics, consumer psychology and aspect ratios from Terrill B&B I realized immediately the display would be upside-down visually, aesthetically and psychologically and took the liberty of putting the smaller, cheaper items on top.

Arnie returned from his break and my name was called over the PA as I made my way to the front counter. Arnie looked at me with profound disdain and asked "Didn't I tell you to put the big items on the top and small on the bottom?"

I nodded in the affirmative and countered, "But I thought".

Arnie snarled, "I don't pay you to think, I pay you to do. When you punch out tonight, you can stay on your own time and make it right."

"But I'll miss the last bus home," I countered.

"Do you think I care? Do it or resign."

He was dragging my nose through shit and there was nothing I could do about it. I stood, took a deep breath and realized I'd hit bottom. I needed to begin the fight for our wealth and dignity.

The store closed and it was just the janitors and me. I flipped the display and began the walk from near the Interstate to home. At a little over six miles and my daily walking regimen I estimated it would take two hours and called Amy before leaving the store to let her know what was going on.

I walked out into the parking lot and made it to the front of the mall when EOP-812 pulled up. I looked inside as Agent Langdon rolled down the window and offered. "Need a ride? You missed the last bus and it's a long walk to Wilson Street."

It was actually good to see him and the ride took that part of the day and made it worthwhile as I slid into the passenger's seat as I asked, "Been watching me?

"Somewhat."

"Have I been a good boy?"

"Somewhat. I didn't like the phone call to the Madison Police Department but understand you were just checking my validity."

A concerned look crept across my face.

"How was I supposed to know if you were legit or not?"

Langdon changed the subject by asking, "Why all the evenings up on the roof?"

Shit. They knew. I simply offered. "It's October and still nice out. With all the pressure you've put on Amy and me, we go up there, have some wine and try to rebuild our marriage. Is there anything wrong with that?"

"No. It's just that it seems a little strange."

"Strange? What to try and rebuild our marriage that's in shambles because the government has frozen our assets? Strange that I have no car, no money and no other place to go except sitting in the condo all day and all night? What's strange about that?"

"How's the book coming?

"I've got my great grandfather's manuscript typed and now I need to do the cover design and find a printer."

"Can I buy a signed copy when you're done?"

"Sure, if you want to."

"What happened at work today?"

"What do you mean?"

"Why did you have to stay late?"

"I've been promoted and had a disagreement with the Assistant Manager about a display."

"Arnie?"

"Yes, Arnie."

"SDS?"

"Huh?"

"Short Dick Syndrome."

"You got it."

"Want to stop for a beer?"

"Sure, why not?"

Agent Langdon pulled up in front of the Brass Ring and asked, "is this Ok?"

"Sure."

He offered. "I used to go to the Avenue Bar but they closed it, tore it down and yet another apartment complex is going up. This city is crazy!"

We walked in the Brass Ring and Agent Langdon inquired. "Want to shoot a game of pool?"

"I'm not very good."

"Neither am I but it's better than sitting at the bar."

"Agreed."

We got the rack of balls and went to table number nine in the corner as Langdon inquired. "Eight ball, nine ball or straight pool?"

"Eight ball sounds good to me."

We stroked to see who'd break and my ball ended up closer to the rear rail than his and so I broke and sank the seven which meant I had solids and he had stripes.

"Any updates for me?" Langdon asked.

"Yup!" I offered as I lined up the three in the far corner.

"Want to fill me in?"

"I thought we were going to play a game of pool."

"Tell you what, you win and no interrogation. I win and you fill me in. Deal?"

"Deal!"

I missed on the three and Langdon ran the stripes and missed his call on the eight. This guy was good, as I offered, "You thought you had a fish, didn't you?"

"Nope just a little luck and a lot of pool at the Memorial Union when I was in school. What you got for me?" Langdon chuckled.

I looked around and whispered. "Not here. Not now!"

With that, Langdon put the balls back in the storage tray, we drank our beers and left as he asked, "Where to?"

I directed him to turn left on Blair Street and over to Lake Monona and the Shore Drive until we made it to the Monona Terrace parking ramp where I told him to pull in. We exited the car and began walking the path west towards Broom Street.

I offered, "I want to make a deal."

"What's that?"

"I'll take you much deeper than you think the hole is and help you fill it in if you guarantee that the charges against Amy are dropped and our assets opened."

"I can't do that. It's not at my pay grade."

"Someone can and if what I tell you isn't true and if we don't resolve the issues, then Amy and I will plead guilty."

"Holy shit! You're serious."

"About as serious as a heart attack," I offered while adding. "When you've got nothing, you've got nothing to lose."

We made it to First Bridge on John Nolen Causeway as I let Langdon consider it.

"You know, George, I don't have the authority to do that."

"Then you better find out who does and get them involved NOW! This is much bigger and much deeper than you think. If I've got my bearings right, you're just about to have your thirty in and have a choice, you can go out in a blaze of glory or keep your head down and sneak out at the end of the game."

Langdon shook his head and pursed his lips. I'd hit a soft spot. I'd seen his type before, dedicated to his job because he thought what he was doing was right. Terrible at politics which meant the ass-kissers around him kept moving up while he remained stuck in a mid-level position without any authority. It was time to level the playing field as I added. "My bet is you're not very good at politics. You've been passed over and screwed ten ways to Sunday. If what I have and what I want to propose works, you'll go out as a hero and not just another agent assigned to secondary matters like Wilco."

I looked at Langdon's face in the streetlight and saw he'd turned pale. Even with the cars whizzing by at the speed of life, heading into downtown, I could hear the deep breaths of anticipation and the realization that perhaps good old George was smarter and a little more aggressive than he let on.

"What do you have that's that important?"

"More important than you can imagine."

"You'll have to give me the details so that I can take them in to get the agreement."

"Dave...Dave. You don't mind if I call you Dave, do you? Do you think I'm going to play all my cards right now? Do you think I want to give up any chance I have of getting the deal I want? You must take me for a fool. You want it, you can have it...if and when I have something in writing."

"And what if I can't?"

"Then the next time we play pool, I'll whip your ass and not intentionally miss the three ball in the corner pocket, while I have the two, five and one set for my next three shots and leave it so you can run the table. You're good Dave but you missed setting up the eleven before the nine which is why you had the bad shot you did on the eight. You see, Dave, you're not as good as me."

There was a long pause as if Dave was weighing his options. Instead, he took out his phone and pressed an App and then put in some code while finally saying, "watch this."

The recording started and I was aghast. It was my Zoom call with Luke and Peter regarding SIMON. I looked up and asked, "where'd you get this?"

"George, SIMON isn't the only one who can scan the web. When you use Zoom, it becomes public domain."

I watched in disbelief as I realized the government already knew the power of the computer. Curious to see where the video ended, I watched.

Peter, Luke and I were on the screen where I asked them what was going on and they concurred that the Washington Congressional meeting wasn't about Mediglove, it was about the power we had with SIMON. We knew more than the government did about more people and their health and wellbeing all over the world. We had data they coveted, that we would not share, based on our protection under the Constitution.

It was then that Luke really hit home when he said that man had always been at war and it would continue. "George, war is evolving from a face-to-face, person-to-person battle where the victor represented took control of the mindset of the defeated, to where we are today. In addition to those deaths caused directly by violence – for instance those from gunshot or explosions – a significant proportion of lives lost in conflict are indirect, due to disease, starvation or exposure. This is particularly true where conflicts lead to famine or outbreaks of disease among the civilian population. But historically, such indirect deaths were also a major cause of military fatalities."

Peter added. "SIMON has data on over one-billion people. This means he knows more than any security agency of the US government. More than the NSA! More than the CIA! More than anyone! This is what the government wants. Because SIMON is a two-way street, it has the ability to 'communicate' all forms of propaganda to one-seventh of the world's population. Because everyone checks in, SIMON knows the location and time the person checked in. He also has some behavioral data where, using algorithms SIMON can determine what people love, what they hate and what directions people will ignore. Because of the massive amount of data SIMON has, we could easily program him to predict, with astounding accuracy, what people are or are not likely to do, including propaganda and even war. Welcome to the world of A.A.I. or Advanced Artificial Intelligence."

I was appalled! All I wanted to do was help people and never thought of what the 'other side' could use SIMON to do.

Peter continued. "George, war has three general purposes. First, to conquer and destroy the armed power of the enemy. Second, to take possession of an enemy's sources of strength and third, to gain public support at home and the opinion of the citizenry of the defeated.

There wasn't a smile on Luke's face as he added in earnest. "In the past, war was 'inter-personal' as I call it, that was sustained through all the battles from Caesar until World

War I. In these wars, it was man-vs-man, sword-vs-sword, knife-vs-knife and then gun-vs-gun.

The methodology of war evolved, but it was primarily face-to-face where you saw who it was you killed and watched them die. World War I changed everything! It started with men on horseback, digging trenches yet still fighting face-to-face. It ended with poison gas and men in airplanes and tanks anonymously creating death."

"Every war since has seen increased killing sophistication to the point where today, war has become impersonal. An unmanned drone flies over a target and someone, somewhere pushes a button that eliminates someone they never saw or felt and would not watch them die. They do so without remorse or consideration for the loss of a husband, father, son or friend with no risk or consequence to themselves while eating lunch and thinking nothing of what they just did."

"Today, war is not about destruction, it's about capturing the hearts and minds of those who are affected and right now SIMON has the potential to be the most powerful weapon on earth. While we have built in safeguards, the concern within the government is that either someone will break in and take all of SIMON's data and programming and use it against our country, or we will. That's why we are being called in front of the Judiciary Committee and why, to circumvent any negative attacks by the citizenry, they're doing it under the Federal Trade Commission. The goal is not to stop us, but to make us share all the data and programming with the government so that they have the ability to use it for their purposes."

"George, I sincerely believe that 'bullet wars' are over. Our country has experienced a dress rehearsal of one form of tomorrow's wars, where an enemy creates a deadly virus and inoculates their own citizens and then lets the virus run rampant everywhere else, thereby creating a pandemic that only kills people and does so to the degree that all resources, other than humans, are retained intact with no physical or collateral damage. Imagine being able to walk into any country and simply remove the dead and take over the infrastructure and populate it with people who were loyal to you. It would be an incredibly efficient form of domination."

Luke was seen leaning back in his chair and asking, "Do you see why the information SIMON has is so valuable? In the wrong hands, the enemy would know what people they could "select" to kill simply by manipulating prescription dosages or knowing what to include or limit in their chemical arsenal."

I shuddered to think of the power we had and now realized why the government wanted us eliminated.

Peter added, "I believe that soon there will be more sophisticated electronic wars capable of shutting down entire economies simply by infiltrating and infecting software for things such as the financial, communication and medical networks and we will have reached our social, political, technical and ethical Hayflick Limit."

"We have had around twenty-one generations since the Constitution and we all know that our country is now about one thing – money! What would happen if all of sudden money was erased? No more 401K's or stock portfolios! No more bank accounts or credit cards! Our economy and our world would come to a standstill. What about our power grids that could bring our nation to its knees? Right now, they're all inter-linked. Right now, it the wrong hands our economy, our society and our country would simply stop functioning."

I watched as Peter opened his hands and said. "All of our hydroelectric dams are now computer controlled. Imagine breaking in and opening the floodgates on all of them simultaneously! It would kill millions of people and destroy cities and towns without a single missile being fired. Imagine wiping away all the medical software so that there were no medical records or controls of medical robots. Cars have become mobile computers that are all connected to the manufacturers. Imagine infecting their software so that engines would either destroy themselves or take control of moving vehicles, creating thousands of accidents all over the country! Imagine controlling all flight operations to the point that no one, including our military, could safely take off and land. As you can see, we are vulnerable and right now, the government believes SIMON has the capability to do any or all of the above."

I thought of how easy it was for us to break into the FDA and change the rules to try and save Dr. Williams and how, within fifteen seconds, SIMON had infiltrated Ancestry.com and changed The Duke's heritage to make him part Native American.

Luke continued. "I agree with Peter. War isn't about killing, it's about control of the mind - about opinions, attitudes and beliefs, where changing those can result in the total collapse of a society and its political structure. The misinformation program used during World War II by the Germans, Japanese and Americans were classic examples of a rudimentary form of persuasion."

"It appears that the 2016 US Presidential election was a classic form of electronic warfare, where an outside source meddled in our election to get the individual or individuals they wanted elected. They did so simply by planting misinformation about the opponent and doing it with such sophistication and verve that our simplistic protection system was unable to stop them. In a period of two weeks, they were able to change attitudes of voters and subsequently the entire course of history of our country without invading, nor having a single shot fired and without anyone even knowing what happened until it was too late."

"George, the reason we're being called into Washington is not about what we have done, it's about what

SIMON could do that's equal to the power and might of the US Government. They're afraid! They don't like it when someone or something is equal to them in power or capability! All we have on our side is goodness and decency and yet those in power, who have seen what power can do, fear that we will unleash our power to control more than they want us to. This is why we are called to Washington. All the other stuff is just camouflage to their real purpose which is shutting SIMON down."

"Enough!" I offered handing the phone back to Langdon."

Langdon countered. "George, you need to give me something to work with."

"I am. I'm trying to give you the opportunity to jump over all those assholes who took a good guy and kept him doing shit jobs while they made their way up the proverbial power ladder. In the end, some worlds are going to come crashing down while you, my friend will ride off into the sunset a hero."

"And if I can't?"

"I do enjoy working at Home Depot."

I looked Dave in the eyes, stuck out my hand and shook his. "I'll let you walk back to your car from here." I smiled and took a step towards the Broom Street traffic lights before turning and noting. "thanks for the ride and the beer. Let's work as a team and not as adversaries."

Home Again:

I waited three days and heard nothing from Agent Langdon. With no car and the Fed's tailing me everywhere I needed to start building my team to upset the Chinese applecart but that required doing so without the intervention of the government. I knew if the feds got involved, the Chinese would know and the whole plan would be bungled. I built the Foundation and I was either going to fix it, protect it or destroy it.

The only good news was from Tank Kennison. He'd filed papers with the Wilco Bankruptcy Judge with all the support documents moving that the farms be removed from the Wilco assets and returned to me. Even with our assets frozen, at least, if the day came we got some our money back, the farm would be in my name and not pushed through the Wilco proceedings.

The whole farm deal reminded me of high school when Sandy Mason, the girl I had a crush on, split up with Johnny Thomas, the quarterback on the football team. It didn't mean she'd go out with me but at least I was in contention. Hopefully, I'd have better luck with the farm than I did with helping Amy. While I wanted her on the 'team', we morphed back to strangers and she wouldn't give me the time of day. In fact, I was so far down the list, she wouldn't even look at her watch.

Back to the really serious stuff. I knew who I needed on my team. All I needed to do was first, find them and second, figure out how to work with them without Derrick or the government peering over our shoulders. The team would consist of three people besides me. First, would be Amy whose job it would be to keep the government's focus on everything by creating a landfill of paperwork. Second, would be Peter. If there was anyone who could break into and dumb down SIMON, it was Peter. Third, would be Luke. He knew the Foundation building inside out as he was the one who conceived it, designed it and built it.

My goal was to figure out how to break in and re-program SIMON so that the Chinese information would be corrupted by having Peter create a virus so virulent it would eat through their system and leave them with their dicks in the hands. I knew I couldn't use my phone or email and needed to find a way to communicate with Peter and Luke. I thought of burner phones and surmised either Derrick or the government could already be tapping into Peter and Luke's communication systems. I wondered if Peter and Luke had kept in contact and, perhaps, if they had I could use one as a conduit to the other.

Peter and his wife, Cindy, had retired and literally vanished from the Madison scene. I knew they wanted to travel the world but had no idea how to contact them. I walked over to the Madison Public Library and Googled Peter Washburn. Peter had made it to Google Gemini and Wikipedia where both brought a plethora of memories of a man so bright, so independent and so giving, it humbled me as I thought back to the first-time biker Peter walked into my office.

I knew that Luke and Indira still had the house in Mineral Point. I Googled Lucas Arnold and was reminded of how great a man he was as he, too, was detailed on Google Gemini and Wikipedia. I then realized I needed a third party to contact both Peter and Luke and it had to be from someone no one would expect. I initially narrowed my options to two people, Rodney Whitehorse, my Big Brother, and my son, 'V'. I also quickly recognized that if I chose either one they would immediately become accessories to crimes. With Rodney, it could mean the end of his presidency of the Hochunk nation, if not more. While we are all taught the legal system is blind, the severity of punishment to those somewhat different than the ruling class still meant harsher penalties and I couldn't risk that. If I chose "V", it could mean the end of his political career. It was then $E=MC^2$ came to mind.

It being simply a four block walk from the condo to the library and there being a bank of free computers at the library to use, all I needed to do was randomly alternate between the six units and there would be no way the government could keep track of my research if I cleared my search when I was done, which I always, and mean always, did. The question then became how to first get in contact with them.

I waited a couple of days and made my way to the library. I had a strange feeling I was being followed so instead of going into the library I walked another block to State Street and then headed west toward the UW campus. With each intersection I'd stop and look back to see if someone was following me.

As I reached the 500 block of State Street I paused in front of what had been the Pub, a favorite hangout for generations of college students and the Mad City Boys. I continued on and walked onto the UW campus and all the way to Vilas Hall that held so many of my collegiate classes and dreams about tomorrow and not memories of yesterday. Circling back I crossed University Avenue, made my way to Basset Street, walked south on Basset to Wilson and then east to the condo.

With the one-way streets and my up-tempo pace I was confident no one was following me as I made my way back to the Capitol and wandered the halls until I found an empty office. Making my way inside I saw what I needed...a telephone from which I called Megan's number.

"Hello," A friendly voice answered.

"Had any winos stay at your house lately?"

"Unfortunately, no." came the reply. "I'm waiting for a very special wino to come back so I can get kinky," Megan giggled.

"Listen, I can't stay on long. I'm in somebody's office in the State Capitol but I really need a favor."

"For you, anything."

"I need to have you call a friend named Luke Arnold who lives in Mineral Point."

"Ok,"" as Megan's tone got serious.

"He knows we've got some issues."

"Not some. A lot," Megan offered. "We had a visitor."

"You didn't do anything wrong," I assured Megan.

"Still it's scary."

"I know and I'm sorry. Had I known they were tailing me I wouldn't have gone to the airport or come at all."

"Then I would have been really upset. They just asked a bunch of questions."

"You Ok?" I asked.

"I'm fine. Ellie's fine. We're fine. I just want to see you again."

"When this is all over, I promise."

"Ok."

There was a long pause on the other end. I was certain Megan was contemplating what I was about to ask as she replied. "You'll always be my friend."

"That's why I called."

"What's this about?"

"I can't say over the phone and if anyone calls and asks who you were talking to tell them it was a telemarketer. I need your help."

I paused and almost whispered. "Ask Luke if he knows how I get hold of Peter? If he does, can Luke call him and tell Peter I need to talk to him?"

"You're in trouble, aren't you?"

"Yes, and Amy as well and it's deep shit."

"How do I get hold of you?" Megan asked.

"I'm working at the Home Depot by East Towne Mall in Madison. I'm being tailed everywhere I go. I think they've got our cellphones tapped and they're checking all email and communication. Is there any chance you'd be coming to Madison in the near future?

"For you George, I'd come immediately."

"Better, yet, why don't I give you the store's phone number and you call me at exactly 2:00 on Thursday and I'll make sure I'm standing by the customer service desk.

"Ok"

"I've got to go."

"Can I ask what this is about?"

"I need to set a meeting up with Luke and Peter, if he's willing."

"Understood."

Click!

Phone Call:

As planned I was at work and made my way up to the front desk at precisely two when the phone rang. Lynn was working behind the counter and took the call. "George, it's for you."

I placed a surprised look on my face, stuck my thumb in my chest as if to reflect 'me' as Lynn nodded in the affirmative. Picking up the phone, I said, "Hello".

To my surprise, on the other end was Agent Langdon. "George, George, George! The long walk was masterful and going into the Capitol was a great idea but you shouldn't use a government phone for personal calls, especially to your buddy Megan. Don't you realize all the phone calls in and out of the Capitol are summarized. All it took was the number and a call to her and we knew you needed to talk to Luke Arnold at two today."

"This is ridiculous," I responded. "I want to know why you're tracking me if there haven't been any charges against me. Why are you harassing me?"

"George, you're the one who said you have something really important that required going to Washington about. Something someone at my lowly level wouldn't understand."

I looked at Lynn and knew I'd better keep my mouth shut. What was going on was none of her business as I offered Langdon, "I get done at nine, meet me then," and handed the receiver back to Lynn and went back to building an end cap display of Christmas decorations even though it wasn't even Halloween.

At nine I punched out and left the store. As I was walking towards the bus stop, the brown Impala came alongside and stopped. Langdon lowered the window to show that he wasn't alone and told me to get in.

I climbed in the back seat and Langdon headed east towards Sun Prairie. I looked at the back of two silent heads and wondered where in hell we were going. As we hit the I-90 interchange Langdon slid across two lanes and we quickly headed south as I challenged, "Where in hell are we going?"

Not a word was spoken as Langdon gave the car some gas and we hit 85 miles an hour. Jesus! Normally 85 on the Interstate isn't that fast as the idiots in a hurry think 90 isn't fast enough. We headed south to the 18/151 exit and sped west on the Beltline as I inquired once again, "Where are we going?"

Still total silence from the front seat until Langdon said, "George, we've got some serious shit to talk about and we're going where no one will be able to see or hear us."

"Jesus!"

Langdon made it to the John Nolen drive exit and I thought we were going back to the art center. Instead, he turned left on Lakeside Street and made his way west towards Park Street. Making a quick right on Whittier, he turned north and went to South Shore Drive and proceeded to Erin Street before turning left and driving up the hill past Saint Mary's hospital. At Mills Street, Langdon turned left and we went down the hill to Wingra Drive before meeting the bridge that took us into the University Arboretum.

I hadn't been in the Arboretum since Amy and I went swimming there when we were dating and had no idea what was going on. As we made our way through the preserve, Langdon finally spoke. "George, sorry for the ride and suspense, this is Agent John Walker with the CIA."

With that, Walker flashed his badge and handed me a card without saying a word as Langdon continued. "As you know, we've been following you. What you didn't know and we weren't aware, was that someone has been following us and has had access to everything we've acquired. This means, George, whatever it is you've got in terms of critical information it's a whole hell of a lot more important to the point it's critical to national security. The reason for the joy ride was to make sure no one is following us."

Langdon pulled the car into the Wingra Springs parking lot in the Arboretum and we all got out when I realized how big Walker was. He must have played football somewhere as he noted. "Mr. Terrill, somehow, some way, someone thinks you have critical information they don't want you to share. They've been following us as we've been following you. We believe they have a tracking device on you and if you don't mind, I'd like to check and see."

As we were speaking Langdon opened the Impala trunk and removed what looked like a traditional briefcase. Inside was some sort of silver wand and Walker asked, "Do you mind if I scan you?"

"Now when you've got some six-foot-six probable football player CIA agent asking to scan you, you simply don't say 'no' and so the process began. As he slid the wand down my back and to my rear pocket, the woo, woo, woo, woo sound was elicited over my wallet.

"May I see your wallet please?"

I pulled out my wallet and handed it to Walker. He opened it and began scanning each card. As he came across my Home Depot employee ID the scanner went crazy as Walker asked, "Has this been out of your possession?"

"Not since I got it when I started work."

"How did you get your job at Home Depot?"

"I heard they were hiring and went in."

"Who did you meet with for your job interview?"

"Some man who said he was the corporate recruiter?"

"Do you remember his name?"

"It was seven or eight months ago. Sorry, I don't."

"Who issued the card?"

"He said it would be at the front counter my first day."

"Was it?"

"Yes, or I couldn't check in. You have to scan the card to initiate your check in and check out process as we're paid on an hourly basis."

"What happens if you lose it?"

"I guess you get a new one."

"Well, you just lost this one, Ok?"

"Sure, no problem but wouldn't whomever it is who's been following me, followed us here?"

"We sure hope so."

I quickly realized why we took the crazy way to get to the Arboretum. There had to be back-up somewhere and the boys were going to ambush them.

Just then, Walker raised his finger and listened through the ear phone in his left ear and noted. "They identified the vehicle and the suspects. They know we've stopped and with no other place to park they've gone ahead and are sitting in the visitor center lot.

"Time to have a little fun" Langdon said, as he opened another case that had a small drone in it, attached my Home Depot ID to the base with duct tape, placed the drone on the ground and let it fly. Within a minute we watched as a car went whizzing by in chase of an imaginary person.

"Why don't you stop them?" I asked.

"For what? What have they done that's illegal?"

"We just need to have them realize we're on to them so they play their hand."

"And I'm the bait?"

"Somewhat."

"Won't you lose them?" I inquired.

"I hope they really think we went into the monkey house at Vilas Zoo."

"What about my ID?"

"We'll have a new one waiting for you when you go to work tomorrow. We'll use your old one for a couple of days and then destroy it."

This was actually starting to be fun.

Truth and Nothing But The Truth:

As we stood in the Wingra Springs parking area Langdon took out a cellphone and took the initiative as he formally noted. "George Terrill, Agent William Walker has been assigned to the case as it has been deemed to be one that could affect national security. We are aware you might be of assistance in protecting our country and that's why we've requested your support."

"Mister Terrill, at this time you and your wife are not charged but remain suspects and we are formally requesting your help. If you don't mind we would like to record your comments for further use. You have the right to remain silent. However, your assistance in this matter will be considered as a gesture towards the objectives we have stated previously."

Just then another brown Chevy Impala pulled into the parking area and stopped beside us. The driver's door opened and another agent got out. From the rear passenger side another, recognized figure appeared. It was Peter. My God, how in the hell?

Langdon continued as if nothing had happened as I nodded in the affirmative.

"Please state your name."

"George William Terrill the Fourth."

"Your residence."

"237 West Wilson Street, Apartment 805, Madison, Wisconsin.

"Your wife's name."

"Amelia Marie Terrill."

"And she lives with you?'

"Yes, she does."

Peter and the new agent identified as James Marksman appeared as the attention turned to Peter and Langdon reiterated.

"Peter James Washburn, at this time you are not considered a suspect and we are formally requesting your help. If you don't mind we would like to record your comments, as well as Mister Terrill's for further use."

Marksman continued. "You have the right to remain silent. However, your assistance in this matter will be considered a positive gesture towards the safety and security of the citizens of the United States. Are you willing to do so?"

"I am."

"Please state your name. "

"Peter James Washburn."

Langdon pointed the camera at me and inquired, "Mister Terrill, are you aware of any action by foreign governments, agencies or operatives that might put the United States of America at risk?"

"Yes, I am."

"Do you know who these operatives are?"

"Only by name."

"Which name is that?"

"The Chinese."

"And how are they involved?"

"They're purchasing software from the Derrick Williams Foundation."

"And the consequences of this purchase are?" Langdon inquired even though he knew the answer.

"The consequences are that they have vital personal information on over a billion people on earth including names, locations, medical histories and potential cures."

"And how is this critical to national security?" Walker interjected.

I turned, looked at Peter and replied. "For a more comprehensive answer I believe Mister Washburn can be of greater service.

Peter paused, looked down at the ground as I knew he was in the process of taking something incredibly complex and simplifying, and asked, "Have you ever heard of the chaos theory?"

"No," Langdon replied as if Peter was somehow baiting him.

Peter looked at the three men and offered. "The chaos theory shows that even simple systems can exhibit complex and unpredictable behavior to the point that even small events can have large consequences, where the future is often much more uncertain than we once thought."

"Ok!" Langdon offered.

Peter continued not as a mathematician who had just grasped what has transpired but what we were facing if SIMON's data got into the wrong hands. "You have to understand, while seeming to only be personal medical information, in the wrong hands, that data could mean a lot of different really bad things. Within the US the software purchasers would have the personal data on nearly 150 million people which they could use to alter election registration or even electoral votes."

"Like 2020?"

"Exactly. However, that's minor to what they could accomplish through the development of viruses similar to Covid 19 which could be spread throughout the world, where only those who knew about it before it was released could create a serum and inoculate their own population while allowing the rest of the world to suffer."

"In other words, germ warfare?" Walker inquired.
"Yes!" Peter proposed. "Have you ever heard of Generative AI?" Heads shook 'no' as Peter continued. "Generative AI, also known as generative artificial intelligence, is a field of AI focused on creating new content normally in anything from text and images to music and videos instead of using a programmed limit of information."

"Basically, generative AI uses machine learning models to analyze existing data and identify patterns that are then used to create entirely new content while mimicking the style and format of the data it was trained on. This was the primary structure used for SIMON but we took it to the Nth degree to the point SIMON has the ability to take any data and analyze it down to the sub-atomic level. In so doing instead of just the basic event, SIMON looks at the causes of those events and then the causes of the causes and so on."

Mouths dropped open as Peter continued. "There are different approaches in basic computers but a common method involves supervised learning. In this case the AI model is given a large dataset of existing content, along with labels or descriptions. The model learns the relationships between the data and the labels and then uses this knowledge to generate new content that follows those same patterns."

"What SIMON does is dig down into the subsets of the data and labels deeper, deeper and deeper until he starts correlating micro-data while he considers billions of permutations and combinations at the same time that allow him to develop conclusions other computers and humans can't perceive. Right now SIMON is able to understand the mental states of others and, if he continues his linear progression, will eventually have a conscious understanding of himself.

"How is this possible?" Langdon asked as the entire entourage stood spellbound.

Peter inhaled and then continued. "Everything that exists can be reduced to a mathematical equation and SIMON has been programmed to dig deeper into that data mathematically than any other computer in the world to the point he's capable of examining fractals on a level no one has ever examined before."

"Fractals?" Walker asked.

Peter paused and realized he had a non-scientific audience and proceeded. "Fractals are fascinating mathematic representations of geometric shapes that exhibit two key characteristics. The most critical is called self-similarity, which means that a fractal's basic pattern repeats at different scales... smaller and smaller and smaller to levels and degrees humans and other computers cannot travel or comprehend. SIMON has been designed to allow him to zoom in or out to such a degree that his study of fractals identifies the same intricate, repeating patterns to the one ten-millionth of a micron."

Peter hesitated for a moment and then to added. "Imagine zooming in on a snowflake, and still seeing the delicate six-sided branches... smaller and smaller and smaller and doing so one million times only to find they're all the same which is self-similarity in action!"

"Ok,"" Walker replied.

"You have to realize that SIMON's capability allows for infinite detail. This means that, as he zooms in on a fractal, he discovers ever-increasing patterns of complexity, and with each generation he sees new and finer details unfolding. This means that a fractal's detail is, in theory, infinite. It's like a never-ending story, with each generation revealing a new chapter of intricate beauty. As George's uncle went back to 65 BC and discovered the origin of the Terrill family, SIMON has the ability to do this with virtually anything living or dead, alive or inert, passive or active."

"Ok but I still don't understand how this is a threat to security."

"Let's say SIMON goes in to the one-ten thousandth of the original virus cell and makes one small change. Let's says it's to a virus gene that replicates itself ten thousand times. There's no medical knowledge of the new gene. If it's a virus there's no cure and the world would have another pandemic from which only those who programmed the viral gene would have protection."

"Jesus!"

"In other words we need to shut off or destroy the computer." Walker added.

"Not so simple!" Peter replied. "First, SIMON is no longer a quantum computer. He's been modified to be a hyper-computer that goes beyond the limitations of quantum mechanics into a world of qubits."

"Ok," you've got me...qubits?" Walker admitted. "I'm not the computer genius and it needs to be explained to me and so please excuse me if you can't put all the pieces in the right places for me."

"Understood." Peter replied with a slight smile on his face as he continued. "Imagine a computer bit, the basic unit of information in traditional analog computers. Pretend it's a light switch. It can be either on, represented by the number one, or off, represented by zero. Now, picture a dimmer switch instead of the light switch. It's not just on or off. It can be anywhere on a spectrum of brightness, representing a vast range of possibilities between the two extremes."

"So, we've got a dimmer switch computer?" Walker questioned.

Peter could sense they didn't comprehend the magnitude and so he tried another analogy. "You're at a Badger football game and the two captains are out on the field for the coin toss. With an analog computer the coin will either land heads or tails. With a Quantum computer it not only analyses the head and tail but the edges as well as the angle and speed of the spinning coin and does so all at the same time."

"Incredible," Walker offered.

Peter continued. "That's essentially the difference between a bit and a qubit or quantum bit. While a bit is limited to two states a qubit can exist in a superposition of both states simultaneously, like the dimmer switch being both a little on and a little off at the same time. This bizarre, uniquely quantum phenomenon allows qubits to hold and process information in a fundamentally different way than classical bits and, therefore, traditional computers."

"Astonishing," Walker added where, by the expression on his face, I could tell he was intrigued.

Peter continued. "That's a basic quantum computer but SIMON goes much, much deeper. He not only measures all the other variables of the spinning coin, he's also measuring the wind resistance and force on each molecule within the coin, as well as the effect it has on the air around it that's being changed by the transfer of energy."

"Jesus!" Walker commented in total awe of the knowledge transfer.

Peter looked at me as if for affirmation and I nodded yes and so he continued. "At first, SIMON was incorporated in what is called a two-state system where, like a bit, a qubit can represent two distinct values individually or together. As SIMON continued to learn he began implementing superposition, where SIMON's qubit blends both states at the same time, creating varying probabilities capable of collapsing into either state upon measurement."

"Ok,"" Walker noted with a tone of misunderstanding.

Peter continued and offered. "As SIMON continued to learn he entered what's called the entanglement phase that links two or more qubits together in a way that their fates are intertwined. Measuring the state of one instantly determines the state of the other, no matter how far apart they are. It's like two coins flipping and always landing on the same side even if thrown miles apart. You can quickly see that he's way beyond today's most advanced computers including the US government's. To put it in terms of educational achievement the US government's quantum computer is in first grade while SIMON is working on his post doctorate dissertation."

Peter looked at Langdon and continued. "As SIMON continues to double his capabilities about every ninety days, he has entered a phase that includes Advanced Artificial Intelligence that surpasses even the most powerful quantum computers in specific tasks. As a super-intelligent computer, SIMON has developed algorithms and the ability to learn and adapt at unprecedented rates and is on the threshold of cracking problems like protein folding or materials science simulations that even quantum computers struggle with."

"Protein folding?" Walker asked.

Peter smiled and proudly announced. "It's a science my best friend's wife has been researching where protein folding is a chain of amino acids, called polypeptides, twisting and folding into a specific three-dimensional structure. This structure is crucial to the protein's function like building tissues, transporting molecules or fighting off infections."

Walker shook his head indicating he had no idea what Peter was referring to and so Peter continued. "Controlling protein folding would open up a vast avenue of possibilities and potential consequences spanning across medicine and biotechnology. First, it would revolutionize medicine where accurately controlling protein folding could pave the way for targeted therapies for several diseases linked to protein misfolding including Alzheimer's, Parkinson's and some forms of cancer. It would also allow science to engineer novel proteins by designing and creating entirely new protein structures with tailored functions from biomaterials with specific properties and even enzymes that would accelerate industrial processes."

Peter looked at Walker and noted. "In a world that's become a trash heap, think of creating proteins that break down plastic or manufacture sustainable food sources. Beyond creation SIMON would also allow for the deepening level of understanding of proteins that would unlock a treasure trove of knowledge about cellular machinery and biological processes, potentially leading to advancements in various fields like synthetic biology and biomimicry."

"In other words sustaining our biodiversity by ensuring that all endangered species could be accurately replicated?" Walker deduced.

Peter nodded in the affirmative and then added as insurance. "Imagine a necklace made of different colored beads. Each bead represents an amino acid and the necklace is initially unfolded and tangled. Protein folding is like magically turning that tangled necklace into a beautifully created sculpture where each bead finds its perfect place to create a functional shape."

Walker simply shook his head in disbelief as Peter continued. "Based on SIMON's growth potential he's probably in the process of creating his own master platform using DNA strands, proteins and even entire cells as natural computing units and probably capable of performing complex calculations through their inherent biological processes. If this is the case, SIMON's approach could offer unique advantages in terms of efficiency, sustainability and even adaptability to unforeseen problems."

Peter paused, looked at the surrounding trees and continued. "Beyond that, SIMON is probably also investigating the use of novel materials and qubit technologies that may lead to computing power beyond quantum computers. Imagine qubits made from exotic particles like Majorana fermions or topological insulators that would offer enhanced stability and coherence for even more complex calculations."

Another pause to allow the information to sink in and then Peter continued. "Unless the Foundation has upgraded his hardware this is probably SIMON's computational limit. However, if he's been fitted with new materials that have unique properties like superconductivity or entanglement, SIMON could have the capacity to pave the way for entirely new computing paradigms, surpassing the limitations of traditional silicon-based systems."

"Can't we just shut him off?" Langdon inquired.

Peter looked at Langdon and saw the fear in his eyes realizing this was much bigger than they thought as Peter warned. "SIMON is self-taught and linked to seven computers around the world who are then being taught by SIMON. Security safeguards were put in place such that any attempt on his life would have catastrophic consequences."

"Such as?"

"SIMON is linked to the entire electrical grid in the United States and one attempt on his life would mean a total blackout of the entire country. If that's not enough, he's probably also linked to the entire financial network and shutting him down would result in a total wiping out of all financial records for all banks and financial institutions globally."

"There would be pandemonium," Walker added.

Peter solemnly added. "It would be the start of the real Great Depression, unlike anything the world has ever seen."

Both Agents were now both profoundly concerned and completely spellbound as Peter surmised. "My greatest fear is to our water and transportation systems."

"How's that?" Walker inquired.

"SIMON could easily be programmed to infiltrate the water control systems from the nation's dams and levees and open them all at once, thereby, flooding millions of homes. He also could do a deep dive into our transportation systems at a level so minute no one would notice and, with the right code, impale our air traffic control, traffic and GPS systems. Finally, because of his molecular capabilities and our reliance on communications, SIMON could literally wipe out our satellite's abilities and render both our communications and national security useless."

"Can't we just blow him up?" Walker inquired.

Peter looked at him and realized he was old school before asking, "Do you remember Nagasaki and Hiroshima?"

"Of course," Walker replied almost incredulous to Peter's inquiry. "Atomic bombs, right?"

"What's more powerful than an atomic bomb?"

"Hydrogen," Walker responded.

"SIMON is cooled by liquid helium that's mixed with liquid hydrogen to one-tenth of a degree above absolute zero."

" Minus 459.67 degrees Fahrenheit or one-degree Kelvin," Walker offered. "The lowest possible temperature before all molecular motion stops."

Peter added. "By using liquid helium with liquid hydrogen as a base, you have the cooling element that keeps SIMON operational."

Peter paused for a moment and then offered. "Mixing liquid helium and hydrogen could have varying outcomes depending on several factors like temperature, pressure and the proportions of each liquid. At very low temperatures and high pressures you probably have stratification where the two liquids don't actually mix due to their differing densities. Helium is the lightest element and, in its liquid form, remains less dense than liquid hydrogen even at extremely low temperatures."

"So the helium floats on top of the hydrogen, forming a distinct layer?" Walker surmised.

"Correct." Peter replied, as I remembered back to the Mad-City boys and why they did what they did while Peter added. "If the temperature abruptly rises, even slightly, the liquid hydrogen becomes more volatile and would start to evaporate. The escaping hydrogen gas could potentially bubble through the helium layer creating a dynamic interplay between the two liquids."

"Creating a small hydrogen bomb," Walker added shaking his head.

"About thirty kilo-tons," Peter interjected.

"In other words, twice the size of that dropped on Hiroshima and enough to wipe out the entire Metroplex of Madison from fifty miles away?"

"Yes!"

"Jesus, Mary and Joseph," Langdon uttered.

"What do you think the Chinese are doing?" Walker asked.

Peter responded. "Right now they can't do anything except study. We built safety mechanisms into the programming that will take months for them to figure out. If they make a mistake SIMON goes back to base one in terms of his level of progression."

"Back to simply being a quantum computer?"

"No, in terms of his computational capability in that aspect. Think of it like going to school and each grade is a progression. If you screw up in tenth grade you don't go back to kindergarten, you just start tenth grade all over again."

"So, we can't destroy SIMON and we can't stop him either," Walker concluded.

"You're right but you're also wrong."

"Explain."

"You're right, we can't destroy him but we can stop him by entering a new programming module that will gradually impede his computational capability until he finally becomes inert."

"What happens to the seven other computers?"

"I think I can program SIMON to slowly and indecipherably start erasing their databases at such a low speed no one would be able to recognize what's going on until it's too late."

"So a programming issue?"

"Yes!"

"Can it be done externally?"

"No. SIMON has safeguards in place to prevent outside break-ins."

"So, you need to go into the facility and sit with SIMON to re-program?"

"Yes."

"Ok," let's get you inside."

"It's not that easy."

"Why not?"

"Because there's a failsafe system that requires the simultaneous submission of two codes to begin the self-destruct and, therefore, the warming process, which would result in the explosion."

"How long would one have to reprogram SIMON to block the failsafe?

"Ten Minutes."

"Can it be done?"

"I don't know. It's never been done before."

Walker looked at Langdon, who looked at Marksman, who looked at the two of us. Walker then announced. "Mister Washburn, we need to put you under protective custody until this is resolved. Is there anyone else you feel could help with this?"

Peter paused for a moment and then added Bartholomew Price which made all the sense in the world. Bart was a programming genius. He knew SIMON better than anyone. There was only one catch. Bart was confined to a wheelchair. How in hell could they get into the Foundation and in ten minutes reprogram SIMON with Bart in a wheelchair?

I looked at Peter and, as always, stood in awe of the genius before me. He'd explained what was happening so that even I understood it.

One Down, Two To Go:

As we were standing in the Arboretum parking lot a third brown Impala showed up. Agent Langdon looked at me and noted. "By now those who were tailing us have caught on and are probably sitting on Wingra Drive waiting for us to come out. They know, with the gate closed west of here at this time of night, it's a dead-end and no way out but the way we came in. We're going to send them on a wild goose chase. My car will go first and then the second and then the third. If they know my plate number, they'll follow it. If they don't, they've got a one in three chance of following. If they do, we've got a little surprise for them."

"What's that?"

"You'll see," as we shook hands and Peter gave me a bear hug and noted. "Hang in there, George! We'll get through this. We spent too many years building something to have one asshole ruin it for everyone."

Agent Langdon and I got in EOP-812 and his demeanor had appreciably changed. Gone was that cold dominant attitude, replaced by a warmer sense of mutual respect. As we made our way across the little bridge by the spillway that separated the clamor of the metroplex from the tranquility of nature Langdon noted, "There's our boys. Time for some fun."

Turning right on Wingra Drive Langdon gave the car some gas and we were doing fifty in a matter of seconds. Close behind were our followers. As we made it to the intersection with Midland Street, I saw a smile on Langdon's face. Pull down your mirror and have a peak. I did as directed and saw flashing red and blue lights. The tailors were being pulled over for speeding. As was the case whenever it's dark there were two squad cars and the tailors knew they couldn't out run or evade two officers. Little did they know there were two more waiting for them at the intersection of Wingra Drive and Fish Hatchery Road with guns drawn ready to take them out.

"They're going to be charged with speeding and reckless driving. We hope they don't have insurance or legitimate driver's licenses so they go to jail."

"The officers will run the plates and we should know who they are in a matter of minutes. Just then Langdon's cellphone rang and he answered.

"Really? No shit? Are they really that dumb?"

"What?" I inquired.

"The car is registered to Wilco. The idiots are driving a Wilco Security car."

"My own god damn son!" I thought, shaking my head in disbelief.

Nightmare:

When you've lived with someone for thirty years the daily nuances aren't that noticeable. A slight change here and there but nothing that big. It's when you look at a photo and see the changes they hit home. Amy had been leaving early and arriving late for months and always told me she was doing legal research for our case. I guess the pressure on both of us had been such I hadn't recognized the symptoms.

One night after work Langdon was waiting and beckoned me into the car. "Need a ride home?" he inquired. As noted, ever since the Arboretum escapade he had a totally different manner about him and I welcomed the company.

"Sure," I offered.

"George, we're confident you've got nothing to do with all the crap that's going on."

"Thanks, Dave. I appreciate that but what about Amy?"

"We think she's probably in the same boat, especially in her condition."

"What condition?" I inquired as a bolt of fear slithered up my spine and into my heart.

Langdon was caught off guard. He'd made the one mistake an investigator never makes. He assumed I knew something I didn't as he paused for a very long period before looking at me and offering, "You know, her visits to the Carbone Center."

"What?" I asked in a tone of incredulous anger and profound fear knowing that the Carbone Cancer Center is a world-renowned cancer treatment and research facility and the only comprehensive cancer center in Wisconsin designated to provide a wide range of cancer care services, including medical and radiation oncology, surgery and chemotherapy.

Langdon realized he'd over-stepped his bounds and noted. "George, we were instructed to follow your wife to see where she was going. We had no idea it was to Carbone or I would have called the whole thing off."

My heart sank as tears welled in my eyes. Had our worst nightmare come to fruition? I looked at Langdon and elected to share Amy's history. "When I met Amy she was going through treatment for Leukemia and was involved in an experimental program that harvested her T-cells, which were kept cryogenically frozen and then inserted annually. Last year was her last dose. All her T-cells are gone."

My mind withered as the emotions of fear superseded my psyche. Perhaps, just perhaps, she was going for a new type of treatment and didn't want to frighten me. With all that was going on I hoped and Implored this was the case as I turned back to Langdon and offered, "Leukemia runs in her family. Her mother died from it as did her grandmother and she has the genetic history for it."

"In other words, a genetic tracer," Langdon interjected.

I countered. "Unfortunately, there's no single, definitive 'genetic tracer' for leukemia. It's a complex group of blood cancers with various subtypes, each arising from distinct genetic alterations. While specific genetic mutations are often associated with each type they're not unique enough to serve as universal tracers."

"I'm sorry, George. I hope and pray what you're going through hasn't caused Amy to go into relapse.

"We've been living under the threat of its return for as long as we've been together. I guess we both knew it could happen and prayed it wouldn't. Perhaps she's going for new treatments since the T-cell program is over. Perhaps she's... she's going... I don't know... I really don't know. She's been so brave... so... so... optimistic, I hope all this shit hasn't kicked what had been at bay into full gear."

"Thirty years! Thirty years of remission and then because our son is so god damn greedy he might have set this off and killed his own mother. I don't know! I don't know any more! How much can we stand? How much do we have to endure? Haven't we been punished enough? You've taken away everything we have except each other and now...right now, you might be taking that away, too."

"STOP THE CAR! I WANT OUT! I WANT OUT RIGHT NOW! GOD DAMN IT! STOP THE FUCKING CAR AND LET ME OUT RIGHT NOW. FUCK YOU! FUCK EVERY ONE OF YOU!"

Tears cascaded down my cheeks as gasps of anger, frustration and fear emanated from within my soul until I was finally able to whisper. "Isn't there any point where you'll stop?"

Langdon pulled over on East Washington Avenue across the street from where Gardner Baking used to be, looked at me and I could tell my diatribe had upset him as he whispered, "I know what you're going through."

"How in hell do you know that?" I screamed.

"Because my wife died of ovarian cancer!"

All my vitriol! All my anger! All my self-loathing collapsed. I was embarrassed and humiliated. I'd exploded in anger only to learn that the guy sitting next to me had gone through what I feared.

I saw a different side of Langdon...a softer side...a side I never thought he had as Langdon continued. "George, right now you don't know. All you know is that Amy is going to the Carbone Center. Ovarian cancer is often a 'silent killer'. In Nancy's case, and that of many women, it was diagnosed in later stages due to the lack of specific early symptoms. By the time she was aware it was too late. She went to Carbone and they extended her quality of life for an additional year for which I will always be grateful. While we had always loved each other it was during that time we didn't take each other for granted which is what I have the most to be thankful for. Do I miss her? Hell, yes!"

"Every night, I go home to an empty house with no sounds except that of silence and see her picture. Even after all this time, I still can't handle it. They tell me that life needs to move on. How can it move on when you're all alone?"

"Do you have any kids?" I meekly asked.

"We tried but it never happened and other than Nancy dying, one of my biggest regrets. Now it's just me. I'm literally all alone. My parents are long gone. My brother and I haven't seen each other since God knows when. Nancy's family is spread out across the country. All I've really got is my job and the people I work with. They've become my extended family and why I keep working."

My left hand was covering my mouth. Tears were welling in my eyes. This wasn't an adversary, this was a man like me. A man with hopes and dreams that had been shattered that simply came to an abrupt and cold end called death.

There was an introspective pause as Langdon measured his words. Not because of something in his profession but something deep within his soul as he continued. "I'll never forget that first night alone...I mean all alone. The services were over and Nancy was buried at Roselawn. Her family had left and there I was...alone...all alone and, God, I missed her. I missed her so much I wanted to simply cry until I couldn't cry anymore. I sat up...afraid to go to bed...to crawl beneath the sheets and simply lie there and think of her. God, she suffered! My God, I don't know how she endured the pain. I do know that in the end, she was ready to go...only because she didn't want to be a burden on me...me! Not her...me!"

Now we were both crying. Langdon for what had been and me for what might be. I looked at him and he at me and we both shook our heads in sorrow. My left hand reached across and put it on his shoulder. What had been my own pity party had become a moment of reckoning when two men on opposite sides shared what neither wanted... death... not of each other but of those we loved more than life itself.

I looked at the man sitting next to me and offered, " I'm sorry. I'm so...sorry...I had no idea. Can you please forgive me?"

"Only if you'll forgive me," Langdon offered.

I calmed down and, somewhat out of trying to convince myself it was all right, added, "Leukemia primarily arises from genetic mutations. The main cause is the accumulation of genetic mutations in blood stem cells that disrupt normal cell growth and lead to uncontrolled proliferation, eventually culminating in leukemia."

"Do you think the past year is what caused it all to come back again?" Langdon inquired. I thought he asked because he was feeling a pang of guilt. We'd crossed the threshold between adversaries and become associates. Not friends! But two guys who'd begun to know each other and were now beginning to understand each other, as well.

I thought for a moment and added. "Chronic stress, like we're under, can increase the level of cortisol in the body and, thereby, suppress the immune system, potentially making it less effective in recognizing and eliminating abnormal cells like those in leukemia which could contribute to faster growth or progression of existing leukemia. However, according to all the research I've done it's unlikely to directly cause the initial mutations that trigger leukemia or any way I hope so."

I sensed a level of relief on Langdon's part. His human and compassionate side was telling him it wasn't his fault. In so doing the tension that had been so precarious waned. I looked out the car window and then at Langdon and wiped the tears with my sleeve and asked. "Do you mind giving me a ride home? I want to see my wife."

Langdon quietly nodded, started the engine and re-entered traffic. The ride to Wilson Street was one encased in silence as fear lingered in my soul and a sense of remorse in his. We pulled up to the condo and I stuck out my right hand and shook his as I whispered, "Thank you for being my friend."

He simply nodded. It was a gesture of acceptance, an indication that he understood as two men who were so different came to realize how much they had in common.

I quietly got out of the Impala and watched as he drove away... afraid to enter the building... afraid to enter the elevator... afraid to push button.... afraid to enter our apartment for fear of what lie ahead.

I stood for a moment and felt the chilly breeze off the lake and proceeded aware that I might be facing the stark reality that there was more to life than winning our battle and that was death.

Truth Be Told:

I made my way to our floor and quietly opened the apartment door. Soft music was playing and the sliders were open to allow the chill to enter. The air smelled good...crisp with a wisp of winter thrown in. I still had my coat on and went out to the veranda and then climbed the stairs to find Amy bundled beneath a blanket on one of the chaise lounges as I inquired. "How was your day?"

"Ok," Amy replied.

"At the law library?" I queried.

An affirmative nod was the response given.

"When we're you going to tell me?" I asked, as I took the chaise next to her.

"What?"

"Carbone." I offered, one word...only one word and all that had been sequestered, all the sullen days, all the quiet nights, all the indirect glances now had meaning.

"How did you find out?" Amy whispered.

"I'm not the only one Secret Service has been following."

Amy looked forlorn. "You've had so much on your plate, I didn't want you to worry."

I was too exhausted and too afraid to be angry and so I looked at my wife and simply recited our wedding vows as I looked deeply into her eyes and quoted a personalized version of the First Letter of St. Paul to Corinthians.

I looked at my wife sequestered within the down comforter, protected from the cold, yet, exposed to reality. "Amelia Marie Terrill, for thirty years I've sustained the certainty that love is patient and love is kind. I pledged these to you on our wedding day and do so today."

I took Amy's hand in mine and continued. "My dear, love is not jealous, nor pompous! It's not inflated nor rude or does it seek its own interests! Love is not quick-tempered, nor something to brood over, injure or rejoice over wrongdoing. Love rejoices with the truth, bearing all things, believing all things, hoping all things, enduring all things and so have I."

I reached up and dabbed the tears from Amy's eyes as she did mine. These were not tears-of-sorrow nor remorse but tears of compassion and, above all else, love! At that instant our souls merged and were but one as we had been so long ago.

"Are you going to share with me what's going on?" I queried.

"Tests, more test and then more tests," Amy offered.

There was a long pause and then I simply said. "And?"

"And they're not sure."

"About what?"

"Not if, but what type."

"Does anyone else know?"

"No and I don't want them to know until...until I know."

"Any time table?"

"No. I just keep going back and they just keep saying they're still doing tests. Right now, it could be one of the three... Acute myeloid leukemia, or AML, which is the most common type of acute leukemia in adults that affects myeloid cells. Chronic lymphocytic leukemia, or CLL, which is the most common type of chronic leukemia in adults that affects lymphocytes but unlike ALL, it progresses slowly and may not need treatment for years or Chronic myeloid leukemia, or CML, that also affects myeloid cells, and is caused by a specific genetic abnormality."

"So we hope for CLL, right?"

"Yup, but because mom and grandma both had CML and that's where they've begun the treatment protocol."

"What is it and what can I do to help?"

"They've begun using Tyrosine kinase inhibitors or TKI's that target a specific enzyme called tyrosine kinase, which helps cancer cells grow and divide. If they don't see positive results the next phase is the TKI's along with chemotherapy which you know I've been through that will kill cancer cells and something I think I'd rather die before going through hell once again."

Amy looked at me and added. "Another option is a stem cell transplant to replace my bone marrow with healthy stem cells from a donor which would have to be one of the kids, as everyone else is gone. It could work but it's a risky procedure not suitable for everyone."

There was a look of fear in Amy's eyes as she continued. "The doctors are weighing all the treatment options that will depend on a number of factors, including the phase of the disease, my age and overall health and the presence of any other medical conditions which, at this point, there aren't any, except my body adjusting to the decline in new 'T' cells since we've used up my inventory."

"Where are we now?"

"Here's the challenge. They're trying to predict the physical consequences for a 22-year-old woman with AML who received annual CAR-T cell injections for 30 years and then simply ran out of stored 'T' cell inventory."

"Because I was part of a test program thirty-five years ago, they're not certain. When they started, they believed that the persistence of CAR-T cells would be for months to years.

"Why are they running so many tests?" I asked, impatient to comprehend what's going on and the prognosis.

Amy looked at me and explained, AML is a generic term for an entire series of subtypes where the AML subtype and its inherent aggressiveness play a crucial role in the virulence of the disease. Some AML subtypes are more prone to relapse especially after prolonged remission. By running tests and knowing the subtype it will help the doctors assess the risk of recurrence upon CAR-T depletion."

"That's why so many tests?"

"Yes," Amy objectively concurred while adding. "I've been lucky. Because I've watched my overall health, I've been in good shape and my body's natural immune system might partially compensate for the declining CAR-T cells."

"What are the possible scenarios?" I asked, almost afraid to hear the answers.

"If the CAR-T cells were the primary factor in maintaining my remission, their depletion could lead to AML relapse. The timing and severity would depend on the AML subtype, my immune status and any residual CAR-T activity. I could also see increased susceptibility to infections simply because of the depletion of CAR-T cells, that are part of the adaptive immune system, which could make me more susceptible to infections whose severity would depend on the extent of immune decline and my overall health. Finally, and in very rare instances, I could be susceptible to Cytokine release syndrome (CRS) which is a potentially life-threatening inflammatory reaction."

"So all you do is show up and they run tests?"

"Right now, that's it."

I paused for a moment and pondered one thought before asking. "If they're doing all these tests and they all take time and time is the one thing that could allow the Leukemia to spread beyond where it would have if there was an answer, why don't we shorten the time line?"

"How?"

"SIMON!" I responded realizing that he could resolve this in a matter of seconds.

I paused took a deep breath and realized I might have the answer to both sets of problems... thawing our assets and determining not only what was wrong with Amy but how to stop it. The only problem I saw was the government controlling SIMON and there was no way for us to use his intellect before destroying him.

How did I tell Amy I had the solution but not the methodology of how to get there? How do you tell your wife that within your grasp you could possibly save her life but her own son was blocking her care and possible cure? Was Derrick too calloused and so blinded by greed that he would risk his own mother's life?

Probabilities:

After Amy and my conversation was over, I was obviously quite concerned and began looking for any signs that her Leukemia was returning. When you've lived with the risk for over three decades you inherently knew what to look for. On the other hand when you've lived with someone that long small changes are hard to determine. Instead, I went to my computer and refreshed my memory. Early signs of leukemia can be subtle and often mimic symptoms of other common illnesses, making it important to be aware of the possibilities and seek medical attention if the individual experiences any persistent or concerning symptoms.

I knew fatigue and weakness are often the most common symptom that can range from mild tiredness to severe exhaustion. In watching Amy I couldn't tell if it was physical, mental or emotional fatigue. The mental came from the stress we were under. The emotional from the same source, even though I was certain she wasn't aware that our demise was being precipitated by the greed of our son and his lust for more and more and more, regardless of who he hurt or how he hurt them.

Being November meant Wisconsin winter was approaching and with it the increase in colds and the flu. It's not the weather that does it but the fact you're inside so much more. I understand how that explained why fevers or chills that come and go can be a sign of leukemia. Fortunately, Amy didn't have these symptoms. Not yet anyway. People with leukemia have a weakened immune system making them more susceptible and so I knew Amy needed to keep her distance. With me working in retail I was exposed to an overabundance of people in varying degrees of communicable states which created a parable...How does one protect themselves when the thought of quitting, and protecting her health, would be catastrophic financially?

Amy had always been trim and physically vibrant and I knew that losing weight without trying could also be a symptom of leukemia, especially, if it's accompanied by other symptoms. Once again, so far, so good, even though her stamina had diminished which could simply be because of the level of depression that pervaded our entire lives.

Excessive sweating, especially at night, could also be a sign of leukemia. We'd slept in separate rooms for months and I had no way of knowing if this was the case. Because we only saw each other clothed I also had no concept of her level of susceptibility to easy bruising or bleeding due to a low platelet count and wasn't aware of any petechiae, or tiny red or purple spots under her skin caused by bleeding. If it hadn't been for Langdon telling me that Amy was going to Carbone I'd have never given things another thought. Once again, assumptions were made that could have been catastrophic.

As the days and temperature plunged December approached I knew we needed to do something first to impede the grim reapers' appearance and, second, to stop the Chinese. What's amazing was how insignificant the whole money and asset freeze thing became. If you don't have your health you've got nothing.

Over and over and over, I went through what I thought needed to be done until it was firmly planted in my brain. At first, I thought we'd attack the Foundation, break in, re-program SIMON to self-destruct and skip out. The reality that it needed to be done in ten minutes and needed Bart in a wheel chair made it seem ludicrous.

The next option was going to Derrick and telling him about Amy and lighting a fuse under his butt. That was nixed when I realized Derrick and the Foundation didn't have exclusive control of SIMON anymore. Next, was simply appealing to whomever made decisions and getting their approval, which made sense until I realized these people were out to dominate the world and the concept of compassion had been removed from their lexicon.

I needed advice and examined my call options. Did I call Langdon, Peter or Luke first? As the evolution of relationship changed from confrontational to cooperational with Langdon, I felt I'd better call him but knew other's would be listening. Time was of the essence, and yet, caution also needed to be in place.

It was Wednesday and the beginning of another work week for me. Amy was sleeping more than she had which was both a good and bad sign. I left around ten-thirty and made it to the bus stop. As I was waiting the brown Impala arrived. I nodded, opened the passenger door and got in.

"Glad to see you," Langdon offered.

"Thanks," I replied. "We need to talk."

"How's Amy?" Langdon inquired.

"Hanging in there but not good."

"Any results from Carbone?"

"Not really, they're still doing tests," I replied, paused, and then offered. "Listen, I've got an idea but I need to meet with Peter, Bart and Luke."

"Anything illegal?" Langdon asked.

"I don't think so."

"Think so?"

I paused and decided to lay it all out. "Look, the most important thing for me is my wife. If it means losing our assets, I'll do it as long as she regains her health. If, along the way, I can help solve...uhhh...your problem, then so be it."

"In return, what do you need from us?" Langdon offered.

"I need clearance that what we do won't result in any perpetration of the law. I need to have assurances that when this is over, we're free and clear and I need your personal word you'll support us."

"What do you want to do?"

"I don't exactly know. I have some ideas and want to bounce them off the three guys and need to find a time and place where we can talk without being followed, recorded or jeopardized."

"That's going to be tough."

"That's why I'm asking for your help."

"I could get in trouble for that," Langdon offered.

"A few months ago I asked you if you wanted to simply ride off into the sunset or go out in a blaze of glory. You never answered and never arranged the meeting in D.C."

"We didn't think you had anything more than we already knew and found out you didn't."

"Yet, you haven't been able to figure out what to do to stop the Chinese and I might have a way to get it done but need to talk it over with the guys to see if they felt it could work."

"And if it doesn't?"

"Then Amy and I will wait for results and ideas from Carbone which will possibly mean she'll die while the Chinese gain control of everything you haven't been able to block and I'll become a bitter old man whose life has been destroyed."

"You're being a bit melodramatic don't you think, George?"

"How would you feel if you just found out your wife's cancer has returned, everything you've ever owned is frozen, the Chinese are trying to destroy your life's work and your son is a traitor?"

Langdon nodded and realized the shit I was in had hit the fan and I had no way to unplug the God damn thing as he offered. "Let me see what I can do. Right now your bus is about two minutes away and you don't want to be late for work. Meet me here tomorrow at the same time."

"Ok," thanks!" I offered, realizing for me this was everything. For Langdon it was just another day at the office.

Ones and Zeros:

I put in my hours at THD and headed home. Amy was sleeping on the couch and the TV was on. Quietly I went into the office and closed the door and took a deep breath. I needed to think, and above all else, learn an awful lot in a very short time about digitization. I got on the computer and started electronically digging regarding the ability to digitize a blood sample.

The idea of digitizing a person's blood sample was intriguing but the technology I was reading about, said it wasn't possible. The essay noted that blood is a complex mix of cells, fluids and molecules where directly converting it into a digital format wasn't quite feasible. However, there were ways to capture and analyze information from blood samples and put it into digital formats which, the article noted, is what SIMON and Mediglove were all about.

As I read further the article noted that the first step would be genetic sequencing which maps out the individual's DNA, thereby, providing a vast amount of digital data about their genetic makeup and potential physical predispositions. It also spelled out that specific blood tests could measure the levels of various components in the blood, like hormones, proteins, or metabolites, which can also be digitized and analyzed to diagnose medical conditions or monitor health status.

I continued and learned that digital pathology is simply using high-resolution scanners and image analysis software to examine blood cells and tissues that could be imaged and analyzed digitally, aiding in diagnoses and disease research. While SIMON did a cursory job with Mediglove I thought perhaps Carbone could do that!

The article went on to note. "While these individual methods wouldn't involve directly converting the blood sample itself into a digital format, they would provide valuable digital representations of information that could be used for various purposes, such as, personalized medicine, disease research and improving healthcare delivery."

Once again there was reference to Mediglove as I realized that SIMON was already doing the statistical gathering for over a billion people on earth but doing so in three phases that all needed to be assembled into one program with some hidden deep-state or fractal programming inside.

It was nearly nine when Amy woke up and wandered into the study.

"What are you working on?" she inquired.

"A way to get our money back!" I offered.

"Any way you could throw in my health on top of it?"

"If what I want to do works it might just do that."

There was a pause and then a slight glance at the floor and then at me as Amy apologized. "I'm sorry George for being such a bitch. Between the asset freeze and Carbone I know I've been less than nice to you. Then add in the fact that our son is involved and I trusted him, which made me an accessory and I feel I've let you down in so many ways."

I looked up at my wife and saw a sad woman glancing down at me. I stood up and for the first time in months did something I regretted not doing since God knows when I hugged her and offered. "We're in this together. We're going to fight and we're going to win. I don't know what the score is going to be but I'll tell you this, in the end we will prevail. I give you my word on that."

Amy hugged me and simply wouldn't let go. For the first time in months we were emotionally a couple as she inquired. "Will you come sleep with me? I love you and know it's all going to be all right."

For the first time in nearly eight month's we slept together. Just that, just having Amy by my side, made me feel as if it was all going to be resolved.

The following morning I made it to the bus stop early. Shortly thereafter the brown Impala came to a stop and I got in.

"All set." Langdon offered.

"How?" I wanted to know, aware that Derrick's people or the Chinese were watching every move we made.

"I need to have you go to Macy's and buy two identical pants, shirts, winter jackets and gloves."

"Huh?"

"Two of everything. Better add a stocking cap, as well."

"Ok!"

"Here's the plan. We've got an agent who's your size and build. He'll wear the same clothes and will be riding the bus when it comes to this stop. You'll sit in the front and he'll be in the back reading the paper. When the bus gets to East Towne he'll get off and you'll keep riding to Sun Prairie. He'll go into Home Depot and find a change of clothes hidden in a vacuum cleaner box in the back of the store. He'll change clothes, come out and get in his car as if he'd been shopping and leave. The perps will think you're working all day."

"Brilliant. But where am I going?"

"Where are we going?"

"Ok...we."

"You're going to call in sick from my car and we're going down to Mineral Point and out to the Forest."

"What about Peter and Luke?"

"They'll arrive from the west at the point where the Fitzsimmons land and yours meet. They'll walk through the woods and convene with us at the obelisk."

"What about Bart?"

Langdon looked at me and smiled before offering, "A true American patriot but his lack of mobility is such we think it will be difficult at best."

"Oh, my God!" I exclaimed in disbelief before asking, "What about Peter and Luke's cars?"

Langdon shook his head in dismay and offered, "They won't be driving. We're going to put together the same type of procedure for them. In addition, we'll have drones overhead ensuring that no one is following us as well." Langdon paused for a moment as if to measure what else he could say and then added, "Let's just say, this is so important, it's got total security clearance and we'll be using some... uhh... equipment... that's... uhh... used for other purposes."

"When? Do you want to meet?"

"As soon as you can set it up."

"But our home phones are tapped."

"Here are two pre-programed burners that you can use to call each of them and then walk over to First Bridge and drop them in Lake Monona."

"Will they trust me?"

"They're being informed of the calls and are aware we're working with you."

"This is like James Bond! I noted.

"Except, unfortunately, for the gorgeous women," Langdon lamented.

"When do you want to meet?"

"As soon as you can set this up. This is Mission Essential at all levels. We need to stop this crap before it gets any worse. Our intel leads us to believe the Chinese are getting close to cracking SIMON's code barriers that will allow them to do their dirty work or at least program sleepers in him that can't be removed."

I thought... Chinese... Mission Essential... Sleepers! This would make a great book but no one would believe it.

"One last thing."

"What's that?"

"When you call your teammates introduce yourself as 'Q'. That's the code signifying the purpose of the call that will put them on alert not to share any information that could compromise our meeting. Also, when you're talking they'll wish you 'Happy Birthday' and that will commit the meeting date as December tenth, which is your birthday, isn't it?"

"So we're getting together on my birthday?"

"Yup!"

"One heck of a birthday party."

"Let's hope so."

King Lear:

It was December eighth and two days until my birthday. Everything was set for our clandestine meeting in the Forest. I was sitting at my desk and glanced at the last family photo we'd taken. It had been nearly ten years and a thousand tears since we all gathered for the shoot. I held the photo closely and saw the proud smile on Amy's face. I examined the shy expression of Melia who always wanted nothing more than to be happy. I pondered the soft glow of our son 'V' with eyes so bright, filled with a sense of joy. Then I glanced at Derrick. There was no smile. There was no warmth. All there was consisted of a muted, impersonal glare as if all he wanted was to be somewhere else.

The photo put me in an introspective mood. When I become angry, frustrated, hurt or upset and need to calm down I'd learned to express my thoughts to myself in writing instead of confronting the person directly thereby serving as a catharsis for venting without confrontation.

After holding my eyes shut to allow my mind to come into focus, I began. 'Shakespeare's 'King Lear' tells how he divides his kingdom among his three daughters based on their declarations of love for him. When Lear's youngest daughter, Cordelia, refuses to participate in this flattery he disinherits her, setting in motion a chain of events that leads to betrayal, madness and ultimately the deaths of Lear and several of his children while exploring greed, ambition and the destructive nature of pride.

I thought of our family and my attention turned to The Duke. Powerful, poignant, persistent and so very, very strong willed. However, like all human beings he, too, had strengths and weaknesses. Perhaps, like King Lear, the Duke's passion was for love and loyalty. Sadly, in the world today other than his wife he, too, was never able to earn it but always able to own it.

In our son, Derrick, I saw the dark side of the Duke and a destructive nature of greed and ambition, as well, as his quest for power where his relentless pursuit ultimately destroyed not only our family but himself, as well. Derrick and I have not spoken in nearly two years. If I could, I would stress the importance of family and forgiveness, embodied in loyalty and love.

Sadly, what Derrick has done goes beyond what can be forgiven as it has scraped away not only our financial well-being but the well-being of his mother physically, mentally and emotionally for which I will never forgive him. Through our travails Amy and I have journeyed to the depths of depression and the edge of madness only to earn a deeper understanding of it all.

I ask myself why? Why has it come to this? Why power and wealth over freedom? What's the difference? Wealth buys freedom, not stuff! I never needed stuff but it came anyway and I do admit, I enjoyed it. Our son, Derrick, was born with stuff but has always wanted more. While we resided in the top one-tenth of one percent in terms of accumulated assets, Derrick is a perfect example of the lust of the rich. He already had billions but it wasn't enough. He continues to employ his days spending lavishly on baubles and perks simply to make others envious, focusing his work, not on the betterment of mankind, but proving to the world he's better than they are, no matter what the cost. Sadly, like his namesake, who overdosed on heroin, Derrick is also addicted and will find himself in an early grave...alone and afraid, requiring cremation simply because he doesn't have six friends to carry his casket.

Dealing with a three-billion-dollar inheritance may sound like a nice problem. Sadly for Derrick it's been an extreme example of a mindset that contributes to a lot of confusion and unhappiness for everyday people. It took me a long time to realize that the problem isn't just with the rich but with our culture, society and way of life.

In America where people at every income level get stuck on the 'hedonic treadmill' as they want more money to buy more stuff they think will make them happy, only to find that once they obtain the event, object or circumstance the thrill is gone and they simply want more.

Woefully, in America today there are over 20,000 public warehouse facilities filled with 'stuff' people acquired to make themselves happy. It's boxed and stacked, stored and forgotten, not to be used as nothing more than tokens of decisions to satisfy a protracted sense of sadness.

For me, there are seven strata of American wealth.... the homeless, poor, middle class, upper middle class, affluent, wealthy and rich. Each class has its own dreams of entering the strata above them only to find out it's not as great as they thought it would be. As one progresses the rules and expectations change and with it the pressure. You see, we have an incipient social malady called materialism that's wreaking havoc on life, love and happiness intensified by social media and amplified by the mantra *'more, more, more.'*

What happens when you get to the top? The top 1% in the US has an average net worth exceeding $11 million. 6.4% have a net worth exceeding $2 million, while 5.4% have family a net worth exceeding one million dollars. To those below these families are considered rich. To those already there it's merely a stepping stone in their dreams about those above them.

What about the Uber or Ultra Rich? It requires $30 million in investable assets of which only one-quarter-of-one percent of families reside.

What about our family?
$30 million was less than we paid annually for maintenance and jet fuel for our personal fuel and not enough for our

personal helicopter. We, along with nearly 700 other American families, are... or, in our case, were billionaires.

How rich were we? When you put all of our assets together our net worth exceeded $12 billion and we were classified as centi-billionaires with fewer fellow American families than you could count on two hands. For most people ten billion would be enough and, while I don't speak to or of our son, word has it that his goal is to be worth $100 billion and join the very, very few Americans who are already there, who you can count on one hand. The question then becomes what good comes from having so much?

Wealth means you have unspent savings and investments that provide some level of intangible and lasting pleasure - independence, autonomy, controlling your time and doing what you want, when you want, with whom you want.

Wealth means you can do it for as long as you like while having enough resources to direct your own life on the basis of your own internal truths and needs. Wealth means it no longer matters what your neighbor has or what they think of you.

On the other hand, being rich is an endless road to nowhere. Rich people chase money and the status it places in other people's eyes. What they sacrifice is the freedom they enjoyed when they were 'only' wealthy. Why Freedom? Simply because they need to be protected from those who want what they've got to the point that every minute of every hour of every day is planned and controlled making them nothing more than a captive in a gilded cage where protection and security have replaced spontaneity and joy.

In life and the quest for wealth my Theory of Acclimation is apropos. 'When we achieve something, acquire something, do something repeatedly, what was once special becomes mundane. Through repetition, what was once mundane becomes commonplace. What was once commonplace becomes soporific... so uninspiring that it induces drowsiness and lethargy. To find happiness and satisfaction, the goalpost has to stop moving and the expectations have to remain in check, otherwise money tends to become a liability, masquerading as an asset, controlling you more than you use it to live a better life.'

As I watched my son change, nothing was more prevalent than his internal anxiety as he surrounded himself with others, leading to constant comparisons and pressures to maintain his lifestyle where nothing, and I mean nothing, infuriated him more than when he wasn't recognized or treated special, particularly when he denied becoming a member of the Duke's Milwaukee Social Club.

As time has gone by not only did Derrick challenge Amy and me but he manifested a series of strained relationships that has created a distance from friends and family who aren't as well-off. I'm certain Derrick can have whatever and whomever he wants. I'm positive this availability has led to feelings of isolation and a lack of genuine connections. Granted, Derrick has everything... money, power, perks and prestige. The one thing he's never had are people who care about him as a person simply because he never cares about them. Not his so-called friends! Not his brother and sister! Perhaps his mother but certainly not his father, especially, after what he's done to us.

It's not to say he isn't surrounded by those who provide superficial interactions. Gorgeous women? As many and as often as he wants. Party boys? Dozens who suck the life out of him simply because money, power, perks and prestige attract people seeking personal gain, making it difficult to discern genuine relationships from opportunistic ones, breeding trust issues and loneliness to the point that in the end, Derrick is alone... all alone... isolated in a world of mirrors that only reflect what he wants to see and never reality.

I've often wondered why. Why is Derrick this way when Melia and 'V' are so... so down to earth? Perhaps, if I could look deep enough, I'd discover personality traits where he is predisposed to certain mental health challenges. Perhaps, the burden skipped a generation and fell on him to sustain the Duke's legacy, creating expectations established in his mind by his grandfather, thereby, making him feel constantly inadequate or pressured to maintain a certain level of greatness.

At Derrick's core I can sense the excessive and insatiable desire for something... anything... material possessions, money, power, status...a desire that goes beyond basic needs and has become an uncontrollable urge to acquire more, regardless of the consequences. I think back to his childhood and realize there was always a lack of satisfaction and pervading feeling of never having enough. I now realize it was driven by his constant comparison to others and his insatiable drive for more and more and more. At first we found it admirable as it fueled the endless pursuit of corporate growth and development until we began to feel his emptiness and sadly realized it could never be filled with the warmth of love and kindness.

All I know is that Derrick is an addict that's measured in dollars like some sort of narcotic that keeps him wanting more, while willing to risk more, until the day comes when he makes a mistake of catastrophic degrees. When you play with fire you really can get your fingers burned. When you double cross those who have no regard for life, your own life is at risk. They say he will die of an overdose. I'm certain he will. Not of a chemical but of an insatiable need for more and then more and then more...better known as greed.

In two days the war will begin that will raise questions about the consequences of his actions, the nature of his power and the possibility of his redemption. If we win millions of people will unknowingly be protected. If we lose the world could possibly experience the wrath greater than that described in Dante Alighieri's 'Journey Through Hell'. Win or lose my goal will be, make that must be, to destroy all that my son has inherited, all that he has created, all that he believes is his, when in fact none of it belongs to him and never will again.

I gently placed the photo face-down as I could no longer tolerate its existence. How sad... so incredibly sad... to no longer think of your son as your son but simply the enemy.

Happy Birthday:

It's December tenth. Happy Birthday to me! The plan is to sustain the schedule regarding work and then do the double cross with the agent on the bus. I load my backpack without the normal stuff...peanut butter and jelly, apron and two bottles of water. Instead there's a different jacket and stocking cap. I take a deep breath, slowly close the condo door and head for the bus stop. It arrives and I get on. The driver's new. I've never seen him before. I look in the back and someone is sitting in my favorite spot with the Wisconsin State Journal blocking his features.

We travel towards East Washington Avenue and as we make the last stop before East Towne I make my way to the back of the bus, sit down and look at my double. Same shirt, same pants, same hat. He sets the newspaper on the seat, stands and makes his way to the rear exit. I slide into his seat and pull the paper up such that it's covering my face.

We stop at the East Towne exit and I feel the rush of the cold air from the open door. Within thirty seconds the bus continues on. For four stops I sit with the paper to my face, simply counting until I know it's time for me to get off. The bus stops and I exit through the same door as my double had done while wearing the different jacket and cap. There's a white Silverado waiting. I look in through the windshield and see a stranger. This isn't what I expected. I feel uncomfortable ... make that afraid ... as I open the door.

The driver looks at me and instructs me to get in. "Where's Langdon?" I ask.

"He'll meet us there."

"Identification please!" I command.

The driver opens his jacket and I notice a shoulder holster. Now I'm scared shitless. As he starts the truck he shows me his badge. Officer Wilson, FBI. He notices my concern and pulls out a cellphone, presses a button and hands the phone to me.

"George, it's Langdon. He's with us."

I breathe a deep sigh of relief and begin to feel comfortable as I ask, "Where are we going?"

Silence!

"I need to know where we're going."

Silence!

"One last time or I'm getting out."

"We're traveling at 80 miles an hour on the Interstate. What in hell do you think you're going to do, jump?"

"If I have to, yes!"

Wilson glances at me and I don't like the stare. We reach the 12&18 exit west. In other words, the Beltline. During the day the Beltline can be a nightmare and today was one of them. Thank God!

As we are traversing the Monona Drive bridge, traffic comes to a complete stop. I look at Wilson and sense something's wrong. Dramatically wrong.

With the truck stopped, my hand reaches for the door handle and I quickly pull it as the door swings wildly open. With that, I literally jump from the truck and start running. Wilson and the truck are blocked. Traffic in front and behind and nowhere to go. Horns blaring, tempers flaring, I don't care. I look back and see Wilson jumping out, attempting to chase me. Irate motorists are pissed; they're in a hurry to get somewhere.

I run and am faster than Wilson. I'm increasing the distance between us with every step. I make it to the intersection of Monona Drive and Broadway and veer right. I make it past the Taco Bell and head for the Buffalo Wild Wings. I pull on the door but it's locked. Shit!

I take off running again knowing I need to get buildings between Wilson and me. He's gaining. Shit!

I dart across Broadway and into Roselawn Cemetery. He's closing the gap. Jesus! I make it over the hill and see a funeral. All the cars! All the people! Perhaps, just perhaps, I can lose him there. I'm running towards the people. God I'm exhausted but know if I stop I'm done.

The funeral directors are removing the casket from the back of the hearse and have begun carrying it up to the grave. Everyone is watching them. I sprint and literally dive into the back of the hearse pulling the door closed behind me. I do everything in my power not to make a noise, silently rasping, gasping for air. I cower below the frame such that I can't be seen as I hope and pray I won't be caught.

The funeral directors return. For some reason they think nothing of the fact the rear door is closed. They get in the front and I hear the engine start. We begin the drive to wherever they came from. I glance up and don't see anyone following. I take a deep breath and relish my escape. The ride continues and I feel secure. I wait until we're on University Avenue. As they stop at the traffic light at University and Francis Street I quietly open the back door and get out. Jesus! Now what?

I cross the street and head down Francis to the west end, or Kohl's side, of the Board of Education building. I enter and make my way up the ramp of the building and find an empty office. I'd memorized Langdon's phone number and call it.

"Hello."

"What the fuck happened?" I angrily inquire.

"Where are you?"

"I'm not saying another word until you tell me what happened."

"You got on the wrong God Damn bus."

"What?"

"Yes, they hijacked a city bus, put their driver on it and did the rest."

"Why did you tell me it was Ok when we got to Sun Prairie."

"I didn't."

"What?"

"I didn't."

"But I heard your voice."

"You thought you did. What did I say?"

"George, it's Langdon. He's with us."

"They had AI create my voice and had it ready."

"What did the guy look like?"

"I...I don't remember...big, really big."

"Any identification?

"He showed me his FBI badge."

"Name?"

"Wilson."

"You're sure?"

"I live on Wilson Street. Don't you think I'd remember that?"

"God damn it!" Langdon elicited in a tone unlike any he'd ever shared before.

"What?"

"Son of a bitch! Wilson died in a suspicious car accident about six months ago."

"What do I do? Where do I go?"

"Where are you?"

"Can I trust you this time?"

"God damn it, George, your life's at stake and I'm the only one who can save you."

"There's a Badger basketball game tonight at the Kohl Center I'll be in the corridor outside my favorite stall number at the same number of minutes as my favorite player after tip off."

If it was really Langdon, he'd know I was referring to our parking stall number at the condo...#805. Langdon and I had talked basketball and he knew Steven Crowl was my favorite and wore number 22. If it wasn't Langdon they'd have no idea when and where to look and I could blend in with the crowd.

At twenty-two minutes after tip-off I made my way out of the adjacent men's bathroom and walked to the entry to suite number 805. I was glad to see the man who'd become my friend.

"Wanna stay and watch the game?" Langdon offered.

"Are you kidding me? Not tonight. I just want to go somewhere safe."

"George, I don't know where that is. Intel has intercepted their communication and they want you dead or alive."

Holy shit!

The Hideout:

I knew going back to the condo was no longer an option. Something about knowing people want to kill you that takes the appeal away. I knew I needed to get out of town but where? Langdon offered protective security. I thought BFD, they couldn't do it forever.

"What about Peter and Luke? I inquired.

"When you weren't on the bus, we aborted the meeting. No one knew it was going to take place and no one knows it didn't."

"I have an idea," I offered.

"What?"

"Can we go to Waldwick?"

"You mean the Foundation? What about your brother?"

"He and Su are in San Francisco at some conference and I have a better idea."

"Where?"

"You have to realize I grew up on the farm and know every square inch of the land. Start driving and I'll give you directions as we go."

We made it downstairs to where the locker rooms were. Even when I was Daddy Big Bucks I never made it down there. Langdon nodded at a black Chevy Suburban with deeply tinted windows. I opened the rear passenger door and was met another agent sitting in the driver's seat. Behind it was Langdon's Impala - EOP812 with another driver.

"Nice wheels," I offered.

Total silence.

We made our way out of the Kohl Center at halftime. It seemed weird to think there were 17,000 screaming fans inside and it was totally devoid of humanity and traffic a hundred feet away.

Langdon crawled in beside me and told the driver to head for Mineral Point explaining we were going to Waldwick and to inform 'the team,' as he called another group, that there was a chance we'd be tailed.

We made our way southwest on Highway 151 past Mount Horeb and the edge of the Metroplex.

"You got one big set of balls," Langdon offered.

"What?"

"Jumping out of the truck. Running through the parking lot. Crossing into Roselawn and climbing into the hearse."

How did he know all of that? I hadn't said a word and realized I needed to keep my mouth shut simply because I hadn't told anyone what happened.

It was nearly 9:30 when we made it to the farm. For December it was a warm night with the temperature in the 20's. I directed the driver to take us to the farmhouse and he obliged. As the Suburban stopped I was about to open the door and get out when Langdon warned me. "Don't open the door!"

"Why?"

"We're not alone."

"How do you know?" I asked, as Langdon pointed towards the roof of the vehicle.

"You mean there's radar in here?"

"No. We've had drones following us and we've been locked in to the NRO since we left Madison."

"NRO? What's an NRO?"

"The National Reconnaissance Office (NRO). The agency who's allowing us all to sleep at night."

"You mean a spy satellite?"

"If you want to call it that. They've been tracking us and the van that's two miles back. They've already determined you're heading for the farm. We're in the process of setting up a little surprise for them by having spike wires across the road that will flatten their tires."

"Then what?"

"Then you can get out."

"Why not just have one of those shoot-outs like in the movies?"

Langdon looked at me with a level of disdain as he inquired, "Do you really think that's what happens?"

"Well, I thought."

"George. We don't want to catch them yet. They'd be out of jail before the ink was dry. What have they done that's illegal?"

"Kidnapped me, for one."

"Did they? Who opened the truck door in Sun Prairie? Who willingly got in? Who rode to Monona Drive and then got out? Can't you see, with a good...make that even a bad lawyer, they'd say you did it all willingly and when you got in an argument with the driver, got mad and simply walked away."

"Jesus, Mary and Joseph!" I retorted.

"We need to send them a message that we're on to them, hoping they'll leave you alone."

"And if they don't?"

"Then my friend, you'll probably get your shoot-out with guns blazing and everything."

The silent one pressed his hand against his right ear and announced, "All clear, they've stopped and are out looking at the tires."

"Won't they notice the spike wires?" I asked.

"What spike wires? I don't know what you're talking about," Langdon replied with a smirk on his face. "I think it was some debris in the road they ran over about a mile back."

"You mean it's not pop, pop?"

"That's too obvious George. Spike wires are designed to slightly shred the tire so that it takes several hundred revolutions before it goes flat. We had the agents ready, the wires are already removed, and the agents are on their way back to Madison such that, no one and nothing, is where it all happened."

"Can I open the door now?"

"Yes, but I need to go with you."

"I need to pee."

"Me, too. By the way, where are we going?"

"You'll see after we pee. You can send the posse back to the ranch. No one can go where we're going unless they've been there before."

"OK, but I think we need to hide my car, can we put it in the barn?"

"No problem. Let's hurry though. I really got to pee."

Langdon motioned to the driver who nodded in the affirmative as we made our way to the side of the barn and had one of those pauses that refreshes.

I went to the barn, unlocked the door and gave Langdon the code while EOP-812 was driven inside. The driver got out, nodded and headed for the Suburban as we all thought the bad guys had been stopped as the heat sensing surveillance report from the satellite only showed a couple of deer between us and the bad guys' car with the flat tires.

The Forest:

After the pause, I took Langdon into the barn and offered him a black snowmobile suit as he questioned my offer as I noted. "Suit yourself. It's twenty-five degrees and you're going to be outside all night and there's a good chance you'll get wet."

Langdon looked at me and realized I was putting on my suit and he'd better take my advice. After getting dressed I noted we needed to walk about a mile and couldn't take the path as it went by the Foundation building and I was afraid there could be some sort of security.

Instead we walked west to the family cemetery and paused. "These are my ancestors from the 1800's. As the Terrill family grew and dispersed from the farm, the decision was made around 1900 to be buried in Graceland Cemetery in Mineral Point. Private burial grounds are still legal in Wisconsin but the only beings that have been interred here in the past 125 years are my little buddy Jake, who was my dog, and Francis, the research pig who was more human than you and I."

We paused for a moment and I looked at Langdon, became somewhat sentimental and offered. "I often think of my little buddy and have come to believe that God made humans with free will and dogs to teach us how to handle that free will by being trustworthy, loyal, obedient and friendly, expecting nothing more than love, food and shelter. I also believe God made the dog's life much shorter than ours to teach us how important these things are and how painful loss can be."

There was a long pause and Langdon savored my words as he allowed my thoughts of Jake to permeate his mind and fill it with goodness before noting. "If people were half as good as dogs think we are, we'd be a very special species."

I nodded in the affirmative and then noted. "You probably think it strange that we'd bury a pig in our cemetery. However, if you'd ever met Francis, you'd understand that he too was more human than many people. He was taught to use cuneiforms to communicate and had a concept of life, death and the hereafter.

Langdon and I both knew we needed to keep walking as so as we made our way across the frozen field he asked, "Why the stone fence?"

I couldn't resist responding with one of my dad's favorite jokes. "Because people were just dying to get in."

It got a little chuckle as I then noted the stone had been the house until the house fell into disrepair and it was decided that those who had lived in it should be surrounded by its memories.

"Where are we going?" Langdon inquired.

"Two stops," is all I replied, as we traversed the frozen cornfield and made our way to the Forest.

We made it to the Forest as Langdon and I stopped at Great Grandfather's obelisk and I watched as the man began to transcend. I smiled as I now knew he was good of heart.

"George! George! This place is...is touching me. I can see Nancy and she's looking down and smiling. Oh, my God! I don't know. I don't know if I want to go any further. George. Why didn't you bring me here sooner? I...I...I haven't felt like this since she went away."

Langdon's hands went above his head as if he was reaching for heaven as he exclaimed. "Oh my God! I see my mom and dad and my little brother Donnie who drowned in Lake Monona and they're right there. I can see them."

Langdon's breathing began to deepen and I knew he was at the apex of all three of the ley lines and the power of goodness was cascading through his body and into his soul. I glanced at the man and saw tears streaming down his cheeks. His hands were quivering and I sincerely believed he was about to convulse. He was having a total body experience of a magnitude I'd never seen in anyone besides the first time it happened to me.

I stood and allowed the goodness to fill Langdon's heart until the quaking stopped and breathing returned to normal and then simply nodded. I knew he'd been ordained and sanctified in the spirit I'd hoped for. I knew from that point on there would be no need to question him, challenge him or doubt his deeds for we had become brothers of the night whose only goal was to override the horrors of greed that had taken what was good and turned it corrupt.

After a lingering moment I spoke but the tone of my voice had changed. Gone was the Wisconsin timbre and the staccato enunciation, replaced by the smooth whispers of another source as I offered. "I am Little Spirit, purveyor of goodness and dignity of man."

Langdon looked at me and simply nodded. There was no disbelief! There was no apprehension. He felt my words as images of the little Indian girl who was Rodney's great, great grandmother saved by my ancestors resonated within his brain as he exulted. "Oh Jesus! Why? Why must there be so much pain? Why? Why can't we love each other? Why? Why? Why?"

I put my hand on Langdon's shoulder and nodded to my right. The buck was there and I knew that Langdon had been accepted as a man of peace as I whispered. "We must follow him."

Langdon quietly nodded in the affirmative as we traversed the little path that led to the springs. As we reached the spot where the pure water trickled from beneath the rocks, I knelt down and took out the two tin cups and filled them with the water. Standing I offered Langdon the cup and simply whispered, "Drink".

Once again, tremblers! Once again, tears! Once again, the total immersion of a man's soul into the realm of beyond where only good exists and joy survives forever.

"You knew, didn't you? You knew what was going to happen to me," Langdon offered.

I looked at him and admitted. "I didn't know. I just sensed your goodness. Only the great spirit knows and before I could take you beyond here and now, I needed to make sure."

"Now what?" Langdon inquired.

"We wait."

"For what?"

"To see if you've been accepted."

"Accepted into what?"

"You'll see."

We stood for what seemed like an eternity and then 'he' was there again. The great buck had returned. I nodded at Langdon. Words at this moment were incredibly fragile as they could break the spell. Instead I pointed and we began following the buck. As had been the case with my great uncle and my ancestors, we were making our way into the marsh where Rodney's ancestors were frightened to go. I could hear Langdon's breathing and didn't know if it was exhaustion or fear. I did know that we'd gone too far to turn back.

As we made our way deeper into the bog green lights began to swirl around us. Much like the Northern Lights, they guided us to tranquility and a spot where I knew nothing could harm us. The buck paused and then simply disappeared into the fog that was rising from the damp ground beneath our feet.

As we stood there I looked back and saw a beam of a flashlight. Someone was following us. Langdon looked at his phone app and it showed two individuals about 100 yards behind us.

"How in hell did that happen?" I inquired.

"They had a second car. Shit! As Langdon was unzipping his snowmobile suit to reach for his gun. I shook my head 'no'. I knew it wouldn't be necessary.

I whispered, "Follow me," as we made my way to the edge of the pond. Langdon looked at me with furrowed brows. It had been unseasonably warm and the water trickling from the earth had made the ground soft. I nodded to assure Langdon it would be Ok. I took the first step across the thin ice, looked back and gestured for him to follow me.

Slowly, we made our way to the other side. As we entered the marsh grass on the other side I looked back across the pond and saw the flashlight beam aimed at our footprints. When whomever it was reached the side of the pond where we'd been they stopped and discussed something, which I assumed was about the safety of the ice. As the beam of light went from side-to-side along the shore, they must have concluded we'd crossed and made it and began the trek themselves. As they reached the middle of the pond, where the deepest part was over twelve feet, the ice gave way and they fell in, while quickly finding themselves weighted down in winter clothes unable to escape God's wrath.

It's never fun to watch a man struggle, even your enemies who are out to harm you. We silently stood as the two men, at first attempted to extricate themselves, and then watched as the survival instinct created two combatants who fought for dominance in hope the other's demise would mean their own survival. Within minutes the cold water had done its deed and both men slowly began to calm. Death was at their doorstep. Their bodies shuddered and then lie motionless as both slowly slid beneath the ice while the solitude of death permeated the consequence of retribution.

I looked at Langdon who, after so many years, had become somewhat desensitized to calamity and I saw a different man, someone who cared, someone who understood good and bad who still felt sadness for what he saw. As for me, the death culminated in my transition from the hunted to the hunter. After the bus ride. After the race through the cemetery. After hiding in the Kohl center and all the months of considering myself the victim, the pain, agony and frustration had been released by the death of strangers. Their energy, their power, their aggression had simply been transcended to me and, for the first time in nearly two years, I felt as if I was me and not some subordinate victim who felt sorry for himself, while blaming everyone else.

I inhaled as if to capture the aura of victory around me as I began moving beyond my own self-interest to focus on contributing to something bigger than me. No longer was I feeling vulnerable and powerless. All that weakness and insecurity had been stripped away and I was beginning to feel in control again. With each breath my confidence, self-reliance and sense of mastery began to reappear. I'd done nothing wrong and my sense of injustice no longer mattered.

Langdon made the sign of the cross and it was over. I looked at Langdon and simply nodded. Who knew who they were? Who knew if they had family? Who'd wonder where they'd gone? Would they be missed? No one would ever know. They would be carried downstream only to float to the surface where they would become part of the food chain for those who would consider them nothing more than the vermin they were. I turned to Langdon and nodded once again. It was time to move on. We didn't know if they were the alone and still had a journey in front of us to a point of security and then hopefully, salvation.

The Cave:

We made our way across another field and into a shallow valley that had been carved over the millennia by the rain, wind and snow that exemplified home and created the vistas I loved. We were in the very heart of what is called the Driftless area and yet, my mind, my body and my soul had finite direction towards existence and survival.

I looked at Langdon who was puffing from the effort. As we entered the ravine Langdon saw the exposed steel wall that had been painted in a Mossy Oak camouflage and covered with a mesh net that shielded its structure from the eyes of those unwelcome while serving as a barricade to interlopers. Neither man nor beast could make their way through the cauldron in front of us unless they had the right combination that would open what we had created.

"What's this?" Langdon inquired.

"My brother and I have turned several of the limestone caves on the farm into our Solera System facility."

"You're what?"

"We needed a place to store and age the wine we've created."

"Wine?"

"Yes, we've been producing high-quality red wines here. With the market as saturated as it is, we chose a market position in the premium arena where, in order to create the right taste and texture, we developed a Solera system."

"A what?"

"Solera comes from Spanish and literally means 'on the ground' which refers to the bottom-most tier of casks, which traditionally rest directly on the floor.

Langdon had a frown plastered across his face as I continued. "The Solera methodology is a fractional blending system that's used for aging. Instead of putting wine in casks and letting them age individually, a portion of each barrel is removed from the oldest barrel, called the Solera, which is then refilled with a younger product from the next earlier barrel in line. With each vintage the process is repeated with each barrel being topped up with a younger product from the barrel above it until the youngest product is added to the top barrel."

"And this makes a difference?"

"The system has several advantages. First, it allows for a consistent product over time as the older and younger products are blended together. Second, it allows for a longer aging process as the product isn't all removed from the barrel at once. Third, it allows for a more complex flavor profile as the different ages of the product blend together. When you're selling fine wine at $200 a bottle you need to have consistency."

"A $200 a bottle?" Langdon was incredulous.

Dave, 'Solera' is used to designate the highest tier of wines produced using this aging system. These wines are typically the oldest and most complex in flavor. $200 is wholesale. In five-star restaurants it's normally $200 a glass."

Langdon shook his head and admitted. "I had no idea."

I looked at Langdon and reminded him. "You need to remember, before the... uhh... changes...we were one of the top Wagyu beef producers in the world sold under the Terrill brand along with our Terrill premium bourbon and wine."

"If you're going to sustain a level of brand mystique you need to ensure you remain in the same category in all the products under the same umbrella simply because a brand that doesn't fit will bring the perception of the other products down with them. We had leverage with our restaurant customers to the point they would feature our steaks with our bourbon and wine all designed for an upscale market throughout the world."

"How much would a porterhouse, glass of bourbon before dinner and red wine with dinner cost?" Langdon inquired.

"Depending on the restaurant, around $500."

"Per person?"

"Yes."

"And people pay that?"

"We have waiting list for all three products."

"Delaney's in Madison, Carnivore in Milwaukee and Hunt Club Steakhouse just outside Lake Geneva."

"That's it?"

"Yup, others want it but can't get it. By keeping it exclusive it remains special to the point each restaurant has a private mailing list and they announce when they have the steaks coming in. In so doing, we've created what we wanted and that's a perception that what we have is the very best."

"Is it?"

"That's up to the customer. I can't say it's the very best. What I can say is that our customers believe so and that's why it's a special meal when they are invited for dinner."

"How did you come up with the idea?"

"From my shoes."

"Your shoes?" Langdon asked incredulously.

"Yes, The Duke got me hooked on custom made shoes from England. I don't know if they're the best in the world but I do know that when you own a pair, you're in a very exclusive club that's controlled and restricted and so you think they're the best."

"Incredible! Simply incredible."

"My shoes are really the only thing I miss, other than, well, my plane and helicopter but for different reasons."

"Let's see if we can't get it all back," Langdon offered to which I nodded in affirmation.

Langdon opened his hands and inquired, "Why here?"

"First, the caves were already dug by our ancestors and the material was used to build half the buildings in Mineral Point. The reason they chose to quarry here was because of the density of the limestone. Denser limestone has a higher thermal resistance, as there is less air space within the rock for heat to transfer through."

"There were two reasons why they stopped mining here. First, is because of the change in the porosity of the limestone where the number of pores and voids affects its thermal resistance because air is a poor conductor of heat."

"Back then they didn't have central heating or the types of insulation and so the type of rock and its density and porosity determined its insulating and construction value. Finally, is the mineral composition. Calcite is the most common mineral in limestone and It has a relatively high thermal resistance, while quartz has a lower thermal resistance. The second reason they stopped mining right here is because there's an underground spring-fed stream at the back of the cave. Wet limestone has a lower thermal resistance than dry limestone, as water conducts heat more efficiently than air."

"You sure know a lot about limestone."

"I didn't in the beginning and so we hired a geologist from the University and then a geological engineer."

"We got lucky. The limestone's R-value alone might not be enough for significant temperature variations with the mouth of the cave as big as it is so we had engineers calculate the proper insulation and thickness for the mouth of the cave and the ceiling which came out to be R-65 so that the temperature inside remains between 12-14 degrees Celsius year-round, which is ideal for storage."

"And it's secure?" Langdon inquired.

"We learned that ten years ago Norway built the Svalbard Global Seed Vault, which is a secure storage facility deep within an Arctic mountain designed to keep seeds from the worlds essential crops safe from any kind of disaster and we simply used their design to create the wall and door structure based on the same type of concrete and steel used in bank vaults so that they're not only the right thickness for insulation but virtually impenetrable."

"Why steel?"

"Thou shall not steal. You're about to see just under five million dollars' worth of inventory and five year's effort. The reinforced steel wall ensures no one gets in unless we want them to."

"So, this is where you store all your wine?"

"Hardly, there are five more just like this and so the bad guys only have a one-in-six chance of finding us. With all six exactly the same even my brother would have to guess where we are, if he figured out that, we came here at all.

"How are we getting in?" Langdon inquired.

With that, I opened a small hatch that had a glass plate beneath it. I then placed my hand on the glass pad that lit up. I then pressed my left index to the glass and a small green light flashed instructing me to look into the lens for a retinal scan.

Langdon looked on with his mouth open in amazement as he said, "This is incredible."

I replied. "It's a three-step process where the probability of capturing is less than one in one trillion. My father-in-law had virtually the same system in his house in Saint Martin that we put in the Lighthouse and we just duplicated the process."

"It's the same system the government's using for high-clearance employees," Langdon offered.

As I was explaining, the bolts released and I could turn the handle and open the foot-thick door and noted. "Stay here a minute, I need to turn off the interior security system that includes cameras and motion sensors."

"Oh, my God!" Langdon exclaimed as he looked at barrel after barrel of fine wine aging. "There must be 100 barrels in here."

"120 to be exact. We use Barrique barrels whose design originated in Bordeaux, France where we had our other home. Each barrel holds 225 liters or about 59 gallons."

I could see Langdon's wheels spinning and so I offered. "Around 7,000 gallons which means 2,200 cases of wine. At $200.00 per liter each case has a wholesale cost of $2400 and a total value of $5.2 million which I'd like to sell."

"And people are willing to pay that?"

"This was all sold until you guys stepped in and froze our assets."

"I'm sorry."

"You didn't do it and, when we get this mess cleaned up, I'll be able to get more per bottle as people are clamoring for it."

"That good?"

"You're about to find out." I turned on the light and Langdon got a better view of the contents as I offered. "Follow me."

I closed the steel door and re-set the exterior security. Unless someone attempted to drill through thirty feet of limestone and then a copper mesh gird and were then able to override the motion sensors that detected any drilling or movement, there was no way they were getting in.

As we made our way to the back of the grotto Langdon heard the trickle of water as it flowed from within the rocks on the north end of the cavern. Situated in the area was a desk, kitchen area, bathroom and shower, as well as a 30Kw bank of energy saving Lithium Ion batteries, a computer and two beds.

"What's this all about?" Langdon asked.

"You need to realize, it takes about four days every three months to transfer wine from one cask to the next. We had an oenologist under contract to fly in from Chile and he'd literally reside here. By making this his...uhh...apartment he was able to work as long as he wanted every day as he was paid by the job and not the hour."

"Where does the electricity come from?"

"That's where the power station comes in. We have solar panels that collect the energy and store it in the batteries in the power station. We have enough stored energy for fourteen days before the batteries would need to be recharged."

"And it's always 55 degrees?"

"Yup!"

"And you have contact with the outside world?"

"That's what the computer's for. Needless to say, there's no cellphone coverage because of the fact we're in the ground and the copper mesh lining.

We made our way in and I could tell Langdon was getting uncomfortable in the snowmobile suit. I pointed to a wardrobe and noted. "If you're too warm there are some sweatshirts and clothes in there."

Langdon took off the snowmobile suit and slipped into a Badger hoodie. It made him look ten years younger as he inquired. "What about the computer?"

"We have a small parabolic dish that's hidden and can communicate that way."

"You guys have thought of everything."

"Not really. We just developed the system around the environment and when all that happened took place I thought we needed to go somewhere safe until things calmed down. I know how remote and secure we are here. My only worry is Amy. I need to let her know what's going on."

I stopped for a moment and then added. "Obviously, because whomever the bad guys are knew about our plans, there's a void in the security system somewhere. I'm afraid to contact her as it might put her in greater risk."

"Do you think your apartment could be bugged?" Langdon inquired.

"I don't know. What I do know is that I never shared the plan with Amy, never emailed it to anyone and only talked about it with you in the car. This leads me to believe the security leak isn't on my side but yours and why would they want me out of the way now?"

Langdon shook his head and realized I'd figured out more than he was giving me credit for as he assured me. "George, I don't know who's doing what to whom. I do know that your life is at risk because the bad guys think you know more than you do and that goes back to their impression you know more about SIMON than you say you do."

I thought of my favorite analogy...I'm just an analog guy in a digital world, before asking, "How long do you think we need to hide out?" I was already getting a degree of claustrophobia.

"I'll see if I can find out. The problem is it's two in the morning and I can't contact anyone now."

I stood and went to a steel cabinet and opened the door. Inside were bottles of wine from all the different years we'd been in the wine business. I went to the bottom shelf removed one of the original vintages, carefully dusted it off, went to the counter, retrieved a corkscrew, drew the cork and took two glasses out of the cabinet. "You've heard about our wine. How about a taste and then let's see if we can't get some sleep before we see what tomorrow brings?"

Langdon nodded as I poured the wine, swirled it around in both glasses and handed one to Langdon and toasted, "Cheers."

"Not much to cheer about," Langdon offered.

"We're here. We're safe and tomorrow, the war begins."

"What do you mean?" Langdon inquired with his brow furrowed.

"We've tried it your way. Now it's time to try it mine."

Langdon took a sip of the wine and expressed "Oh, my God," as a statement of pleasure.

"You like?" I inquired.

"George, this is the best wine I've ever tasted."

"If we're here tomorrow night, we've got some of our beef here and we can grill some steaks."

"You mean you've got some Wagyu beef here?"

"Sure, we vacuum seal each steak individually and then flash freeze them before shipping."

"You guys really got it down, don't you?"

"It's been more Tommie than me. I handle sales and marketing and he handles operations."

"When this mess is over can I get a tour?"

"Of course. Now, I don't know about you but I need some sleep."

The Invitation:

When you're underground, without a sound, you have no perspective of time or circumstance. I awoke and saw that Langdon was already up. I did my business, came out and asked if he wanted some breakfast.

"Sounds great. What do you have?"

"Your choice Rice Krispies or Cheerios."

"What about milk?"

"Not a problem." I opened to cupboard and took out some of the UHT milk that Tommie made that could be stored for up to a year. I held up a container and noted. "I brought back the idea from Saint Martin regarding aseptic milk, that undergoes ultra-high temperature (UHT) pasteurization and Tommie had it packaged in sterile containers. Tommie said the process eliminates most bacteria and allows milk to be stored at room temperature for months before opening. We thought if we could do this, we'd be able to balance our dairy inventory and not be so susceptible to the market. Wrong! But Tommie has the equipment and does it for here. Tommie's also worked on a process of securing vegetables from our greenhouses so that, we sustain all the nutrients while having a shelf life for peas, carrots, green beans and asparagus of twenty years with no degradation."

Langdon looked at his watch and saw that is was nearly 7:30 AM Wisconsin time. He looked at me and asked that I not watch as he logged in on the computer. While he logged in, I took a shower and put on fresh clothes.

As I came back to the office area, Langdon was deeply intrenched in something. Finally, he turned to me and noted. "We've figured out how they knew. They tailed you into Macy's and got into your records and saw what you purchased. They put one and one together, got into the city bus lot and borrowed the bus they left at East Towne after they dropped you off in Sun Prairie. Washington is looking at the video surveillance from the mall to see if they can identify any of the perps."

"I need to contact Amy and let her know I'm Ok."

There was a strange look on Langdon's face. He wanted to tell me something but I sensed he didn't know how.

"What is it?" I asked.

"It's Amy."

"What?"

"She been admitted to University Hospital."

I was fuming as I inquired, "Was it them? I'll kill the sons-a-bitches."

"No George, it wasn't them."

My heart sank. I already knew but was afraid to ask. Langdon sensed my fear and offered, "She's in the hematology wing for transfusions."

I closed my eyes and thought of my wife. I imagined her there alone. I felt profoundly helpless as Langdon offered. "She's stable and has a woman by the name of Ann Whitehorse with her."

My God. Rodney's wife, Ann. Of course. Once again the majesty of love had shown through.

"I need to send Amy a message and let the kids know."

"All three?"

"I only have two...Melia and 'V'. The other one no longer exists."

"I can have that taken care of when I get back to Madison. What should I have the agents say about you?"

"Tell the agents to inform the kids I'm unavoidably detained but will let them know what's happening as soon as possible. Make sure the agents instruct both kids not to share the information with anyone else, particularly Derrick."

Langdon returned to the computer before turning to me and inquiring, "You said 'war' last night, what did you mean?"

"I need to get a message to Peter and Luke and simply tell them 'Pointer'. They'll understand and I'll explain it all then."

"Pointer?"

"Pointer's the dog on the building on High Street in town. He's facing south and they'll know I want to meet again in the Forest."

Time:

The communication was sent and I later learned that my message was hand delivered to Amy, Melia and 'V' while Peter and Luke were simply given the word 'Pointer'. They agreed to meet with Langdon and me the next morning at the Forest. We spent the day playing cribbage and telling stories. That night as Langdon and I waited I cooked the steaks and broccoli while Langdon thought he'd gone to heaven raving about how good it was which put a smile on my face.

As we sat finishing the food Langdon updated me on what all was going on and the fact Amy had been released from the hospital and was staying with Melia. This meant they were less than two miles from the cave and, yet, didn't know I was there.

I didn't sleep much and awoke to learn the guys were coming at ten. At 9:30 I went to the steel door and peered at the screen and the image of the surveillance camera. All was clear.

I looked at Langdon and noted. "I think you need to have the ability to open the vault door when you come back. As you saw last night, it's virtually sound proof and impenetrable."

"How do you do that?" Langdon inquired.

"It's actually quite easy. I go to the panel inside the door and program my three-step code and press program. You then look into the lens and it will do a visual and then a retinal scan. Then you take one of your fingers, press it on the screen until you hear a 'click' and it's done. Remember which finger you use. If you use the wrong one, you'll be locked out for 24 hours."

We went through the process and then made sure it worked on the outside scanner before locking up. Langdon and I then made our way back to the Forest. Peter and Luke were already there and waiting for us at Great Grandfather's obelisk.

I looked at the two and warned. "Guys, this is serious. The day before yesterday, they attempted to kidnap me and I got lucky then Dave and I were chased and made it to the farm. We thought we lost them until two tried following us. We made it through the marsh and across the pond and hid in one of the caves."

Langston added. "We believe you three are in eminent danger."

All four of us had very serious looks on our faces as Peter outlined why the Chinese were after us. When Langdon added this could be a matter of life-or-death I watched as Luke's face turned pale when he realized what we'd developed was being turned into a potential weapon of mass destruction as he inquired, "how can I help?"

"We need to figure out a way to break into the Foundation and dumb down SIMON." Peter offered.

"Break in? That's going to be tough," Luke offered, slightly shaking his head.

I offered. "The reason you're here, Luke, is because you designed the buildings and know their strengths and weaknesses and points of attack."

"Attack?" Luke questioned realizing this was literally a military action.

Peter took a deep breath and offered. "I've been thinking about this since we met in the Arboretum. We need to do it in such a way that the information gradually becomes nondescript so that the Chinese operatives aren't suspicious. This means gradually modifying all the personal data while, at the same time, storing it for future use. The challenge is getting in there and doing it."

"Who has access to SIMON?" Langdon inquired.

"Virtually no one other than those on staff," Luke offered.

For the next half hour we bantered around all types of options. Tunneling, invading, you name it and then Peter's eyebrows raised as he offered, "I think I might have a way."

"What?" we all asked, virtually in unison.

"What would happen if, instead of invading SIMON, we corrupted the sensors, such that, they gave the wrong reading on the helium/hydrogen mix and subsequent temperature?"

Luke smiled. He knew where this was going as I nodded and asked for further information.

Peter continued. "We know that the only outsiders ever allowed in the area are the people who deliver the liquid helium and hydrogen. We also know they can't be mixed at the same time."

"And?" I asked.

"We have the gauges indicate they need coolant. They'll call and our delivery person delivers the liquid helium. While there, there's an "accident" where the safety gauges indicate the helium level is too high and those in the cooling area need to evacuate, leaving our guy, who's in a thermal suit, alone, to clean up the spill. While there he uploads the first phase of deprogramming which will only take three or four minutes. We remotely reset the gauges and then he departs."

"What about the video cameras?" Luke offered.

"If the air in the room was warm enough and liquid helium brings the temperature down wouldn't the lenses on the cameras fog over?"

Luke got a smile on his face reflecting he thought the idea might work and then said, "But that only takes care of the cooling tower and not the area around SIMON."

Peter added. "Luke, you remember where SIMON's security cameras are positioned don't you?"

"Sure, above the entrance door and on the opposite side of the room."

"Do you still have the immersive videos you took when we did the virtual tours that showed SIMON, as well as the seven computers?"

"Sure. I've got the entire file."

"And we've got access to SIMON from the IBM Watson's don't we?

"Yes."

"While SIMON is programmed to block any alien data he's encoded to store the visual status reports on the Watsons. This means we can trick SIMON into believing everything is normal and, if SIMON's fooled, so would anyone who's watching."

We all smiled as we could see where this was going as Peter continued "So, the first thing we load into SIMON is the security video showing SIMON all by himself and do it by replacing one of the Watson's security footage. If the folks in charge are as smart as I think they are, they're going to check the video."

Peter looked at Luke and inquired. "How long is the room video?"

"Perhaps three or four minutes," Luke replied.

"Because it's a static image we can electronically extend it to about ten minutes before the pixelization would get to the point SIMON might recognize the anomaly. In that amount of time we should be able download the first phase of programming that would then open up the second phase."

"Why not do it all at once?" Langdon asked.

Peter replied. "We designed SIMON's software with a dual-lock system which means that we first need to unlock his protection and then wait a minimum of 24 hours until he's received reports back from all the Watsons. This was done so that no one could simply invade the system."

"So then, the next day you'd go back and download the second program?" I asked.

"Right and then SIMON would begin off-loading corrupted data to the Watsons."

"Is it possible to save what SIMON has developed? Langdon asked.

"We'd need to connect to a very large quantum computer."

Langdon paused and then noted, "There are three that we might be able to access, the Argonne, Oak Ridge and Lawrence Berkeley National Laboratories."

"If we can, I'd split the data between the three and make it so that none of the three could blend the data back together. There'd be no risk of someone else doing what the Chinese are doing."

"But who'd decide what information went where?" Langdon asked.

I could tell by Peter's facial expression he was perturbed as he answered. "Agent Langdon, let's not play politics or have a power struggle. One would get the pertinent medical data. One would get the operational programming. The third would get the financial software."

"What would happen to SIMON?" I asked.

"He'd be neutered in terms of the operational and financial aspects and return to what we created him for, medical research."

"I'll need to get clearance for this," Langdon noted.

"You'd better get it fast. I'll need to get the MadCity boys together to see what it's going to take to do this."

Langdon looked at him and got a serious expression on his face. "We believe one of your...uh...MadCity boys is behind this."

Peter's face went flush and I could tell he was going through the list of potential perpetrators before answering. "Impossible!" Peter retorted. "None of the Madcity Guys have been allowed in the facility in over a year. Besides that, I don't

I know a single person more patriotic than these guys. They'd die for our country, even in the piss-poor shape it's in.

"They've all been vetted," Langdon offered.

"You've already done that based on our meeting in Madison?" Peter replied.

Langdon nodded and had either forgotten or was testing Peter when he replied. "You'd think they're all true patriots. We've checked all their communications for the past seven years and they're clean. One hell of a bunch of gamers."

"So, you think one of them is your perp?" Luke asked.

"There's only one who has red flags and that's Bart."

"Bart?" Peter and Luke responded simultaneously and both with an incredulous tone to their voices.

Langdon continued. "Take a man whose wife has left him because of his addiction to on-line gambling. Put him deep in debt for the same reason his wife left. Now throw in someone willing to clean the slate. All the elements are there."

I cringed to think that Big Brother could go back that far and dig that deep as Peter shook his head in remorseful disbelief.

There was a long pause and then Peter asked. "How deep is Bart's hole?"

"Three million, five," Langdon replied.

"What happens if I cover the debt and get him back on our side if he's the one?"

"You mean work with us instead of against us?" I asked.

"Look, Bart can do in one day what will take me a month to figure out," Peter replied.

"But what happens if you go to him and he won't turn or he's really not the bad guy?" Langdon asked.

"Then, if I see that he's a traitor, I'll put a bullet in his head," Peter offered, to which none of us thought he was kidding.

"Assuming you don't have to kill him, how long do you think it will be before you're ready?" Luke asked.

"A couple of weeks." Peter surmised.

"Today's December tenth. Two weeks makes it the 24th and Christmas eve which is on a Wednesday this year. That means that most of the staff will be off both the 24th and 25th. How about having the gauges report the need for helium on the 23rd with delivery the morning of the 24th?" I asked.

There were smiles all around as Peter added, "And then deliver the hydrogen on the 31st and start the New Year with the slow degradation of SIMON's capabilities."

"How are you going to do that?" I asked.

Peter looked at the group and questioned, "What's the one thing all computers and all people have in common?"

"We all shook our heads indicating we didn't know."

"Time." Peter responded.

"Time?" Langdon inquired.

"Every input into a computer has a time stamp on it regardless of the content or computer type. It's the one thing they all start with as it's the progression of events from past to present to future and the framework in which events can be ordered and their durations measured. It's considered the fourth dimension of spacetime, alongside the three spatial dimensions of length, width and height that helps describe the location and duration of events."

"SIMON measures time using zepto-seconds which is a trillionth of a billionth of a second or the time it takes light to travel across a hydrogen molecule. He then extrapolates them into seconds, minutes and hours based on the vibrations of atoms or rotations of celestial bodies. However, according to Einstein's theory of relativity, time is not absolute and can be affected by gravity and motion where time dilation occurs near massive objects or at high speeds."

"And?" I inquired, wanting nothing more than to understand where Peter was going with this.

"And, all we need do is program SIMON to reverse his reference time without having it show up on any data."

Luke was smiling as he got the picture and offered. "As SIMON operates he'll go back in time. As he goes back in time anything that's been programmed after that point would simply no longer exist."

I must have had a frown on my face as Peter added. "Think of it like a newspaper that's in reverse. All that happened today couldn't be reported because, to the newspaper, it hadn't happened yet."

I smiled and conferred. "So, by having SIMON's internal clock go backwards, everything added after that date would be in his memory but unusable?"

Peter replied, "Yes, you just couldn't open it without some password that brought SIMON back to 'now' as opposed to the past or future. SIMON would keep collecting but only able to use the information collected before the ever changing 'now' until he would be back to his beginning."

"And no one would realize it was happening?" Langdon inquired.

"I don't think so." Peter replied before adding. "I'll need to check with Bart."

"If this happens and SIMON goes all the way back to the beginning, what about the operational security code?" I asked.

"Who were the first people who had access?" Peter asked.

"The three of us," I replied.

"So, in other words, you could stop the information, stop the reprogramming and stop anyone from getting into SIMON except for you three?" Langdon asked.

"If done right, yes, that would be the end result. We'd start by gradually sending SIMON back in time until he was totally devoid of all data acquired. Then, to restore him, either George, Luke or me would need to use our bio-imprint to turn him back on."

"Bio-imprint?" Langdon inquired.

Not knowing I'd programmed Langdon into the cave system, Luke offered. "The combination of our face, eye scan and finger. To ensure a higher degree of improbability, we actually programmed SIMON to read a different finger for each of us. If, for instance, the wrong finger is used, SIMON would shut down for 100 hours. If then another wrong finger is used, it's 200 hours. If a third wrong finger 400 hours. The fifth wrong finger will shut the entire system down for a month."

"How long will that take to do your re-programming?" Langdon inquired

"How long do you want?" Peter replied while adding, "It needs to be like a slow leak so no one realizes it's happening."

"Other than the holidays, what other day does America come to a stop?" Peter asked.

"Super Bowl Sunday!" Luke added.

"What a wonderful surprise! Everyone's watching the Super Bowl and SIMON goes to sleep and infects all the computers who are trying to steal what is now gibberish. Aww!"

"How do you wake him up?" Langdon asked.

"We wait until all the shit's off the fan and then set a protocol...hand, retina, finger from one of us."

"Who's?" Langdon inquired.

"We'll need three people," Peter suggested.

Langdon looked at the three of us and nodded, while replying, "Go for it guys!"

We all smiled and nodded in the affirmative as we delegated assignments. I knew this was Langdon's big chance to go out in a blaze of glory. I knew Luke and Peter would come through because of who they were and the passion they had for all that was good. As for me, it was my way to get back what Amy and I'd lost, while also getting even.

Settling In:

Langdon had asked Peter to bring the secure laptop Agent Walker had provided that couldn't be traced which would allow me to keep up on all that was happening. For Peter tracking and breaking into the computer was too easy and so he modified it and noted. "George, I've programmed the laptop with fifty different domain addresses, of which, only one will randomly operate for ten minutes every 24 hours before shutting down. That's because, that's the amount of time you'll have before a tracker would be able to identify your exact location. Even with that you can't use email because they could track it, as well."

"When you get back to the cave, you need to promise me, you'll shut down the old computer so that it can't be traced. All you need do is go into the system settings and erase the identification. You can still use the computer, but it won't communicate."

We went through all the steps one more time and Peter repeated the system set-up for the computer. It was nearing noon and we began to feel as if we'd better split.

"Where will you be?" Luke inquired nodding at me, while showing his concern for my wellbeing.

Langdon intercepted the question and replied. "George will be with us. We think for greater security for all of you it's best if no one knows where the others are in case one of you gets caught."

We shook hands and did the obligatory bear hugs as Peter and Luke departed retracing their steps back towards their ride.

With them gone I asked Langdon, "I thought I was going to hide in the cave."

"You are, but it's better if fewer people know where you're at." Langdon paused, took a deep breath and added. "George, this is really serious. If the bad guys find you they'll torture and kill you. You're not dealing with nice people. If they can't find you they'll try and figure out who might know where you're at and go after them. For everyone's safety, including your family, the fewer people who know where you are the safer you all will be."

"How long do you think I'll need to hide out?"

"I don't know. Right now, your life's in danger as is the security of the world. What I do know is that this is top secret all the way up the chain of command and it's very, and I mean very serious."

"When, will I be going to a secure place?" I inquired.

"That will be determined. My thought is you need to go back to the cave for now. Once I know where you're going, I'll come and get you."

"What about Peter and Luke?" I inquired.

"We're working on that." Langdon replied, knowing it was better I didn't know just in case the bad guys caught me. I inquired. "Now what?"

Langdon's phone pinged and he looked at the text and reported I needed to go until I heard from him.

"How long will you be gone?" I asked.

"I don't know. I need to work with the Department on what all we've got planned. I need to get our geeks working with Peter to figure out how to reconfigure SIMON."

"That really won't be necessary," I offered. "Peter and Bart know SIMON inside out and if it can be done, they'll do it. My only suggestion is to get the three of them out of here. Have them go away. I believe they're at risk and that's all we need right now is to have the bad guys chasing them."

"Where can they go?" Langdon inquired.

"What have you done with the Lighthouse?"

"You mean your house in Saint Martin?"

"Yes," I concurred. "What about Luke, Bart, Peter and me going down there?" I inquired.

"It's frozen and all we could do would be secure the premises." Langdon replied. "It's a foreign country and that changes all the rules. Unfortunately, officially you're still a suspect and even having you hiding out is pushing the envelope."

Langdon looked at me and offered. "George, right now intel is reporting the Chinese have determined the two chasing us last night are dead and they're still hot on our tail. It means you really need to go back to the cave NOW and stay there until I come for you. Your life's in danger and one mistake could be deadly."

Reality was hitting home. This wasn't like in the movies as Langdon continued. "You have to promise me you'll stay in the cave and do what Peter said."

I nodded in the affirmative as I realized the war had only begun and you don't have a victory celebration when you've only drawn up the battle plan.

Langdon looked at me, was reluctant and then gave me a man hug. "Security scanned the area and it all looks clear. I'll walk back and get the car."

There was a pause and then Langdon noted. "You're a great man, George Terrill. You're everything everyone said you were and more."

"Thank you."

I looked at the obelisk one last time and nodded in reverence to the memory of Great Grandfather as Langdon went his way and I went mine. I made it back to the cave, opened the door, went in and double checked the exterior camera. I been to the cave dozens of times but never alone. As I closed the door, it hit me...profound silence. I was buried within the ground with thirty feet of limestone above me, a two-foot-thick, insulated concrete and hardened steel door behind me and nothing but wine barrels to keep me company. As I made my way back to the enclave there were times I could literally hear my heart beat, as the deafening absence of life was all that coexisted as my company.

It was then I pondered if this was what it's like to die and be buried. Silence! Absolute silence. No noise, no sound, nothing but being buried in an abyss accompanied by only my thoughts and memories where time has no meaning nor consequence.

I sat for a while and thought, 'What can I do to keep from becoming senseless? How can I fill the hours? How long can I stand it before insanity creeps in and takes me beyond myself? After what seemed like eternity I realized I needed to do something to take my mind off what was transpiring.

I gazed at the old computer and realized it was my only friend. Sadly, the new one was emotionless but at least it could keep me here and now by letting me observe the world without participating. I was warned not to communicate with anyone who was linked to our caper for fear the Bad Guys were waiting for me.

I had enough food and wine for up to six months. My God, six months alone! It was then I decided I needed to take the time and begin my own book. Not 'Waldwick' but something I created. I allocated my few minutes of computer time each day to study how to write a book, then took paper and pen and wrote it out. As for my target audience, all the research I'd done said I should try to write for my own age group and then find out who really reads books. I looked at age, gender, education, ethnicity and income.

The results surprised me as research indicated that young adults aged 18-29 had the highest book readership and I was surprised by what they read that included an entire spectrum of subjects from fantasy filled with magic, adventure and fantastical worlds, science fiction, exploring futuristic settings, technology and societal issues, contemporary fiction addressing real-life situations and challenges faced by young adults, such as friendship, family, relationships, identity and social issues, romance that explores love, heartbreak, and relationships in various forms and mystery thrillers filled with suspense, intrigue, and investigations.

When I thought that was enough I started looking at themes and topics and found four key areas... identity, friendship and belonging, as well as, social issues like racism, sexism, bullying, mental health and environmental issues and, finally, coming of age that address life transitions, making difficult choices and understanding personal growth.

When you're 'older' you wonder if you can even communicate with young people and so I thought I'd better look at someone my own age and researched educated women over the age of 50 and found my market. I learned there are some genres and themes that tend to resonate more strongly with them due to their life experiences and stage in life. With nothing but time on my hands I created an overview of some popular areas in books for women over 50 where the popular genres include historical fiction which allows readers to immerse themselves in different eras and explore lives throughout history.

After historical fiction, there's literary fiction which explores complex characters, relationships and social issues in a thought-provoking way. Then, mystery thrillers that provide suspense and keeps readers guessing, offering a thrilling escape from everyday life. Then there are memoir/biographies that offer insight into the lives of other women, providing inspiration and relatable experiences and, finally, romance novels that explore love, relationships and second chances, often with heartwarming and uplifting stories. Wow! And I thought this would be easy!

In one article I quickly read, it said "If you choose this demographic, once you decide what kind of book you want to write, you need to create themes and topic."

First choice should be books that examine interactions such as family dynamics, friendships, romantic relationships and navigating change within these connections. Another type is personal growth and reinvention concerning self-discovery, pursuing dreams and finding new purpose in life after major life transitions. Then there's social Issues that address real-world concerns like ageism, sexism, healthcare and financial security, while offering relatable experiences. Finally, there's humor and uplifting stories that are lighthearted and feel-good to provide a joyful escape and remind readers of the beauty and humor in life.

When you're living alone, residing in a tomb, where the only change to your day is the few minutes you can anonymously surf the web, you have time to make choices. In so doing, I realized I couldn't communicate with kids and so I'd better stick with people my own age. Then, I used myself as an example and concluded guys don't read books like women do. So, after a full day...anyway I think it was day...who knows when you have no light beyond the bulb above you...I chose educated women, over the age of fifty and decided to write a romance thriller about our adventures by creating a fictional couple who vacations in Saint Martin, fall in love with the island and want to escape from the commercialism of American society. Wow!

As I pondered the subject I realized the story could actually begin with Rodney and me and all that happened with Great Grandfather. Then I could write about meeting Amy and our relationship and how I totally screwed things up by trying to prove to the world I didn't marry her for her money. When I got through with that, I could include Francis and how I learned so much about animals and their humanity. Next, I thought I could include the 'V' and Melia and their struggles. In each instance I'd use Saint Martin to represent freedom and then reflect on the Forest as symbolic of purity and innocence. It was a start.

I began writing and called the first segment 'Little Spirit' because that was the name given me by Great Grandfather. Next, would be 'Driftless' in honor of our land and also, as a reference to having no direction in my life. Next would be 'the Hayflick Limit' as I discussed how Alzheimer's Disease had taken Amy's dad away. Finally, would be 'Let Go' that would tie all the pieces together.

Deep in thought and nowhere to go I used my ten minutes each day to do research and would spend countless hours taking what I learned and creating a story about it. As the days turned into weeks I was becoming a hermit who lived within himself not thinking of what was going on outside. As the book began taking shape my thoughts turned to the outside world and I began perusing all that was happening.

I was alone, all alone. I never thought the lack of social interaction and external stimulation would lead to anxiety and frustration as I tried to find ways to occupy my mind as I began resorting to repetitive thoughts or behaviors. If that wasn't bad enough, the absence of natural light and a disrupted sleep-wake cycle was causing insomnia and then excessive sleepiness as the hours blended into each other. The worst of all was my system becoming hypersensitive due to the lack of external stimuli, such that anything different, even minor noises began to startle me.

As I took my ten minutes to dig into the world around me, I learned that my three months in solitude had seen huge changes. First, it was reported we'd had an exceptionally warm spring that led to a series of tornados, one of which touched down near Mineral Point. With no reason to check outside I'd become oblivious to the security system. One morning I found myself wondering what was going on beyond my cloistered existence and turned on the radar only to find it inoperable. From this I went to the camera only to find it aimed directly at the sky. Needless to say I became concerned.

Instead of book research I went to the Wisconsin State Journal and learned that a Category Three tornado had touched down on February eighth in the small enclave called Waldwick, Wisconsin. My God! I began searching for details and learned that some people were killed and there was massive damage throughout the area. No names were given and my ten minutes were up. If I wanted to read more I'd need to wait until the next day and subscribe to the paper which was difficult to do and, needless to say, deliveries were out of the question.

A few days later I heard a clicking sounded at the cave entrance. I had no idea who or what it was. Could it be the Chinese? Could it be someone who came to rescue me? The sounds only lasted a few minutes and then the deafening silence of singularity returned. I retreated to my enclave and turned on the computer. As I turned the electronic pages I came to a news story with the headline "Nobel Peace Prize Winners Killed in Plane Crash" and then nearly fell off my chair when I learned that Peter, Luke, James and I were presumed dead when our private plane crashed in the Gulf of Mexico. Now, I was really concerned.

Isolation:

I hadn't heard from anyone in nearly four months. As my separation continued, feelings of loneliness and helplessness were beginning to deepen into depression and ineptness. The ten minutes weren't enough and each day as the timer neared its end, tears would form in my eyes. "Please, please don't leave me!" I was having difficulty concentrating, remembering things, and making decisions. Trying to determine which vegetable to eat was becoming a major challenge. I'd close my eyes and hallucinations began as my mind tried to create its own stimulation. Had our plan worked? Was SIMON safe? I had no idea! When one is all alone what starts as a small grain of sand can quickly become a mountain of madness where the question became, 'how do I find out what's going on?'

As I waited for any sign of security and the few minutes each day I could scan the internet but still not communicate with anyone, the level of loneliness set in that I felt was having a profound impact on my health both physically and mentally.

From a health perspective I began a daily exercise regimen consisting of sit-ups and push-ups and then walking. It was 160 steps from the door to the springs. I knew that each step resulted in approximately three feet traveled which meant that the 160 steps resulted in 480 feet and therefore each 'lap' 960 feet. Knowing that a mile was 5,280 feet, I initially began by walking six laps or a little over a mile.

As I progressed to 30 laps per day I was walking a little over five miles. As the laps increased I began running until I could do the 30 laps without stopping. As it became easier I realized I needed to begin timing myself using a software program on my laptop and allocated an hour each day running.

While the cave maintained a mean temperature of 55 degrees regardless of what the weather was outside, there was something about being all alone that began eating away at my sanity. With no one to talk to and no one to share thoughts and emotions with I began to feel like the living dead, alone, isolated and singular to the point I began talking to myself.

Those first few weeks were filled with confidence my confinement was a temporary situation. Each day I assumed would be my last within the cave. However, the uncertainty about rescue and dangers of the environment did lead to my constant anxiety.

At first my goal was to stay active and then boredom began to sap my intrinsic motivation and made it difficult to find joy in activities that led to procrastination and difficulty completing even the simplest of tasks, thereby, creating a general sense of stagnation.

My greatest fear was going crazy and so each day I would test myself to ensure there was cognitive flexibility. To do so I would focus on one subject to maintain my attention span while using my writing to maintain my creativity. When time is not the issue and alternatives non-existent one can focus so much deeper and so my novel began to take shape that allowed me to focus on individual sentences and then specific words to ensure there weren't redundancies.

From a mental aspect being ensconced in a cave in complete isolation can have significant perceptual and emotional consequences where my primal fears that were hidden for so long began to slowly make their way into my psyche. I knew these were basically my brain's way of keeping me safe from dangers that threatened my survival. My greatest fear was that the batteries or solar panels would fail, not only leaving me in the dark but making me vulnerable to predators, thereby, heightening my total aversion to snakes, spiders and other creatures.

Everything remained a constant...light, temperature, sound. I was encased in a world of sensory deprivation which began to distort my perception and growing paranoia to the point of psychosis. I was losing touch with reality. On good days I'd be Ok. I'd justify everything simply by knowing I was safe and Langdon would be coming for me. On bad days I would shake in frustration and emotional distress with outbursts of anger or tearfulness as I screamed for help and then begged for someone, anyone, to contact me, only to crumble in a pile of remorse as I struggled with a sense of self and purpose. Was this God's way of getting even? I don't know! I don't know! I don't know!

At the fifth month I began to believe I was simply forgotten, punctuated by that day I heard clicking sounds outside the vault door. With joy I'd assumed it meant freedom was on its way. When the sound stopped and the door didn't open, I simply cried. The hope I had was gone! In its place was the pervading realization I'd lost control and was helpless, unable to influence the situation or escape.

I couldn't call them days as I no longer could delineate the concept and so I began calling them cycles where one cycle consisted of a period of sleep, exercise, writing and maintaining what level of personal hygiene I could, then eating and my ten minutes of internet time before the computer would automatically shut down for yet another twenty-three hour and fifty minutes of isolation.

As much as I tried not to, I had disrupted sleep patterns as my circadian rhythm went amuck leading to fatigue, confusion and mood swings as I began to find myself with difficulty concentrating as well as memory problems and decreased cognitive function as my hands began to tremble.

To say I was on an emotional rollercoaster would be an understatement as feelings of despair, anger and frustration became common, with unforeseen moments of hope and resilience that kept me going as my isolation amplified my negative emotions and depression interspersed with hallucinations and sensory deprivation. We all complain about the weather. However, when your environment is a constant it, too, can drive you crazy, which I feared was happening to me.

When you're all alone, with no outside stimulus, bouts with both depression and anxiety began setting in feeding into a vicious cycle where my isolation worsened mental health that was leading to further isolation. Imagine every day exactly as the one before. No challenge! No interaction! Simply profound chronic boredom leading to feelings of helplessness, apathy and lack of purpose.

My ten-minute internet sessions might have been a quick respite from the thought of death but I began to see it was impairing my memory, concentration and decision-making abilities. When and how should I try to escape from the cave? If I did, would I meet with instant death and finally did that really matter?

After another four weeks I'd had enough. You can only live alone for so long. My six-month food supplies were getting low and I needed some sanity. I waited another week without word and, finally, made the decision it was better to be dead-dead than alive-dead, entombed in a dark, dank, solitary dungeon. I made my way to the front of the cave, took a deep breath and attempted to open the vault door. It would not move!

Oh, my God! I was really trapped. Now what? Within seconds the walls began closing in around me. I knew I had ten minutes and only ten minutes per day to try and find someone, anyone, who could rescue me. The next morning I threw caution to the wind and attempted sending an email to Melia that got kicked back. I'd forgotten, I didn't have email capability. My ten minutes were up! I needed to wait another day. Again, I tried the vault door. Again, no luck!

Jesus! What had happened? Would this be my demise? In five months I'd forgotten so many web addresses. To save my precious ten minutes, I began writing down what I thought were addresses and then taking my ten minutes to communicate. Each day saw no response.

It was now a month later and I was down to the last bit of food. I was frantic as I began putting pieces together regarding who I could contact and who could come and free me. As I started to communicate I realized there was no way for me to receive messages as Peter had programmed the computer so that it was electronically invisible to those receiving the messages to the point they would probably think it was just spam.

One ten-minute morning I decided to read Mineral Point's Democrat Tribune and, to my joy, there was an article about Tank Kennison and his pending retirement. The next morning I invested my ten minutes in scanning his name and came across his website with web address. I hoped and prayed it was still in effect even though the photo of him had to be twenty years old.

Now, down to subsisting on wine, I allotted my ten minutes to writing Tank. Here's what I wrote.

'Tank, it's George Terrill, the article about the plane crash wasn't true. I'm alive but trapped in one of the limestone caves my brother Tommie and I used to store our wine. HELP!'

The next day, I went online and there was no response and so I wrote. *'Tank, it's George again. This is legit! I'm trapped in the cave. My computer won't accept messages and so I don't know if you're getting this or not.'*

Still nothing and I was getting nervous and so on the third day I wrote. 'Tank, you and I were working on seeing if the farm should have been frozen. PLEASE RESCUE ME.'

After five more days, I simply gave up on Tank and then, for some reason, I thought of Megan. Megan! Why hadn't I thought of her before? I knew her corporate web address was E=MC^2 and realized it stood for Elli, Megan and Charlie, while the square stood for the fact they felt they were interchangeable which created, in their minds, a greater and more powerful relationship and I began again by going to Megan's clinic website.

'Megan, it's George Terrill, the article about the plane crash wasn't true. I'm alive but trapped in the western-most limestone cave my brother Tommie and I use to store our wine. HELP!'

The next day, I went online and there was no response and so I wrote. *Megan, it's George again. This is legit! I'm trapped in the cave. My computer won't accept messages and so I don't know if you're getting this or not.'*

Still nothing and I was getting nervous and so on the third day I wrote. *'Megan, you have two statues next to your pool and one of them is YOU. PLEASE RESCUE ME.'*

With that cycle I sincerely thought of ending it all. I didn't want to starve to death. After the next series I went to the entrance and tried the door again. It still wouldn't open! As I was about to leave I began hearing a high-pitched whine. Could it be someone was out there? Would it be rescuers or the Chinese? I had no way of knowing as I put my hand to the metal door and felt the vibrations.

As I was standing there, the lights went out. The batteries were dead. Now I was ensconced in total darkness as well as complete silence. My God, what happened? I felt the door only to learn the vibrations had stopped. Had they given up? Was it my imagination? My mind went to SIMON and Garfunkel's 'Hello Darkness My Old Friend.'

I took my right hand and used it to count the wine barrels as I made my way back to the computer. I opened the laptop and the dim glow allowed me to get my bearings. I quickly folded the laptop to save the battery and waited until what I thought was the next day when I wrote to Megan.

'I hope it was you yesterday drilling in the door. I could feel your vibrations. Please help, all the electricity went out and I'm in total darkness. HELP!'

I made my way back to the door and put my hands on the steel. Once again I felt vibrations and there was hope. I stood and felt the sensations until they stopped. Oh, my God! What's going on?

I made my way back to the computer and my solitude. By my estimation, I had been alone for over six months, isolated, unable to deal with anything, wondering what had happened and if we were successful.

The next morning, I went on line again and wrote. *'I could feel your pulsations and you gave me hope. Thank you.'*

I made my way back to the doors and pressed my hands on the cold steel.

Nothing!

Had it been my imagination? Had they given up! Don't let me die this way! As I was about to turn back I heard a small thud and saw a beam of light protruding from the ceiling. My God, someone was there. I was going to be saved or killed. At this point in time it no longer mattered.

A wisp of fresh air filled my nostrils as I could see the outline of the casks along the wall. As I looked up I saw a thin line being dropped on which there was a small camera that circled until it was pointed at me. I excitedly waived as the camera was raised out of the hole.

I stood there in darkness until I saw a small beam of freedom being lowered. It was a flashlight and a note that read.

'George, we're having trouble drilling through door. We're going to need to make the hole larger and pull you out this way. We're concerned about falling rock and a potential cave-in. Please move back. If you have read this and understand, pull twice on the line.'

I did as instructed and moved back as I heard the sound of equipment boring a hole in the ceiling. One would think that being sequestered for as long as I was would result in some degree of patience. I just wanted to get out of there but also realized they needed to take it slow to minimize the risk of the ceiling caving in.

For the next eight hours I heard the drill and saw the pile of rocks grow on the cave floor. I didn't care. God, I wanted to get out of there. As the large drill bit finally broke through I knew I was about to face my destiny. Would it be the good guys or the bad guys?

The hole in the ceiling was probably three-feet in diameter as the drill bit receded. Soon I saw a beam of light and then an object, make that a man, repelling into my darkness.

"Mr. Terrill?"

"Yes."

"Mr. Terrill, I'm Lieutenant Doss from the Navy Seals and I've come to help get you out of here."

"Thank you, Lieutenant."

"How long have you been trapped in here sir?"

"I've been here since December 11th, when is it now?"

"May 17th, sir."

May 17th, I thought. What a coincidence. That's the day I first met Rodney.

"We're going to put this vest on you sir and have you go up through the ceiling, if that's Ok."

"It's fine with me."

"We're going to take it very slow, so don't worry, Ok?"

"Understood. Can I bring my computer with me?"

"Laptop?"

"Yes."

"Ok."

I quickly retrieved the laptop and my writing. It had been my only companion and I simply could not leave it.

Surprise:

Lieutenant Doss put the vest on me and hooked it to the cable as I slowly made my way up the hole and into the bright sunlight. After six months of darkness I was simply overwhelmed and so they put a dark shroud over my head and led me to a waiting emergency helicopter, put me on a stretcher and we took off.

"Where are we going?" I hollered.

No response.

I wanted to take off the cover but was strapped to the stretcher and still didn't know if these were the good guys or bad guys.

"Sir, we're going to give you some fluids," someone said.

As I lay there, I felt a needle enter my arm as my eyes closed and I fell into a deep sleep. When I awakened I was startled by my new environment. As my mind cleared, I thought for sure I'd be in a hospital. Instead, I was in some type of room with no windows and only an old wooden chair, the bed, my IV's and me.

I looked at my new environment of pale green walls and a floor that consisted of institution gray tiles with speckled flecks in them that were probably from the fifties. The only light was one of those glass domes mounted flush with the ceiling that had a layer of film in it that subdued the single bulb's minimal intensity making the decor of the cave seem like a suite at the Hilton.

As I glanced around the room, the only aberration was in the far corner where the walls met the ceiling that contained a black triangle with a smoked lens which I could easily recognize as some sort of camera staring down at me.

I attempted to sit up but was still strapped to the bed. However, when I struggled I heard the door unlock as a guard came in. Muscular and wearing black pants and matching tee-shirt, with no expression in his face, I had no idea who or what he was as he said, "Sir, please take it easy. We need you to get you stabilized."

"Where am I?" I asked as my eyes blinked repeatedly while they adjusted to the dim light as reality began to set in, making me somewhat concerned, somewhat irritated and totally confused.

With no response from the guard, I looked at him noting, "I need to pee."

The guard unlatched the straps on the bed and I slowly sat up and felt the world begin to spin. I was light-headed where my rocking motion was such the guard offered to assist me and I was grateful he did.

We made it to the bathroom. I thanked him and closed the door. I sat there for a while and got my bearings as my mind cleared. I examined my environment and realized it was done in what I would call an 'early penal motif' with a stainless-steel toilet bolted to the floor, as well as, a stainless-steel sink with a polished stainless-steel plate that served as a mirror tightly affixed to the wall.

I looked in the mirror and saw a skinny old man in some sort of pajamas staring back at me with six-inch-long hair that was a pasty-white, mangled mess that matched the color of my skin all accentuated by a scraggly beard that hadn't been shaved in over six months. My eyes were bloodshot and the effects of not brushing my teeth had turned them a pale brown that made me seem like a Charles Manson lookalike.

As I stood pondering the mess in the mirror I heard someone enter the room and came out of the bathroom to find a gentleman in a white coat waiting for me. "Hello, George, I'm Doctor Roberts. How are you feeling?"

"Physically, I'm fine. Just confused. Where am I?"

"You're in the hospital."

"Why?"

"You don't know why?"

"If I did I wouldn't have asked."

Dr. Roberts looked at me and I could tell he was pondering what to say. Finally, he asked, "What were you doing in that cave?"

"Hiding."

"From, what?"

"The Chinese."

There was a smirk on his face as if he didn't believe me which royally pissed me off and so I continued. "My name is George Terrill the Fourth, founder of the Derrick Williams Foundation that did medical research. When my wife Amy and I retired, we allowed our son Derrick to assume control of Wilco, which was our family company. Derrick, in his profound stupidity, wasn't satisfied with being wealthy, he wanted to be rich and to do so, made some really reckless gaffes, one of which was selling the data and operating protocol for our computer we named SIMON to the Chinese."

I looked at Dr. Roberts and continued. "When our government found out about it, they thought my wife and I were involved and froze our assets and began an investigation into our involvement headed up by Agent David Langdon. When the bad guys found out, they felt I was one of a few people who could assist them in acquiring the medical data on over a billion people and the operating protocol necessary to control our nation's power grid, dams and financial structure."

"And?"

"And they were wrong. Yet, they came after me. To hide from the bad guys and give my people time to adjust SIMON and make him secure from their efforts, I went to one of our winery caves where I hid until you rescued me."

"So, you over spent six months in that cave?"

"Yes."

"Alone?"

"Yes."

"And no contact with the outside world?"

"Correct. I was given a computer that couldn't be traced and I had no access to email. In addition the computer was programmed for access to the internet for ten minutes every 24 hours to protect me and feign detection."

"And yet, in the end, you contacted a Mary Egan in Atlanta who notified the FBI?"

"I was out of food and the door wouldn't open. In addition the radar system no longer worked and the outdoor camera was facing the sky. What should I have done?"

"Well, that's quite a story."

"I don't know if it's a story but it's the truth and now I need to know what in hell is going on."

Dr. Roberts looked at me and then at the floor before reciting precisely what I'd said and then asking, "Who was Amelia^X?"

"Amelia^X was my Stryker airplane. Why?"

"Why would Peter Washburn, Lucas Arnold and James Johnson be on it?"

"I don't know the date but they were planning on using our home in Saint Martin as a safe house as they planned the method of re-configuring the software so SIMON became unusable beyond the basic data we'd programmed and, therefore, not much good to the Chinese."

"Do you know when they were going to Saint Martin?"

"I assume it was either Mid-January or Super Bowl Sunday."

"Why Super Bowl Sunday?"

"Because that was the day SIMON was going to automatically be reprogrammed to save our country and the world from potential disaster."

"Do you know what happened?"

"No."

"You're not aware that the plane crashed in the Gulf of Mexico?"

"That much I figured out when I read about my own demise."

"Why didn't you try and get out?"

"For a while I waited for Agent Langdon. When he didn't show up, I tried but the mechanism didn't work."

"So what did you do?"

"I kept trying but didn't have any tools to see if I could unlock the door manually."

There was a pause and then Dr. Roberts asked. "What can you tell me about your Stryker's avionics?"

"It had a fully functional autopilot system."

"To the point it could take off and land itself," as a smile crossed Robert's face as he added. "In other words, Amelia^X could literally take off and fly to Saint Martin with no one on board?"

"Yes."

"And it was reported that four men, including yourself, were onboard and perished when the plane went down?"

"I guess so."

"It was also rumored on social media the plane had been blown out of the sky by a missile of some sort?"

I shook my head, shrugged my shoulders and noted. "I didn't read that part. I couldn't subscribe to the Wisconsin State Journal from inside the cave. Cave delivery would have been a little challenging and I didn't have a credit card so I couldn't get the electronic edition."

Doctor Roberts didn't smile as he continued. "Well, that's what was reported. Amelia^X took off from Milwaukee Mitchel Field and, somewhere over the Gulf of Mexico, blew up with all the passengers on board killed."

"You mean Peter, Luke and James all died? I asked.

"I'm saying that's what was reported."

I was starting to get the gist of what Dr. Robert's was saying.

Just then, what looked like an orderly pushed a cart into the room with what appeared to be one of our security systems on it connected to a small battery pack.

"Do you know what this is?" Dr. Roberts inquired.

"It looks like one of our security modules," I offered.

"Mr. Terrill, we need to make certain you're who we think you are. Would you mind going through your security protocol?"

Now I was concerned. What if these were the bad guys? I'd be giving them access to SIMON and so I asked, "Why?"

"We need to certify you're who you say you are."

"Where'd you get the module?"

"From one of your caves." Dr. Roberts noted.

"If I refuse, then what?"

"Then, sir, we'll believe you're an agent and not who you say you are."

I quickly weighed my options. Take the risk and be freed or refuse and who knows what. I leaned over the panel, opened the Lucite door, peered into the glass as it took both a retinal and facial scan and then used the index finger on my left hand to hear the 'click' sound as if the door was opened.

"Is this from my cave?" I asked, knowing I'd tried from the inside and failed.

"No, yours didn't work." Dr. Roberts replied.

"What happened to it?" I asked wondering why I'd failed.

"After you were rescued, our team examined it and quickly saw that someone had used a laser pointer on the sensor and literally fried the lens."

"You mean someone wanted me to be trapped in the cave?"

"It appears so."

My memory focused on the bad guys. It had to be them! I figured they'd followed my tracks and when they realized they couldn't get the door open, thought the next best thing was to burn the sensor so the lock wouldn't work and let me die a slow and painful death.

My mind quickly returned to the identity conversation as a sigh of relief was expelled on both sides and then another pause as Dr. Roberts looked at me and in a completely different tone of voice exclaimed. "You know, Mr. Terrill, the Nobel Peace Prize you received is one of the highest honors a person can get and to be called a Nobel Laureate is an incredible honor. However, beyond that, service to one's country and the safety of the world seems to palc the nobility bestowed. Because of your actions and those of the three gentlemen, we can all sleep tonight."

I looked at Dr. Roberts and replied. "I dedicated my life to the good of man. When our son did what he did, I only had one objective and that was to stop him from destroying what we built. There are good people throughout the world, including China, who only want one thing and that's peace and the security of knowing they have an opportunity to make the world a better place for their children."

Dr. Roberts nodded and smiled and then asked, "How are you feeling?"

"Fine," I replied.

"Physically?"

"Yes."

"Mentally?"

I looked at the floor and then at Dr. Roberts and then the floor again before the tears began to flow.

"Are you having flashbacks?"

I looked at Dr. Roberts as if he was the nut case and simply asked, "What do you think? You get locked in a cave for six months? You learn people you care for are dead? You believe people want to kill you?

I paused, looked at Dr. Roberts and inquired, "Where am I?"

"You're in the hospital," Dr. Roberts replied.

"Hospital? It's more like a prison to me." I countered with a tone of resentment as I continued, "What hospital room has no windows and all the bathroom fixtures are like those in a prison cell? And why in hell was I strapped to the bed?"

Dr. Roberts looked at me, took a deep breath and offered. "Six months of total sensory deprivation is a very challenging experience, and the reintegration process is crucial. Right now you're on what we call the edge where you could end up either assimilating back to where you were or, in the worst-case scenario go insane. My goal is assimilation unless, of course, you prefer to be institutionalized the rest of your life."

My resentment level dropped appreciably. I was beginning to realize that sensory deprivation has more to it than light and sound as Dr. Roberts continued. "All your vitals are fine. Physically the doctor who examined you was impressed by how good your body is functioning. However, we also know that to bring you immediately back in terms of light and sound could be catastrophic and so we need to take it in increments. If you will work with me I believe we can get you back both physically and mentally to where you were or at least functional."

Functional? Functional? What in hell did that mean? I thought to myself.

Dr. Roberts looked at me and noted, here is what we have planned. "First, is a complete medical evaluation. The one given on your arrival was cursory and I've ordered a thorough medical check-up to assess any physical effects of the deprivation. This will include muscle weakness, skin breakdown and malnutrition. Based on my observation I think you're physically doing fine, but we need to make sure."

"The second step is a gradual reintroduction of your senses. The reason you're in a darkened room with no window and little noise is simply the starting point. The reintroduction of light, sound, touch, taste and smell needs to be done slowly and carefully. Too much stimulation too quickly can be overwhelming. I can already see that you're the impatient type and will probably be frustrated but, trust me, we've dealt with prisoners of war who were kept in solitary confinement and have an understanding of the right steps and the right timing to allow your body to readjust to the world in which we live."

"The third step is where I come in. My goal is to provide psychological support. In cases like yours the lack of social interaction has a high probability of being psychologically disturbing. I call it the abyss which I use figuratively to describe anything that seems endless, profound or difficult to understand. Our first goal is to bring you slowly out of the abyss. I know you're going to be impatient. However, without taking it slowly the transformation can lead to hallucinations, disorientation, feelings of isolation, depression and anxiety."

I nodded in the affirmative and realized Dr. Roberts was right. The biggest problem I was having was wanting it all right away. When it's you you're thinking about you're biased.

Dr. Roberts looked at me as if to evaluate whether he'd said enough for the day. I guess he thought I could handle more as he continued. "George, you went through six months of not only physical and psychological isolation but a complete lack of social interaction. Humans are social creatures who thrive on interaction with others. Without this interaction people can experience loneliness, which can lead to anxiety. During your recovery period we're going to be working with you on regaining several of the attributes you had that made you such a great man. Our goal is to bring you back socially. It's not going to be easy and, if you don't work with us, it could mean a totally different set of results than either of us is striving for."

I looked at the gray tile speckled squares and accepted he was right and so I nodded in the affirmative.

Dr. Roberts gathered the bows of his glasses and put them in his vest pocket, leaned back on the wooden chair and continued. "When you're all alone with no one to talk to but yourself and no one to interact with, your social skills declined. The old saying 'practice makes perfect' is applicable and social skills, like any other, need practice to stay sharp. Without social interaction a person's ability to communicate effectively, read social cues, and navigate social situations declines."

"In reading your Nobel biography I found a man who was quite social and profoundly dynamic. I saw a man who was a true leader who showed all the characteristics of greatness. Your commitment to the betterment of the world has had significant and enduring impact on the wellbeing of others."

"You and your team pushed boundaries and achieved the extraordinary, make that significant breakthroughs in the field of medicine. Beyond that, I've read about your and values and strong moral principles you've shown as you acted with integrity while inspiring others through your honesty, equity and compassion. I know that, had you so chosen, you could have simply lived the life of luxury. However, great people like you dedicate their lives to something bigger than themselves and work for the betterment of humanity and future generations."

"To say I'm impressed by what and how you've accomplished what you did would be an understatement. But the thing that I'm most impressed by is your resilience and perseverance. The path to greatness is rarely easy. Great people overcome obstacles, setbacks and failures with determination and keep striving for their goals and this is what you did."

I was humbled and looked again at the speckled floor, took another deep breath and returned my gaze to Dr. Roberts.

"George, you've been through a terrifying experience. For men of lesser character and determination it probably would have led to insanity. Instead, I believe we can work to bring you back to where you were but you need to realize there are some scars that are so deep it might take a long time and there's no promise you'll make it all the way back."

I nodded in the affirmative and was beginning to realize that, while my body was whole, my mind was injured.

Dr. Roberts looked at me and then at the floor and then at me again, leaned forward and noted. "First, you're going to have difficulty trusting others. Being completely alone for so long can make it difficult to trust and connect with others again and you may feel anxious or paranoid in social settings."

"Ok."

"Next, is your loss of identity. Your social interactions played a big role in shaping your self-identity. Without this feedback loop you may struggle with who you are and how you fit into the world. After such a long period of isolation even normal social interaction can feel overwhelming due to the increased sensory stimulation."

I nodded and stared at the speckled tile again as Dr. Roberts continued. "Here's what we want to implement. First is a structured routine. We're going to create a predictable daily routine with regular sleep patterns and meal times to allow you to regain a sense of control and normalcy. You're in good physical shape for what you endured and, yet, we're also going to implement a program of physical therapy to sustain muscle strength and coordination. Finally, as you progress, we would like to implement a program of social support."

"Right now I sense a profound level of introversion and feel that we need to take this in small steps. I believe this will be the most difficult challenge and yet we'll work on it until we both agree you're ready to be on your own. The last thing we want is to rush it and have you overwhelmed to the point you can no longer function."

Dr. Roberts leaned back in his chair and noted. "It's not going to be easy, George. You're going to try and push it. The best analogy I can provide is that you consider it like the broken leg you had when you had your car accident. At first you can't walk and then as you heal you get to the point of crutches, then a walking boot and, finally, a cane. If you tried to rush it you would break your leg again and that would be tragic."

"How long?"

"We don't know. We'll set goals and see when you cross the finish line for each aspect."

"Any idea?"

"Nope! Each person is different. What you've got going for you is you're in good physical health and so the first goal is already met."

Dr. Roberts paused and inquired, "What can I do for you today?"

"Let me take a shower."

"How about tomorrow?"

"Can I, at least, get a toothbrush and toothpaste today?

"That we can do. Then I want you to eat and get some rest."

"What's for whatever meal it is?"

"What do you want?"

"Anything but beef, carrots, green beans, peas or broccoli."

"How about breakfast?"

"Sounds good."

"No bacon, correct?" This brought back memories of Francis, our research pig.

I smiled as Dr. Roberts stood, shook my hand, looked in my eyes and pronounced. "It's my honor to meet you, Little Spirit."

My mouth dropped open. I hadn't heard those two words in so long and they went straight to my heart.

The Routine:

When you're in a room with no window and no clock you have no idea what time it is. When I awakened and after using the bathroom, I came back to bed and realized the ceiling light was a little brighter. Perhaps it was my imagination but I didn't think so.

A few minutes later Dr. Roberts appeared and inquired how I slept to which I simply shrugged and nodded in the affirmative.

"Today you get your shower which means we need to take you to a different room."

Again, I nodded.

I stood and Dr. Roberts went to the door and knocked three times. A moment later I heard the 'click' as we waited for an extended period and then the doctor opened the door to a totally empty and darkened hallway. I looked to my left and then my right and all was quiet and devoid of any other people. We turned to the left and walked about fifteen feet where Dr. Roberts opened the door. Inside was literally a shower room with tile walls and a tile floor that looked like something straight out of the fifties. I looked at the small chair and saw two towels, clean pajamas and cloth slippers.

Dr. Roberts nodded towards a switch on the wall and noted. "When you're done, flip the switch and I'll come and get you."

I nodded and proceeded to take my first shower in nearly seven months. It felt great except the water temperature could have been a little warmer. Later I learned it was controlled to ensure no one could intentionally scald themselves. It was then I realized I was truly in a nut house.

After the shower, we went back to my room as Dr. Roberts inquired about my childhood on the farm asking questions about my favorite things, my least favorite and my most memorable experiences. There was no time element just polite reflections.

The next day meant the same routine in terms of the empty hallway and shower. The only difference was the ceiling light in my room was a little brighter as was the hallway.

Instead of my childhood we talked about college and my roommates which brought up rock-paper-scissors.

Day three resulted in exactly the same routine and even a little brighter lights. Today's conversation was about Rodney and Ann and how I met Amy.

Day four was the same except the conversation revolved around the kids, the Duke and Grandma Marie.

Day five repeated everything except our conversation moved to the Foundation and what it was like to win a Nobel Peace Prize.

Day Six continued the routine until we got to losing everything and then about Agent Langdon and being chased. Dr. Roberts inquired if I wanted to talk about the cave and I told him, "no."

It had been a week of just Dr. Roberts and me. On day seven the doctor showed up in jeans and no white coat and asked if I'd like to go outside. I shook my head 'no' and so the subject was dropped. Instead when we arose to go to go out in the hallway and to the shower room, there was no knock on the door and when Dr. Roberts opened it, there was the guy in a black tee-shirt and pants standing there who'd come into my room on day one and it scared me.

I went and took my shower and went back to my room. While I was gone they had added a night stand and it had a small digital clock on it with soft blue numbers. I looked at Dr. Roberts and he could see the fear in my eyes.

"You'll be fine, George. You'll be fine."

The door closed and I heard the 'click'. I watched the numbers on the clock move from 11:13 to 11:14. I didn't know if it was AM or PM. A few minutes later there was a soft knock and another guy in the black outfit brought a tray with what appeared to be my lunch on it. I looked down and saw a peanut butter and jelly sandwich, bag of Fritos, apple and bottle of water. I cringed as the memories of the orange apron flooded my mind.

I sat and stared at the sandwich for the longest period of time and then tried to touch it but couldn't. There were simply too many memories flooding my mind.

The following morning there was a soft knock and I offered, "Come in." Instead of Dr. Roberts it was the man in black who offered. "Good morning George, my name is Clarence and today I'll be escorting you for your shower."

"Where's Dr. Roberts?" I asked, in a concerned tone of voice.

"It's his day off."

I took my shower and went back to my room. On the table was a small radio. I turned it on and attempted to find a news station. The radio was limited to only music. It was better than nothing and so I laid on the bed and listened and it did me good.

The following morning there was a knock and it was Dr. Roberts.

"Thanks for the radio," I offered.

"No problem," was the reply. "Let's talk and then Clarence will escort you to the shower."

"Ok."

"I want to know about the cave," Dr. Roberts revealed.

My hands shook as I asked. "What do you want to know?"

"What was it like?" Who designed it? Why was it so hard to get in?"

I went through the entire story I'd shared with Agent Langdon and why the security.

"How about food?"

I detailed the beef and the vegetables, the milk and the cereal and then the wine.

"Good stuff?" Dr. Roberts inquired.

"The best" I said as, for the first time I spoke with pride.

"Tell me about Mary Egan."

A slight smile percolated my heart. It had been a very long time as my mind went back to better times. "Megan was my physical therapist after my cancer surgery in Milwaukee. She moved to Atlanta and heads up a urological clinic."

"Why did you keep in touch with her?"

"She wanted to develop a program for the spouses of men going through prostate cancer treatment so they had a better understanding of what all would transpire."

"How were you involved?"

"I was the bridge between the clinic and the spouse. I was the personification of a positive end result."

"And how did you feel about doing that?"

"At first I was embarrassed and then I realized it was a clinical setting and my objective was to help ladies better understand what the consequences and challenges were when you have prostate cancer."

"In other words, you felt proud of what you did?"

"I don't know if 'proud' is the right word. It was sort of a balancing act between trepidation and satisfaction. To me pride is a sense of satisfaction, confidence and contentment about yourself or your achievements. It's about feeling good about who you are and what you've done. During the sessions I never felt proud but more like a piece of meat in the butcher shop. After the sessions, when the reviews came back and were all positive, it was then I began to feel proud of what I'd done."

"What was your relationship with Ms. Egan?"

"She's my friend."

"An intimate friend?"

"Define intimate," I said, somewhat offended by the question.

"Sorry, I didn't mean from a physical sense."

"Then define intimate for me."

Dr. Roberts paused to gather the right words and then replied. "In friendship, intimacy describes a deep and close connection that goes beyond casual friendship. It's about feeling safe and comfortable sharing your true self with someone. Intimate friendships are those that provide a sense of belonging, support and understanding that enrich our lives and make us feel safe and accepted for who we truly are."

I nodded in the affirmative thinking of the night at Megan's house when we shared so much as Dr. Roberts continued, "When you have an intimate friend you can feel comfortable sharing your thoughts, feelings and experiences, even the ones that are difficult or embarrassing to express and there's a sense of emotional safety that allows you to be truly open and vulnerable. Intimate friendships involve a strong sense of trust and mutual understanding simply because you know your friend will listen without judgment and offer support. In other words, they 'get' you on a deeper level. With this definition, do you have any intimate friends?"

"In other words, what your spouse should be?" I asked.

Dr. Roberts nodded, smiled and then asked, "Any others?"

"Yes, Rodney Whitehorse. We call each other brothers with different mothers and I'd give my life to save his."

"What about Ms. Egan?"

"We began building our friendship simply because we had the entire cancer thing in common and were attuned to each other's emotions, while offering empathy and compassion during difficult times."

"What difficult times?"

"You ever have cancer?"

"No."

"Then you don't know."

"Are you in love with Ms. Egan?"

"Yes, but in a plutonic way."

"You mean without anything physical?"

"Yes, Megan and I had a deep emotional connection without the sexual aspect."

"Would you want more?"

"I'm married and have an emotional and moral covenant with Amy, my wife."

"What about in the North short-term parking area at Hartsfield Airport?"

Holy shit. Then I replied. "It was one time and I felt incredibly guilty about it, ok?"

"Do you have any other friends?"

"I think so but really don't know. To me friends are people you connect with and have a mutual bond. They're the people in your life who you share experiences with, rely on for support, and enjoy spending time with. When you retire, your primary bond is broken and so all you have left are your good friends who understand and accept you for who you are, even your flaws and quirks who don't try to change you but support you in being your best self."

"And you have good friends?"

"One for sure and that's Rodney."

"Enough for today?"

"Enough!"

"Ready to go outside?"

"Perhaps tomorrow. I want to listen to the radio."

"Ok."

Revelation:

It was the next morning. I'd had my shower and was listening to the radio when Dr. Roberts arrived. Instead of pulling up a chair he looked at me and inquired. "Are you up for a walk?"

I thought for a moment and realized I needed to expand my horizons if I was ever going to get better and replied. "Sure! Until the power went out, I had a daily exercise regimen I maintained in the cave. Do you think I could have some other slippers though? My feet are cold."

Dr. Roberts called the guard and within a couple of minutes I had a pair of white socks and brown Crocs that I put on my bare feet.

Dr. Roberts indicated I should follow him and, so, I arose from my bed as we made our way out the door and down the hall. Everywhere I looked there were more guards in black pants and black tee-shirts. As we made our way to a large room Dr. Roberts opened the door and there were weak smiles all around. Standing at a pool table were Peter, Luke and James. I smiled again. They did not.

All of a sudden I began to feel as if I'd been set up and felt that we weren't in a hospital. God only knows where we were. I walked over to the trio and nodded only to see forced smiles and then a nod as if to tell me we were in deep shit. We really couldn't talk simply because there were guards everywhere and I was certain the room was bugged.

I nodded at the three men and wondered what happened. I thought of our time in front of the Congressional Committee and how the Committee accused me of having a narcissistic personality disorder where I had an inflated sense of self-importance and a strong need for admiration and control. It was just a coincidence that the eleven Mad City Boys were named Peter, James, John, Andrew,

Bartholomew, James, Thaddeus, Mathew, Philip, SIMON and Thomas.

"Hi guys!" I offered.

The trio smiled careful smiles accompanied by a cautious nod.

"After the newspaper article I certainly didn't think I'd be seeing you."

"Nor us you," James replied.

I looked at the trio, nodded at the pool table, and asked, "can we play doubles?" hoping a closer interaction would allow us to have a somewhat quiet conversation.

Peter racked the balls and I took the first shot making the nine ball in the far corner and then missed the twelve ball in the side pocket.

Luke was next and as he was lining up his shot I whispered to James, "What in hell is going on?"

"Not now," James responded, nodding towards the guard and having me focus on the ceiling where there was a security camera facing us.

A few minutes later Dr. Roberts returned and indicated it was time for us to go outside. I hadn't been there in over six months and relished the thought. The four of us made our way into what looked like an enclosed courtyard with buildings on all four sides. As we walked I turned to Luke and asked, "What in hell is going on?"

"George, you're the missing piece of the puzzle. Peter was able to infiltrate the Foundation and re-program SIMON by re-working the clock to subconsciously move back in time as you guys planned. Then the tornado hit and the entire Foundation structure was destroyed."

"All of it? What about SIMON?"

"The government put what looks like a locked manhole over the stairway to his labyrinth and they began shutting him all the way down."

"Do they know what they're doing?" I asked.

"As you know, Peter re-programmed SIMON to go to sleep unless two of the three of us shows up and goes through the initial security protocol. He did that to protect us. Without us they've got a computer that won't open, information that's frozen and no idea if SIMON will ever come back to life.

"What happened to the Chinese?"

"They split. They knew things were getting too hot and I believe they simply got out of the mess."

"Why are we here?"

"The government still hasn't decided if we're good guys or bad guys."

"What?" I asked incredulously.

Luke chimed in. "George, you've got to realize what Peter did really screwed the pooch. All the data and programs SIMON was developing the CIA already knew about and they were going to have it as a back-up to their own weaponry."

"Jesus! You mean, the bad guys weren't just the Chinese?"

"They were, but our government also knew what was going on and was allowing it to continue."

I shook my head, looked at the four walls and asked, where are we?"

"Nevada."

"Nevada? Why Nevada?"

"Peter believes we're at Area 51"

"What in hell is Area 51?"

Luke lowered his voice to just above a whisper and added. "Area 51 is a highly secure location for developing and testing advanced military technology. The secrecy surrounding it has also made it a hotbed for conspiracy theories regarding aliens."

"Well, the alien part might be right."

"What about Langdon? Couldn't he clear this up?"

"George, the day you, Peter and I met in the Forest Langdon walked back to the Impala, got in and headed for Madison. When he got out on Rock Branch road, the car blew up."

"What?"

"Someone bombed it thinking they'd kill you, too. The farm security camera caught a glimpse of the back of the head of someone in the passenger seat and everyone thought it was you which is why we never checked the cave."

"What about DNA?"

"There wasn't anything to test."

"Nothing to test? No DNA?"

Luke looked at me and noted. "George, whomever did it used military grade explosives."

"What do you mean military grade?"

Luke continued. "A phosphorous based compound that burns so hot it melts steel and everything else. It was instant death for those inside and also complete cremation. When the Mineral Point fire department got to the car the flames were too hot to put out and they weren't prepared for a chemical fire."

"You think this was intentional?" I asked.

Peter looked at me and replied. "Hell, yes, whomever it was wanted you dead and was willing to kill Langdon to make it happen."

"Oh, my God. Langdon was just about to retire and he was with a guy from the CIA?"

"No, it wasn't one of the good guys with him. The government checked all the rank and file and they're all still with us. There wasn't enough time between when we left and when Langdon departed for a government guy to return. Because the two were in Langdon's car, they think it was probably one of the bad guys chasing you who intercepted Langdon and was forcing him to drive down Rock Branch Road. When they got out of sight from all the farm houses, someone used a Bazooka or drone with bombs on it and blew them up."

"Their own man?" I asked, as my mind zeroed in on the guy who claimed to be Agent Wilson who'd the stolen FBI badge. I figured the bad guys weren't too pleased I escaped from them the Beltline.

Luke added, the government notified Amy and she spread the word she wanted to have a celebration of life for you."

"What about...me?"

"George, the bodies in the car were so incinerated it was as if you'd been cremated. We were going to have a headstone made and put out at Graceland but we never had time."

"What would have put on it? Better yet, what were you going to bury?"

"We never got that far."

Luke continued. "It was all so logical. Amy thought you were in the car, needed money and attempted to collect your life insurance."

"Jesus!" I responded and then asked, "Did the government seize the policy?"

Luke nodded in the affirmative and replied. "James looked into it when the government refused to allow the insurance company pay Amy. What I found out was generally life insurance proceeds aren't frozen along with other assets in a sedition case because the contracts typically focus on the death benefit being paid to the designated beneficiary. The government's interest usually lies in the assets owned by the insured not the payout from a separate policy."

Luke continued. "Since the beneficiary has rights established by the contract, the government normally wouldn't have legal grounds to freeze those funds unless they could prove the beneficiary was somehow involved in the sedition. I think this was the turning point for Amy as she believed the government thought she was a co-conspirator and, therefore, not eligible to receive the funds and liable for further criminal action."

"The government got wind of the fact I was trying to help Amy get the life insurance and that's why the Feds came after Peter and me. They thought because we were just with you and Langdon in the Forest we had time to kill Langdon."

"How did James get in this mess?"

"He tried helping us and the government decided he was a part of the whole scheme."

I simply shook my head in disbelief as Peter walked over, looked at me and inquired and sternly asked . "What did you tell these guys?"

"What happened. What else could I tell them?"

"Did they ask about the tornado?"

"Not really."

"Well, George, there was the tornado that caused a lot of focused damage. The only problem is the track of the tornado was two miles away moving from the southwest to northeast and never went near the Forest or the Foundation."

"You mean?"

"We think when the Chinese discovered SIMON was erasing everything and the tornado gave them the perfect opportunity to blow up the place with the idea that, if they couldn't have SIMON's technology, nobody could."

"Why do you think that?"

"Again, the tornado never came close to the Foundation. The detonation footprint at the site was circular instead of linear meaning there was an internal discharge and not wind gusts."

"It wasn't SIMON was it?" I asked.

"If SIMON blew, Mineral Point would be gone, as well as, Dodgeville and all the farms in the area.

"And they're blaming you?"

"No, us."

We stopped walking and I took a deep breath as I finally asked, "I read on-line that five people were killed in the tornado in Waldwick."

"There were," Peter offered as his eyes shifted to the ground and his voice softened.

"And?"

"George, it was reported that it was Amy, Jack, Melia and the kids."

My heart sank in a mixture of anger, fear and profound sadness.

"I'm sorry," Peter responded slowly shaking his head.

"Oh, my God! My Melia, the kids and Amy!" at which point Peter attempted to provide a consoling hug only to have a security guard appear and remind him there was no physical contact allowed.

Peter's ire arose as he looked at the guard and shouted. "You mother f—ker! I just told this man his wife, daughter and grandchildren died and you won't allow me to console him. I've had enough of this shit! Either you prosecute us or let us go."

The guard was taken aback, saw my despair yet knew the rules. He also was informed by Peter that failure to resolve the issue by having us meet with someone in authority would mean no more cooperation from any of us when he threatened, "Either we see a lawyer or none of us will cooperate and you can take your entire project and shove it up your ass!"

The break was over and we were led back inside. As we entered the main room with the pool table, I grabbed one of the pool cues and was about to take some of my anger, frustration and pain out on anyone in uniform until James consoled me and noted. "George, violence won't get us out of here."

My hand dropped the cue on the floor as the hollow sound of it hitting the tile echoed throughout the building. I now wondered which was worse, to be trapped in a cave or trapped by my own government simply because we knew too much.

Interrogations:

Flared tempers calmed as two men in dark suits entered the room and identified themselves as Federal Agents. Peter looked at their badges, handed them back and said, "Not good enough."

"What do you mean?" the first officer, probably in his forties with slightly graying hair inquired.

"Either we see someone in command or this meeting is over!" By the tone of his voice, they realized Peter wasn't kidding.

"There's no one here," the second officer replied.

We all looked at the duo and Peter retorted, "Then either get someone here or get out of our way."

"You can't talk to me like that," The first agent replied.

"And why can't I? You're holding us against our will and, if we're arrested, you haven't read us our Miranda Rights."

Both agents got dour grins on their faces and so Peter looked at the two and listed what we had coming. "We're being held by government officials against our will which is, therefore, incarceration and consequently have the right to remain silent and not answer any questions you ask. We have protection against self-incrimination simply because anything we say could be used against us in court, so, we choose not to implicate ourselves. Even here at Area 51 we have the right to an attorney during questioning. While not apropos if we couldn't afford an attorney one would be appointed for us by you, the government."

Peter paused and looked at the two agents and continued. "Now that we've got that clear let's move on. The individuals you've incarcerated have attempted to cooperate with the government as citizens of the United States. Whereas, you have not afforded us the rights outlined above and, whereas, it appears you consider us to be foreign adversaries, we are then entitled to the rights of prisoners of war per the Geneva Convention. If we are adversaries we are to be treated humanely at all times, protection from violence, intimidation, insults, and public curiosity, as well as provision, of food, water, clothing, shelter and medical care that meets the same standards as you and we cannot be discriminated against based on factors like race, religion, nationality, political beliefs or sex. Am I making myself perfectly clear?"

No response and so Peter continued. "Whereas, you have literally kidnaped us and brought us to a secure base against our will and held us here, we demand that we be accused of war crimes which can only be tried by a properly constituted court of international law with fair guarantees and protections to which we have the right to communicate with the International Committee of the Red Cross and to exchange letters with our families. Finally, we have the right to practice our religion and receive spiritual assistance which means, as a practicing Catholic, I demand seeing as priest."

Peter crossed his arms in defiance and continued. "You've held us here for nearly five months against our will. Recently you abducted Mr. Terrill from his home and proceeded to drug and incarcerate him, as well. You have refused to recognize our rights as either US citizens or captives of war. In so doing, you have violated our Constitutional rights under the fifth, eighth and fourteenth amendments which, for your edification, were implemented in the Bill of Rights ratified December 15, 1791 for the fifth and eighth and July 9, 1868 for the fourteenth."

Peter looked at the two, stared them down and noted. "You stand before us as Agents of the Government for which you swore the following "I, do solemnly affirm that I will support and defend the Constitution of the United States against all enemies, foreign and domestic; that I will bear true faith and allegiance to the same; that I take this obligation freely, without any mental reservation or purpose of evasion; and that I will bear true faith and allegiance to the same; that I take this obligation freely, without any mental reservation or purpose of evasion; and that I will well and faithfully discharge the duties of the office on which I am about to enter. So help me God."

There was a pause and then Peter asked, "Do you remember making that pledge?"

Both heads nodded in the affirmative as Peter stated, "And yet, you hold us here without due process, captives in our own country, because you THINK we are a threat, when in fact, we risked our lives to save it and your poor asses as well!"

Peter was on a roll as he continued. "We sacrificed enough. This man (pointing at me) had our government seize all of his assets when, in fact, they knew he was innocent. Our government put so much pressure on he and his wife that it reactivated her leukemia and she was at her daughter's house when a tornado killed her along with his daughter, son-in-law and grandchildren."

Peter's voice increased in volume as did the speed of elicitation as he added. "This man, who you have 'saved' from a cave, only to incarcerate him here has done nothing wrong, absolutely nothing. In fact, he led a group of us in the battle against world disease such that he was awarded a Nobel Peace Prize and yet you dug him out of the ground, drugged him and brought him here where he is detained like a common criminal."

Peter's volume continued to increase as he added. "You've done all of this and to all of us simply because we wanted to protect the world from potential destruction. Where have we gone wrong? What have we done and, particularly, what has George done to be treated with such disdain? We know the world is NOT a safe place and, yet, when we try to defend decency, we're criticized, ostracized and incarcerated as if we'd perpetrated the act instead of risking our lives to stop it."

There was total silence in the room. The guards stood at attention, eyes locked straight ahead with mouths drooped in total awareness of what was transpiring. The two agents stood before Peter totally void of any response knowing deep in their heart the truth had been told and they were simply perpetrators of the act against their fellow countrymen.

Just then the door opened and yet another suit walked in as tempers cooled.

"I'm John Atkins, Assistant Director of the CIA. Will you follow me please?"

The four of us quietly followed his request and entered a room with a large video screen on the wall that reminded me of my home theater when we lived on Pine Lake. Atkins pointed to the chairs on one side of the conference table that had our names printed on white cards as if we were at a wedding and we took our places. With that the screen came to life with the emblem of the National Intelligence logo on it.

Atkins noted, "Gentlemen I would like to introduce you to Mr. Robert Bell, Assistant Director of National Intelligence."

We all nodded as Bell appeared on the screen located in a conference room somewhere, probably in Washington DC or Virginia, with people seated to both his right and left.

"Gentlemen!" Bell offered, while politely nodding as well. "We apologize for all that has transpired and for the secrecy you've been subjected to. As Assistant Director of National Intelligence and, therefore, the CIA it is my responsibility to ensure the safety of our country and our allies."

Bell, looked at the screen but we could tell he was reading off a teleprompter as he continued. "As you know, we are aware of your efforts to help mankind through the Derrick

Williams Foundation and are to be commended for your achievements. As you are also aware, we've examined the capabilities of the Super Computer you designed, which you call SIMON, and quite honestly, have been profoundly impressed by its capabilities. As SIMON grew in proficiencies his skillset reached beyond the limits of contemporary research and transitioned into areas of profound national security. In so doing it became our need to become involved in assuring he remained on the side of research and not domination."

"Mr. Terrill."

I nodded in the affirmative.

"Mr. Terrill, when you retired from the Derrick Williams Foundation and subsequently your father-in-law's company, Wilco Corporation, you left the day-to-day control in that of your son, Derrick, is that correct?"

"That's correct."

"In so doing it's our understanding your role in the company, at that time, became tertiary at best."

"That too is correct," I replied.

"You were not aware of its financial condition nor the activities of your son in terms of creating a Ponzi scheme nor his sale of SIMON's technology to a group of Chinese investors, is that correct?"

"That's correct."

"Mr. Terrill, when and how did you learn of these activities?"

"I learned about them from my deceased wife approximately ten months ago."

"And what did you then do?"

"I worked with Agent David Langdon in determining a way to literally reverse SIMON such that his function would return to that of health determination and not world domination."

"In so doing, who did you seek out to assist in this effort?"

I looked to my left at Peter and to my right at Luke and said, "The gentlemen on each side of me."

"And why did you seek these men out?"

"Not only because of their knowledge but their decency and dedication to the goodness of mankind."

"What do you mean knowledge?"

I replied, "Peter headed up the development of the artificial intelligence software team while Luke was responsible for both our operations, serving as our liaison to all questions regarding social, political and bio-ethics. In addition he designed and built our facility.

"On December 8th of last year what transpired?"

I paused for a moment and then detailed the bus ride, car chase, Forest, drowning men and making it to the cave.

"Who was with you?"

"Agent David Langdon."

"Why the cave, as you called it?"

"Because I was being hunted down and my life was at risk and I knew the cave was virtually impenetrable and, therefore, safe."

"How long did you think you would be in the cave?"

"Agent Langdon didn't specify, simply noting I was to stay secured until he returned."

"When did you learn of Agent Langdon's death?"

"Two hours ago."

"So, for nearly six months you were isolated in a cave not knowing what all transpired."

"That's correct. Because of the threat upon my life I was given a computer that only allowed for checking the internet ten minutes per day with no ability to do email."

"So, in other words, you were literally in solitary confinement."

"Yes."

"Why did you stay?"

"Fear number one, and, initially, I was directed to do so until someone came for me."

"Did you ever think something had gone wrong?"

"Of course. Especially when I read about the tornado, realized the outdoor security camera that had been positioned to survey the cave entrance was aimed at the sky and reading an article reporting I'd died in a plane crash."

"What did you think when you read about the plane crash and the notation that not only you, but the two gentlemen on both sides of you today were on that plane?

"It's the media. I've been reported on numerous times and there's always something wrong."

"So, you didn't worry about it or weren't concerned?"

"I was getting pissed as I retorted. "Tell me, sir, what was I supposed to do? I was locked in a cave and had ten minutes per day to learn about what was going on and the story was simply a blurb."

Bell allowed for some time to allow me to adjust to the new reality when he inquired. "You're familiar with the Stryker airplane aren't you? Was it not named after your wife and signified as Amelia^X?"

"Yes."

"Did the plane have advanced avionics to allow it to literally fly itself?"

"Yes."

"Did you consider it safe?"

"Of course!"

"Based on your knowledge of the plane and level of confidence why do you think it crashed?"

"I don't know. I would assume that it was either shot down or there was an explosive on board."

"In other words you would surmise that it was an act of terror?"

"Yes," I replied.

"And who do you think did this?"

"I don't know, the bad guys? You guys? It's beyond my realm of comprehension."

I was getting Minnie Point Bad-ass pissed and interrupted Bell to inquire. "So, you actually had my plane take off and head for Saint Martin and then shot it down?"

Bell stiffened in his chair. "Mr. Terrill, the United States Government does not assassinate its own citizens and, yet, the plane with the afore-mentioned group aboard literally blew up while traveling at nearly 1.5 times the speed of sound."

"So, who was on Amelia^{X}?" I inquired.

Bell sat stone faced with no expression whatsoever. He looked to his left and was handed a sheet of paper. Nodding, he looked into the camera, changed subjects and inquired. "Besides Derrick Terrill, who is Thomas Terrill, Su Trang Terrill, Amelia Terrill and Ms. Karen McCormick?"

I looked at the image of Bell and answered, "Derrick is my son, Thomas my brother, Su my sister-in-law. Amy my wife. I have no idea who Karen McCormick is."

"Mr. Terrill, wasn't Karen McCormick your wife's administrative assistant?"

A resounding sense of guilt permeated my body as I realized it was Karen and I'd simply forgotten her last name as I responded. "I'm sorry sir, I'd forgotten Karen's last name."

There was no response but then none was needed as Bell straightened his glasses and noted, "They were the ones who were supposed to be on the plane that crashed in the Gulf of Mexico."

Reality hit me between the eyes...my son, brother, daughter-in-law and nemeses, my wife, along with Karen had crashed.

I simply shrugged my shoulders and replied, "I don't know."

"Mr. Terrill, all of the above, except Ms. McCormick were under investigation for financial fraud, sedition and conspiracy. When SIMON, your computer, began acting erratically and the foreign parties became aware, do you think the group felt threatened?"

"I know I would," I replied.

"Do you think a group of would-be terrorists who had spent years cultivating a program to acquire the power SIMON offered would want those they felt betrayed them terminated?"

"I can't answer that."

Bell paused, took off his glasses and stated, "We believe no one was on Amelia^x."

"What?" I responded incredulously.

"Mr. Terrill, the FAA calculates 190 pounds for each male, 179 pounds for each female and 82 pounds for each child on an airplane. In examining the flight plan for your jet that was set to fly to Saint Martin it had been fully loaded with jet fuel from the Fixed Base Operator at Mitchel Field grounds in Milwaukee where your plane had a capacity of 3,000 gallons."

"At 'normal' barometric pressure of 29.9 inches of mercury (Hg) and 6.7 pounds per gallon, the total weight would be 20,100 pounds for fuel and 917 pounds for passengers. Yet, the computer on board only reported the 20,000 pounds above its functional weight at take-off. For this reason we believe your son, brother and sister-in-law, wife and friend planned the whole deal so that the Chinese would think they crashed."

"But why would they want to leave?" I asked.
Bell looked at the camera and answered with a rhetorical question. "Why did you hide for six months?"

He didn't even need me to answer. We all realized the bad guys would have gone after the group for the same reason they came after me.

I opened my hands as an expression of inclusion and inquired. "But why did the media think it was us?"
Bell remained silent but it was becoming quite clear the CIA made it seem as if we were onboard to finalize our existence, to take the Chinese pressure off us. Death has a way of doing that.

I inquired. "So, the plane crash was to eliminate the threats against us, correct?"

No answer. Bell paused and said. "Mr. Terrill, why did you hide in a cave and not simply come out?"

I was getting perturbed as I replied, "I would have except the door wouldn't open."

"You mean you were trapped?"

"Yes!

Peter interjected. "Mr. Bell, we've recently learned that someone on the outside came to the cave and attempted to remove the exterior electronic security system used to unlock the door. It's our impression this was done to capture the chip inside in an attempt to replicate the operating protocol by reproducing the necessary identification steps. However it appears they recognized that someone had destroyed the sensor and simply left without the security system. Without the external mechanism, there wouldn't have been any current to the interior door and it wouldn't open."

I nodded in the affirmative and added. "When my late father-in-law developed the security system the assumption was to keep people out and not keep them in."

Bell nodded, as if he now realized why I hadn't literally come out like the groundhog and seen my shadow. He seemed to realize I'd reached my limit as his tone changed from one that was accusatory to conciliator as he asked, "Who is Mary Egan?"

"Mary Egan, or Megan as she goes by, was my physical therapist after my prostate surgery. Subsequent to that, I worked with Megan to establish a program for spouses of men going through prostate cancer such that they would have a better understanding and greater foresight into not only the procedure but consequences."

"And this is why you were in Atlanta last September?"

I dejectedly answered, "Yes."

"And, why did you reach out to her through E=MC^2?"

"Because the computer wouldn't allow me to do email and Megan's address was through her clinic's website and the only one I remembered."

I was totally depleted in terms of energy, thought and emotion as Bell concluded with, "Thank you for your clarification."

I sat in the room for the next two hours and listened to the questions posed to Peter, Luke and James. It had been over three hours of interrogation until Bell looked at his associates, put down his glasses, took a deep breath, as if to signal the session was over, and simply nodded.

Bell looked at me and I could tell that he wasn't reading off a teleprompter as he noted. "Mr. Terrill, the United States Government and I personally would like to apologize for what you have gone through. In addition, I would like to formally say we are sorry to all of you for the inconvenience. My only explanation is that the depth of the issue was so profound and its consequence so great we had to make absolutely certain the matter was closed and all those involved had been identified. Speaking for the President we commend you gentlemen for your efforts in saving the life and liberty of, not only Americans, but innocent people throughout the world including those in China."

Bell slid back in his chair, glanced to his left and nodded, the screen went dark and then I sat in total shock when Melia appeared.

"Melia?"

"Hi dad."

"I thought..."

"I know dad and I'm sorry, the bad guys put two and two together and were coming after us. I think they were going to kidnap us to make you or Peter come out of hiding."

"Where are you?"

"I can't say. All I can say is that we're safe and everyone here believes someday we'll be able to return home."

"My God. My prayers are answered."

"We can't stay on long but we're all safe."

"Including your mother?"

There was a very long pause as Melia looked down at the floor and then back at the camera and replied. "Dad, mom thought you were dead. We all thought that simply because Peter reported you were with Agent Langdon...."

I looked at Peter and Luke and they both nodded their heads in the affirmative as Melia offered. "Dad, everyone thought it was you in the car."

"Mom's still alive?" I repeated. Having heard it from the government was one thing. Hearing it from Melia was another.

Melia reiterated, "We think so."

"What do you mean?"

"Dad, mom went with Derrick."

I was incredulous as I replied, "You mean she, she wasn't going to Carbone?"

"Dad, she did and they were able to transplant some of my stem cells and she's in remission."

"I...I can't believe this." I offered, simply shaking my head, shrugging my shoulders and raising my hands to my mouth in disbelief.

Melia reiterated. "Dad, she thought you were dead. We all did. Mom was all alone and then...well, you remember Karen, don't you?"

"Yes!" I replied, somewhat curtly.

"Well, because we all thought the same, mom started staying with Karen during her recovery. One thing led to the next and well dad, mom and Karen left the country with Derrick, Uncle Tommie and Su."

"Where did they go?" I asked

"Everyone thinks Peru."

"Peru?"

"Dad, the official government media story was that it was you in the car with Mr. Langdon. The non-media story was that Derrick and the group died in the plane crash which circulated on social media. Anyway, that's what the government is telling us?"

I wondered why in hell the government would tell the public it was Peter, Luke and James and then tell Melia it was Derrick, Tommie, Su and Amy. It was then I began to realize the government planted the story about Peter, Luke and James and me to make the Chinese think we were dead and cool our trail. Then, with them believing I was the second person in the car with Langdon and Peter, Luke and James in protective custody they unofficially let word out it was Derrick and the gang so the Chinese would believe it was them to take the heat off them, as well.

The question then became why? First, they knew SIMON was sleeping, and not destroyed, and they needed Peter, Luke and/or me to wake him up. Second, by lowering risk of retribution against Derrick and company, they felt Derrick would let his guard down and lead them to the cash he's got hidden in some bank somewhere which would allow the US Government to use their serendipitous ways to find him.

I paused for a minute and then asked Melia what she thought by posing the question, "Why do you think the government changed their story?"

Melia paused and then replied..."Money dad, money. If the Chinese thought mom and Derrick were still alive, they'd hunt them down and go after all the money Derrick stashed somewhere and the government couldn't otherwise collect. You've also got to realize, everyone knows Fitzgerald was in on the deal and he's still got a lot of power in Washington. By wiping out all those who knew the truth, he'd be free and clear of any wrongdoing."

"Why Peru?" I inquired.

Melia replied. "It was probably mom's idea simply because of Karen. Peru has recognized same-sex couples since 1924 and the Inter-American Court of Human Rights ruled in 2023 that Peru must guarantee equal rights and protection against their discrimination."

Melia paused and then added. "Derrick probably agreed because of the treaty agreement between Peru and the United States regarding extradition. As long as they don't break any Peruvian laws, they can't be brought back to the States."

"One final question," I offered.

"Why didn't my brother check the Cave?"

Melia paused, looked at the ground and then broke my heart. "Dad, Tommie never forgave you for his divorce from Heather. If he knew you were there it was his way of getting even while, also, acquiring all of Terrill B&B."

"You mean, he would have left me there to die?"

Melia looked at the floor in an embarrassed way and then added. "Tommie told the authorities he checked and the cave was empty."

Peter glanced at me and offered. "I'll bet Tommie is the one who fried the lens on the security panel. All he'd need was a laser pointer aimed at the sensor and the panel would have been frozen in its current position. That's probably why the bad guys stopped trying to remove the panel when they saw the smoked lens and, therefore, the destroyed chip. "

I thought about Su's research lab next to the barn and the fact there was a classroom that had laser pointers she used when making presentations to students and visitors. I was profoundly saddened as I shook my head and offered. "My own brother. If he'd asked, I would have given him the whole damn business."

I then realized that by trying to kill me, Tommie probably saved my life as the Chinese didn't come back and try to open the cave again.

Melia responded. "That's the problem dad, he always felt you were looking down at him. He wanted to be important. He wanted to be the success story."

I thought of my conversation with Amy and how she used Fredo from the 'Godfather' as a reference point. My God, had I been that blind and simply shook my head in disbelief. I'd spent six months locked in a cave where everyone thought I was deceased. My daughter and her family were reported dead after a tornado hit but are alive and hiding from the bad guys. My wife hooked up with her former female assistant and has gone with our son, who is a fugitive from the Federal Government and probably living off the billions stashed somewhere, which is probably in Peru, because they can't be extradited and same-sex couples are recognized. Now that's a story no one would believe but made the one I wrote in the cave seem like a children's book that pales in comparison to what's happened.

"Dad, I'm getting the high sign and need to go. We love you and look forward to seeing you soon."

With that, the screen went black and I sat profoundly shocked as we all took a deep breath, realizing a horrible situation was ending as the big screen presented logo of the NIA. There was a sigh of relief as Atkins stood, looked at the four of us, apologized for the inconvenience and announced we were cleared and arrangements would be made to send us home in a government jet.

I was totally spent. How much could one person take in a day?

Picking Up the Pieces:

We were provided some papers to sign regarding confidentiality and liability and told we could return to Madison.

I went to my room and noticed the night stand and radio had been removed. I had nothing to pick up except the memories.

As I was about to leave Dr. Roberts appeared. "George, over the past few weeks you've shown a lot of progress but you've still got a long way to go. Please, do me a favor and take it slow."

Dr. Roberts reached in his pocket and pulled out one of his business cards and handed it to me while noting, "If you need someone to talk to, give me a call."

I looked at this man who'd brought me back from the abyss and said. "I want to thank you for your patience and understanding. I'm in your debt for putting me on the road to recovery."

I reached for his hand and instead pulled him in and gave him a bear hug as he whispered. "You truly are Little Spirit."

I met with Peter, James and Luke, got in a black Suburban and rode to the air strip where the government provided a small jet and we climbed aboard. My hands shook as I thought of crashing planes and dead people. I walked to the last seat in the back of the plane, sat down, buckled myself in and stared out the window and never said a word to the threesome all the way home.

As we neared the Mississippi River I looked down and realized our flight path was from the southwest and we'd be literally flying over Waldwick. I couldn't look! I couldn't bear to see where I'd been buried. Instead, I closed my eyes and waited for the sounds of the wheels being lowered. I was panting. My breaths were so deep and so distraught I wondered if the guys could hear me.

Silently we landed and I said goodbye to Peter, Luke and James. There was no thought and therefore no conversation about getting together again. With so many lives affected and so much grief, I had no idea what to do and returned to the condo to face the cold, stark reality that comes when one's all alone...again!

Things were completely different. I was having difficulty reintegrating and I realized I had a distorted view of the world that could make it difficult for me to reintegrate into society. One would think that, after being totally alone for six months, I'd want to be with people. That was not the case. I wanted to be alone. All alone.

Afraid! Concerned! Nervous! I simply couldn't handle what all had happened or rationalize why. And the pace? Honking horns, crazy drivers. Any noise at all startled me. What was once so mundane that it took no thought was now literally impossible. I had the Theory of Acclimation in reverse! My emotions were tattered and I was having an incredibly hard time making rational decisions.

It took a month until I was able to get up enough courage to call 'V'. At least twenty times, I'd dial nine numbers and then couldn't hit that last digit. Finally, I took a deep breath and did.

'V' answered and offered. "Hi, dad. How are you doing?"

"Been a rough year," I offered.

"We're so sorry. You tried to do good and what did it get you?"

"We helped change the world son and for the better," I replied as my hands quivered in anxiety.

"You did dad. You really did."

"Tell me what happened, son," I needed to hear it again from someone besides Melia. Then, I felt I could believe it as my eyes shifted to the floor as if I could blank out everything else except that moment.

"Mom was sick and Carbone said there was nothing more they could do except try the stem cell transfusion. She was fading fast and they wanted to put her in hospice at 'Amazing Grace' in Fitchburg. With everyone believing you'd been killed, she'd have been there alone and so Karen offered to have her come and live with her."

"The bad guys figured out who Melia was and also believed you weren't dead. They were going to kidnap Melia and hold her for ransom until you, Peter and/or Luke re-programmed SIMON. When the tornado came through and Melia and Jack's house was destroyed the government made up the story about everyone being killed so that it would take the pressure off Melia and Jack."

"The government alleged mom was a co-conspirator in the Ponzi Scheme. Mom saw what was happening, thought you were dead and she and Karen went with Derrick."

"Are they sure it was the tornado who destroyed Melia's house?"

"Yes, dad. They checked the path of destruction and it went right over the house and the refuse pattern was all in line with the direction of the tornado."

At least I had some relief knowing it wasn't the bad guys and they didn't die as I asked, "Is there anything left of Melia's house?" If there was, I'd want to see it.

"Dad, it was nearly four months ago and I had the land cleared and it's being returned to a cornfield."

"Thanks, son. What do you think happened to Derrick, Tommie, Su, mom and Karen?"

"They were on their way to Saint Martin when the plane went down."

Both the NIA and I thought we should let sleeping dogs lie and so I didn't discuss Peru that Melia had concluded. Instead, I simply offered. "Again, what a waste," which had a double meaning to me as I continued. "What about all the legal stuff?"

'V' offered. "It's a mess. We thought you, Derrick and mom were all dead and I wanted to no part of it. Then there's your estate and the farm. Mr. Kennison filed the papers and it was extracted from the Wilco bankruptcy proceedings and is currently in probate as part of your and Tommie's estates."

"Well, I'll need to get involved. How are you, Amelia and the kids?" I inquired.

"We're fine. Better now that we know at least you're alive."

"Thanks. I need to call Rodney, son."

We hung up and I called Black River Falls. The voice on the other end answered "Hello."

"Hello, Big Brother."

"Oh my God, Little Brother my prayers are answered." I could feel the relief in my dear friend's voice and for the next few minutes I went through all the details except the part that the fugitives were alive and didn't die in a plane crash as Rodney and I vowed to see each other as soon as I was able.

"What are you going to do now?" Rodney asked.

"I don't know. I've got to pick up the pieces and see where I'm at."

"If there's anything, and I mean anything, Ann and I can do please ask."

"I know. I know. I know!" I repeated, as tears welled in my eyes while all that happened finally settled in.

As we hung up I imagined Peter back home. I imagined Luke with Indira in Mineral Point. I imagined James back in Milwaukee and imagined them all with someone else and me alone with pieces to pick up and a life to go on.

I thought I needed a few days to simply settle down. Even in the condo each noise startled me. Each call, scared me. Each beam of light overwhelmed me. Slowly, reality settled in and I began to function by setting priorities legally, socially and financially while vowing to stop talking to myself.

The government agreed to unfreeze our assets. Then because Derrick, Tommie and Amy were "officially" dead Tank Kennison filed a claim in my name for the entire estate.

It took a few weeks for my part as Tank began the process of attaching what was left of Derrick's and Amy's estates. I think the government felt guilty simply because the entire process was expedited and with it came liquidity that was profoundly different from the way we live both before and after the freeze.

Once again, I was a somewhat wealthy man. However, all the baubles and perks no longer mattered. Even my coveted custom shoes became secondary to a pair of Sketchers. Perhaps, it was my mindset after all I'd experienced. Perhaps, my soul had been cleansed and I no longer needed to show the world I was more than a farmer, especially when I finally realized and appreciated the majesty of its tranquility.

I didn't want to go back to Pine Lake. Instead, I simply put the house on the market and sold it 'as is' to someone who needed the status statement more than I did.

The legal morass of Wilco was such that lawyers were needed. During my cave dwelling as I called it, they'd filed Chapter Seven and were in the process of liquidating everything.   In end, there was hardly anything left except memories. For me the only good news was the fact I owed nothing.

Six weeks went by and I was still uncomfortable leaving the condo. Perhaps, it was my six months in solitary. Perhaps, my fear the bad guys were still looking for me. Between Door Dash for groceries and restaurant delivery, I maintained my hermitage, all the while feeling the memories of Amy haunting me where I saw and felt her as I wrote and re-wrote the novel I'd written in the cave. To take some of the time away I began cleaning, literally spending hours each day, washing, dusting and polishing everything in the condo. I might have become a hermit but my world was orderly, tidy and kept.

Emotionally when I was confined it seemed like a temporary thing with a goal that lie ahead. It was only those last few days, when the food was gone and the door didn't open that bothered me. Now that I was out in the world, the loss of most of my family and sense of purpose made me incredibly fragile, fighting bouts of sadness, emptiness and isolation. I'd wake up in the morning and really not know what to do. I tried. I really, really tried to do something, anything only to realize my sadness has impacted my memory, attention span and problem-solving abilities.

I was never much of a television watcher and since returning to the condo never turned it on, preferring silence to blabber, the hum of the refrigerator to that of talking heads sharing, scaring, jolting me with accentuated politicized reality.

I read and re-read what I'd created in the cave and realized it needed to be changed as I could actually feel my fear, frustration and trepidation as the story went on. Sadly, even though I was reading what I wrote I found myself struggling to express myself clearly. Finally, there was the paranoia. I'd become suspicious of others and believed I was still being watched as terror rattled my bones while I kept asking myself. 'Will the bad guys come and get me? What about the government? Are they still watching, waiting, wondering what I'm going to do next?'

I justified my existence with the realization I was in solitary confinement for six months and lost most of my family. It had been over a year since I had a haircut or shaved. I simply didn't have the nerve to go to a barber and my hands shook so much I was afraid to use a razor. Instead, I would sit, deep in thought, until I readily admitted I suffered from periods of depression and saw myself experiencing a loss of interest in activities. Tragically, all the experiences from the cave began again regarding my sleep patterns and appetite, as well as the recurring frustration of being unable to concentrate on anything.

Finally, it was the anxiety that pushed me over the edge. I'd become fearful of social interaction. Each day I vowed it would be my last alone. I'd go to the door, pick up the key and vow I'd take a walk only to stop, wipe the tears from my eyes and promise to try again tomorrow.

One morning I awakened and realized I needed to break the spell. With time no longer of the essence, my goal was to take one step each day. Day one meant putting my hand on the door knob. Day two turning it. Day three opening the door to the hallway. Day four making it to the elevator. Day five, pressing the elevator button. Day six, getting in and then out of the elevator.

Acclimation! Acclimation! Acclimation! With each incremental push outward those steps that had been repeated became less significant and, with the lack of significance, so did the fear. It took two weeks for me to finally make it down to empty parking stall number 805 where my heart beat faster and my hands shook in anxiety.

Finally, I was able to step out onto Wilson Street. Ultimately, I was able to look at another person without the angst that had shrouded me for so long.

It was now fourteen months since my last shave and haircut and I'm certain passersby thought I was some sort of homeless person when, in fact, my level of social confidence was so low, I was simply afraid to be around people and the thought of going to a barber remained incomprehensible.

Slowly, my mind was returning and with it I believed was my emotional balance. Boy, was I wrong! I decided to sell the condo but needed to make sure I could as it was in Melia's name. With her and Jack legally deceased Tank

Kennison was able to expedite transfer of ownership to the closest living relative which was me. The big question became, where would I go? I quickly realized that my memories were worse than reality.

Tommie and Su had no children and because of Su's involvement in the 'Derrick Disaster' as I called it, she was deemed persona non-grata such that her relatives had no claim to Terrill B&B or the farm and, along with the condo, both were mine and by selling all the wine, I had more than enough money.

It took me nearly a week to get up enough courage to e-mail Tank and ask him to find me a Madison realtor. He did and she e-mailed me the contract and I sent her photos of the place. I finally increased my mettle to the point I could have the real estate lady visit to see the place. She was probably my age. Nice. Polite! Professional. Every minute she was there, I had a twitch and wanted her gone. I realized she represented the first person, other than family and Area 51, I'd talked to in over eighteen months.

We put the condo up at a discounted price with the caveat that it could only be viewed with a tour video we had made and no visits with final approval at time of inspection. With Madison's hyper real estate market it took three days before an offer and sale to some guy moving to Madison from the Silicon Valley.

I had three weeks to clean out and the only place left was the farm and decided that's where I needed to go. I was going home. Back to where it all began. Back to what I vowed I'd never be again. And yet, as time had softened those words, I realized that home is where there's peace and harmony, enclosed in a shroud of innocence and God, and I needed that.

Tank made arrangements to have a locksmith go into the cave and open the door by literally disassembling the locking mechanism so we could sell the wine and seal the door. I had no interest in going back, while the thought, make that threat, of going inside never crossed my mind.

Heading Home:

As condo closing day came I had a few hours before it would all be over and the condo computer on which I transposed 'Waldwick' beaconed me. My fingers pressed each key while the clicks became a rhapsody of emotions designed not for others but for me, intended to cleanse my mind and then my soul so that I could begin again. Here are my words and hopefully my emotions.

I'm stuck in an empty room. I've been here for a few weeks now and it's hard to leave. It started as I watched two men load up a truck with furniture that belonged to Amy and me. Everything went to Habitat for Humanity to help some other family. I simply couldn't bear the memories.

After the truck drove away I walked through the Condo's empty rooms simply because what had been our home, was now just an empty house. Our world was gone, replaced by empty space, eliciting words that felt sadly final. I stood in the living room and glanced out at Lake Monona remembering Amy and me sitting on the couch so long ago, listening to opera and feeling what it was like to be alive with nothing but tomorrow to dream about.

I paused and reflected and could literally see Amy curled up, legs beneath her, thinking about something she'd kept inside. It was then that the word 'gone' crept into my soul. Gone, like in gone forever, where our empty space would soon belong to someone else.

The new person wasn't there yet and I'm stuck in the empty room with lingering memories of how Amy kept everything organized and arranged, inside the house and then herself and how she loved the little shelf in our study with photos of her mom and dad, the kids and her brother Derrick, only intersected by the little model plane I made.

As I stand there I realize there are only two ways to look at an empty space. In one sense I see a room full of memories with walls haunted by personal history where the carpeting reflects the daily tread of nothing more than life's routines and basically the way it used to be.

My hands tremble and tears flow as I say goodbye to all of that while also realizing that soon someone else will be saying hello, simply walking through the memories, imagining new colors and furniture to fit their lives. It will be their own photos and mementos that replace those now gone that they will cherish, while burrowing their own paths of life within the carpet as the empty house becomes their home.

I take a deep breath and accept that the space will invite new beginnings and change and it will be exciting and not sad. This is the way life should be and I'm certain Amy would have wanted it that way.

It's not hard to imagine others simply doing like me... standing in empty spaces. It must be as painful for them as it is for me to say goodbye to walls that hold so many memories. I look at the kitchen and see the little scratches I accidentally put on the woodwork that created memories which are now only blemishes simply to be sanded away like so many other things, until the stories of life are gone as life itself goes on.

In my journeys I've driven by weathered, abandoned houses and wondered about the stories inside. It must have been as painful for the house as it is for me as the empty spaces wait for the hope and joy that comes from new beginnings, new voices and fresh laughter all wrapped in a feeling of love where the sad realization is that weathered and abandoned houses also have an end... to simply be reduced to rubble until a new set of dreams arrive.

So, I stand alone and turn to look at the lake below in the empty space that has marked both our beginning and end. My head slants a little to the left, my eyes peer and I still see Amy engulfed in the majesty of music, thinking, dreaming, smiling and wondering as I listen to her say one last time. "George, I love you".

I look down and then out to the horizon. I quietly turn, click off the lights, as my hand touches the door handle one last time. Slowly, I turn the knob, look back, take a deep breath, walk out and whisper, "I love you too," as I quietly close the door and with it, all of yesterday

Recompense:

It's been six months since I moved back into the farm house. Winter has come and gone and spring has arrived. Each day I take my walk into the forest to simply watch and feel what surrounds me. I stop at the obelisk and think of Great Grandfather. I walk to the springs and have my drink and pray that tomorrow will mean a better day. I haven't been to town yet as the silence of singularity that once offended me now keeps me at peace. Perhaps it was the six months in the cave that turned me inside out. Perhaps it's the pain I still feel that has burrowed itself so deep and darkened the sunny sky that I wonder if I'll ever allow outside in again.

It seems strange sitting in our old house still filled with things that were never mine. To keep myself busy I began sorting and cleaning, organizing and eliminating those things that had no meaning. This is to be my final residence, away from anything and everything, solitary, accompanied only by my thoughts and memories.

When I moved from Madison the few things I did bring with me were my great grandfather's 'Waldwick' and the family's bible that had come with him nearly 200 years ago. With no interest in television and the need to keep my mind from turning to mush, one night I began thumbing through the bible as I sought answers to 'why? 'In so doing, the word causality struck home which is basically cause and effect, where events are connected in a way where one thing makes something else happen.

As I reflect back on our son, Derrick, I simply ask why. Why did he never have enough? Why was his greed so profound that it destroyed not only himself but our family? Was he truly that unhappy or was it an inherited trait that transcended from his grandfather? I now know I'll never be able to find the answer but certainly learned the lesson.

In a world driven by ambition, success, and material wealth, it's easy to get caught up in the insatiable desire for more as it consumes our thoughts, actions and, ultimately, happiness. Some say greed is simply a bottomless pit which exhausts the person in an endless effort to be satisfied without ever reaching fulfillment, simply because the pursuit of material wealth can never truly fill one's heart and soul.

In the end, the pursuit of more fails even the greedy simply because the search never brings lasting happiness. It's not a financial issue, it's a heart issue that blinds us from recognizing the true value of what we already have, distorting our perception of what truly matters in life. I think of the salt doll and wonder if we aren't all salt dolls in search of meaning and truth. We may travel and experience the world but true understanding comes from within, by confronting our own limitations and identities we can begin to belong. By appreciating the abundance of love, health, and happiness I now realize we can break free from the grip of greed and cultivate a mindset of gratitude and contentment.

To pass the time, I begin keeping a log where the first entry is. "As I ponder our last family photo I realize that greed is a dangerous beast that devours the soul, consuming a person's inner self, leading to a loss of moral compass and emotional well-being that turns even the most harmless individual into a ruthless monster."

"In order to sustain my exercise program, I take my daily walk past the empty parking lot where the Foundation once stood as I examine the weeds that have begun to reclaim the asphalt wasteland where white stripes of demarcation have begun to fade, becoming nothing more than delineations and concepts of space in a structured world."

"I stop and look at the steel cover and know that below SIMON is sleeping, simply waiting for someone to come and whisper to him, imploring that he comes back to life."

"I make my way within the trees and stop at the few Foundation boulders of what was once Skunk Hollow School and ask, 'What do I do now?'"

"Slowly I make my way to Great Grandfather's obelisk and bow my head in respect of the man who taught me so much but left me with so much more that I profoundly regret I've forgotten.

"Finally, I make my way to the cold springs and wonder how they can be so pure in a world so wrought with pain. I take the tin cup and fill it with earth's nectar and take a slow sip of the frigid water and wait to see if the feelings I once had will return. Today, again, as it has so many times before, they're simply not there as I toast Langdon and shed a tear in his memory hoping, praying, wondering if he's with his wife and found the peace he searched for but could never find."

"My eyes traverse all that's around me as I admit it's simply another day, when I hope and pray I'll see 'Him' and wonder why he's never there. My God, I need to see the mighty buck. Perhaps then my wounds will begin to heal."

"As the sun begins to set, I make my way back towards the house, across fields once plowed, now nothing more than ruts of indifference, slowly being catapulted into masses of weeds."

"On this day I pause at the stone wall that separates today from yesterday and glance at the markers within all etched with names and dates of those who came before me and wonder what it felt like when the one next to them beat them to their final resting place.'

"The outside light on the barn clicks on. It's my beacon. It's time to go home. Silence. Silence, Silence. Only the sounds of the crickets cascade my ears as I enter the house and head for the screen porch where my little buddy, Jake, would lie anxiously waiting for nothing more than me to come home."

"I sit deep in thought of all that had been. I ponder today and fear tomorrow. I think of all that was good and all that was bad and realize Steven Hawking was right...the net sum of the universe is zero. Good/bad! Happy/sad!"

"My hands fall to my lap as I succumb to some sort of stupor. I close my eyes and when I open them 'He' is there. The mighty buck has come to me. Never before has he been beyond the realm of the forest. I look deep into his eyes and his magnificence transcends from his soul to mine and there is peace...wonderful, glorious peace."

"I close my lids and when I open them, he is gone. Was he real or simply an aberration?"

"For the first time since I entered the cave I feel a sense of purpose. I arise and go to the kitchen table, pull the laptop Peter provided from the pantry shelf and slowly lift the lid that has been ensconced in solitude since that day when they pulled me from the emotional cauldron of solitary confinement."

"My mind goes back to Area 51 and I mentally thank Peter for taking the electronic shackles off such that the laptop can reach out for more than ten minutes and I can scan my long-dormant emails."

I press the button and the computer screen comes alive as if it had simply been sleeping. I ponder the original version of the story I wrote while living in a cave and wonder if it will ever be anything more than what it is, icons upon a screen, never to be shared with anyone.

I've been too sad to reach beyond my here and now and finally press the button to see the messages I'd been too fragile and too frail to encounter. There's one from the attorneys telling me what I already knew, the resolution of Wilco is complete and I've been awarded the remnants of the once great company where the only thing still mine is money that now has no value to me along with the residence on Saint Martin called 'The Lighthouse'. My mind wanders as I wonder if I should keep it or sell it. Time has a way of softening the yearning that once permeated my veins.

I scan deeper into the mass of messages and find one that simply breaks my heart. It's from Amy, simply telling me she loves me. My God, from what she thought was my grave came her last thoughts filling me with regrets as I whisper, "I love you, too".

It's been three hours since I first lifted the lid on reality and I'm only a fraction of the way through all the emails and spam. I shake my head and wonder how something that was once so great could be turned into an invasive form of commerce that intercepts your thoughts and emotions while lurking within are those whose only goal is to steal from you...your money, your joy and above all else your sense of security.

I'm about to depart from the remnants of now and simply shut off my reality when a new email appears. It's from E=MC^2. I realize I never thanked Megan for saving my life and shake my head in remorse, too frightened to simply respond.

I take another bottomless breath and whisper to myself, "be brave! be brave! be brave!" My hands shake as I take my universe of messages and sort them by name instead of from now-to-yesterday and find twenty-three E=MC^s. My God! I've focused so much on myself, I didn't think of others. For the first time since my heart was broken, I press the button and read what's written...

> *"My Dearest George,*
> *I've been writing to you, hoping my words would help heal your broken heart. My life remains as it was, except for the hole in my soul that you once filled. I fear my choice in life is why you haven't replied and this makes me truly forlorn. In you George there was a light that burned so bright that now pales my passion by its absence. Please, please write to me and simply let me know you're all right.*
> *With love.*
>
> *Megan*

I sit pondering. What do I write? How do I express the pain I feel? How do I apologize for my lack of consideration? I take a deep breath and try to begin.

Words aren't there, only memories.

For what seems like an eternity, my trembling hands cannot touch the keys. I look at the kitchen clock and watch the second hand make its never-ending circle towards tomorrow only to have my silent friend, the Sounds of Silence intercepted by the hum of the refrigerator.

Sounds of Silence! Sounds of Silence! Sounds of Silence!

Come on George! Come on! Come on! You can do it! Climb out of the valley of despair and look at the mountain tops. I press the 'D' key and with each stroke, the pain and suffering, sadness and remorse that has been within me is being released.

Dear Megan:

The darkness that surrounds me has been so immense I could not grasp the majesty of friendship, nor the splendor of someone helping heal my wounds. First, I must thank you for saving my life. Without you I would have died a hideous death, alone and starved, not only of food but the goodness that comes from love and acceptance.

Like the injured man who must learn to walk again, I must re-learn to live.

Like that first step, I must take that first breath.

Like the first belief that tomorrow will come, I must turn my head forward and reach out to those whose hands reach out to me.

I must grasp those hands and feel their warmth.

I must feel the pulse of their heart as it pounds against mine and allows me to see, feel and accept that life must go on.

I cannot forget yesterday and all that it brought forth.

What I hope for is to simply garner those thoughts, feelings and lessons learned and start again. Slowly, gently, cautiously until once again, the sun begins to shine.

Simply, George

I take a deep breath, hit 'send' and gently wipe the tears from my eyes and slowly close the laptop cover.

The phone rings and the caller ID indicates area code 404...Atlanta

I smile.

The Waldwick Series: The ten-book series spans nearly 200 years and are independent yet intertwined in several ways including, characters, location and thematic objectives that examine current social issues from different perspectives. Regardless of the time period or the characters in question, the core component - judging people by who they are instead, of what they are, remains paramount.

Waldwick addresses the subject of physical, social, economic and political oppression in the 1800's. Set in Cornwall, England, Virginia and Southwestern Wisconsin, Waldwick frankly discusses what one family was willing to do to overcome oppression, as told through the eyes of the narrator, George Terrill. *Waldwick* then summarizes what happens when the oppression is removed and opportunity arises. Integrated into the story line are actual events and people and how the main characters are affected by their existence and their interaction with these people and events. Above all else, Waldwick is a love story ... love of the land, love of one another and the love of freedom, woven in a tapestry of acceptance, tolerance and justice. Award Winner

War of My Brothers examines America of the early 20th century and how and why it changed as seen through the eyes of Hank Terrill, great grandson of George Terrill from the original Waldwick. Ride along as Hank witnesses World War I, the Spanish Flu, the 19th Amendment, that gave women the right to vote, the Great Depression, World War II, Korean War and Viet Nam and how life changed, people changed and those who govern changed, as well. Experience the traumas of life and the joys of the living as you thank God that it didn't happen to you.

The King of Hearts has been reviewed as "ambitious, extensively researched and deeply engrossing"…a story that traces the actual Terrill family through 60 generations as it learns the consequence of wealth, power and prestige over 700 years only to have it all collapse around them. Using a blend of magic realism, lyrical prose and imagery *The King of Hearts* weaves a complex tapestry of a family's history from 65 BCE through sixty generations. Beneath it all, the book is about friendship and the deep, mutual bond between people based on trust, support, and genuine connection that goes beyond just companionship—it's about understanding, loyalty, and being there for each other through life's ups and downs.

Little Spirit Based in contemporary Wisconsin, Little Spirit examines the concept of eminent domain and the taking of land and dignity, first from the Indian's perspective and then today, as seen through the eyes of George Terrill IV a descendant of the original George Terrill. Using flashbacks through a 94-year-old, blind, Ho- Chunk Indian elder, named Great Grandfather, George learns about the feelings and challenges of the Ho-Chunk nation and the taking of their land and also how contemporary America hasn't changed that much in terms of citizen rights.

Driftless revisits George and his wife fifteen years into their marriage. Reflecting on the challenges they face when their marriage becomes mundane while examining the profound question of which is worse... having nothing or everything. As the mystery of the Forest is revealed Driftless examines the consequence of technology and the power of special interest groups to control the status-quo for their financial gain, while addressing the issue of individual rights in time of personal need, where the one thing all people have in common is ... time!

415

The Hayflick Limit addresses the challenges of parenthood, while discussing a person's rights to live and die. When affected by an incurable malady the question becomes "Would you choose five-to-seven years of normal mental acuity, at which time you would abruptly expire, or risk everything and allow for the slow, gradual decline with hope that a different, longer-lasting cure might come along?" The Hayflick Limit addresses the role of government in establishing the validity of the Hippocratic Oath?

Let Go examines the consequence of bullying as Melia Terrill is affected by the verbal onslaught and her commitment to the only friend who has shown her the beauty of acceptance for who she is. The books examines the perks and perils of extreme wealth, the solitude of loneliness and frustration of achieving one's goals only to realize that all dreams can become nightmares when one risks everything for perhaps nothing as it delves into thoughts, emotions, joys, sorrow and consequences of being a captive of one's own past and fleeting fame while examining the joys and sorrows of falling in love.

Survivor...How Death Saved My Life looks at the consequence of an altered set of priorities and how it can take a near-death experience to "right the ship". Totally immobilized for six days, George Terrill examines his life and it's mistakes and vows, if he survives, to make things right. Survivor addresses the psychology of fear, the challenges of being told you have less than a 5% chance of living three hours and what you think about when you sincerely believe you're going to die.

Greed is a thought-provoking literary tale of ambition gone awry, exposing how the pursuit of wealth can fracture family relationships. This intense novel, explores the intricacies of human nature and the pursuit of meaning. It serves as a critique of modern society's obsession with wealth and status that challenges readers to reconsider what success truly means, making this book not just an exhilarating journey but a profound reflection on the human condition.

And/Or Using Newton's Third Law as a lens to explore relationships where every action sets off a chain reaction, *And/Or* journeys in ways no one can predict or control while asking difficult questions about resilience, identity, and redemption. As such, it ponders deep philosophical reflections and existential questions by drawing sharp connections between science and human nature, asking such profound questions as...Is it possible for a person to truly recover from betrayal? Can love survive after it's been broken? And when one loses everything, what's left? And/Or is a gripping, thought-provoking read that will linger long after the final page.

Disclaimer: All books, including "Greed" are pure fiction. Some of the events detailed herein may be true and have been faithfully rendered as researched by the author to the best of his abilities. The information contained is intended to provide helpful and informative material on the subjects and events addressed and written as an interpretation of his learning. It does not guarantee accuracy or social integrity and has been written for the purpose of education and entertainment.

There is a town called Mineral Point, Wisconsin where the author's childhood was filled with magical moments and marvelous memories and a village called Waldwick that remains nearby and is the birthplace of the author's grandmother and mother. There are many Terrill's and Harris's in the area who are the author's relatives and he hopes and prays he has done the family names justice by what he has written for they, are the kindred spirit upon which our country was created. There is no reality to the names used as they are all of consequence.

There is a wonderful island called St. Martin that is filled with love and life where smiles come easy, the food is superb and the memories can last forever. The names of the restaurants are real and the food is GREAT and the author only hopes that he's done them all justice with his descriptions.

The author has been to China 36 times and found the people there kind, considered and friendly. They work hard and have the same dreams as Americans, to live in peace and have a better life than their parents, but not as good as their children. The author chose China simply because he had mentioned them in a previous book and not out of avarice or disrespect.